THE POLITICAL ECONOMY OF THE
EUROPEAN CONSTITUTION

The Political Economy of the European Constitution

Edited by
LUIGI PAGANETTO
University of Rome Tor Vergata, Italy

Routledge
Taylor & Francis Group

LONDON AND NEW YORK

First published 2007 by Ashgate Publishing

Reissued 2018 by Routledge
2 Park Square, Milton Park, Abingdon, Oxon OX14 4RN
711 Third Avenue, New York, NY 10017, USA

Routledge is an imprint of the Taylor & Francis Group, an informa business

First issued in paperback 2018

A Library of Congress record exists under LC control number: 2006100205

Notice:
Product or corporate names may be trademarks or registered trademarks, and are used only for identification and explanation without intent to infringe.

Publisher's Note
The publisher has gone to great lengths to ensure the quality of this reprint but points out that some imperfections in the original copies may be apparent.

Disclaimer
The publisher has made every effort to trace copyright holders and welcomes correspondence from those they have been unable to contact.

ISBN 13: 978-0-815-39807-3 (hbk)
ISBN 13: 978-1-138-62115-2 (pbk)
ISBN 13: 978-1-351-14576-3 (ebk)

Contents

List of Figures

List of Tables

Part 1

Chapter 1

The European Economic Constitution

Luigi Paganetto

A Constitution, at least in a liberal version, is a set of laws and procedures aimed at protecting citizens' rights and individuals from the will of Government.

The European Economic Constitution has to create a coherent architecture within this definition, set out principles and define the precise meaning of concepts such as vertical and horizontal subsidiarity, market liberalisation and market surveillance, as well as the regulation of capital mobility and budgetary balance.

The issue of the European Constitution therefore refers not only to a simplification of the Community Treaties – an exercise that the European Convention has done essentially in the second part of the new Treaty establishing a European Constitution – but also, and most of all, to the relationship between the system of the European Community and constitutional system of the Member States within the prospect of a common constitutional order. A political Constitution should be complementary to the existing economic Constitutions, and consistent with Community Treaties that created a common market and currency union.

The real, never-ending central concern, relates to the allocation of policymaking prerogatives between national and European authorities. Some authors think that a 'European Constitution' should be adopted as a basis for the establishment of a future European Federal State. Being in favour of such a Constitution often means being in favour of the establishment of a Federal or a Confederal European State. A confederation of states, however, does not constitute a new state, just an association of sovereign states, while a federal state, as its name indicates, is both state and federation.

The nature of European Union has long been debated and there are many definitions regarding such a Union. According to Alberta Sbragia 'the European Community is [...] unique in its institutional structure, it is neither a State nor an international organization [...]' to use Helen Wallace's words, 'a part-formed political system'.[1] To Keohane and Hoffmann[2] 'If any traditional model were to be applied, it would be that of a confederation rather than a federation [p. 279] [...] However, confederalism alone fails to capture the complexity of the interest-based bargaining that now prevails in the Community [p. 280] [...] the European Community [...] exemplifies what sociologists refer to as a *network form of organization*' [p. 281].

---

1   Sbragia, A. (1992), *Euro-politics: Institutions and Policy-making in the 'New' European Community* (Washington, DC: Brooking Institutions).

2   In Wallace, W. (Ed.) (1990), *The Dynamics of European Integration* (London: Pinter).

Philip Schmitter once proposed five models based on the domination/integration relation: *national state, confederatio, condominio, federatio, supra-state*.[3] Otherwise the EC/EU has been defined as 'a loose federation',[4] 'une entité post-étatique',[5] un 'objet politique non identifié',[6] 'a multi-tiered system of governance',[7] 'a multi-tier negotiating system',[8] 'a multi-level European system',[9] 'a mixed polity',[10] 'a polity creating process in which authority and policy-making influence are shared across multiple levels of government'.[11] In Wessels and Maurer's words: 'Whatever the language used, political scientists and lawyers classify the EC/EU as a system for joint decision-making in which actors from two or more levels of governance interact in order to solve common and commonly identified problems'.[12]

Indeed, the institutional design of a federation is the fruit of a compromise between two different objectives: the internalisation of externalities amongst countries and the adaptability of policies to different national preferences. The benefits from internalisation of externalities increase in the degree of interdependence between countries, while the benefits from adaptability of the policy increase with heterogeneity between countries. A union in which every country independently chooses its policy maximises the adaptability to local differences, but minimises the internalisation, and does not take into account heterogeneity between countries (Alesina *et al.*, 2001).[13]

The analysis of the relationship between corporatism, institutions and growth has recently been performed by a coincidence of theoretical and empirical research initiatives which have focused the debate on different perspectives and heterogeneous analytical paradigms.

Some theoretical contributions (Freeman, 2001, and Phelp, 2000), for instance, have examined the supposed convergence of the western European system of

3   Schmitter, P.C. (1991), *The European Community as an Emergent and Novel Form of Political Domination*, Working Paper 1991/26, (Madrid, Juan March Institute).

4   Wallace, W. in: Wallace, H. and Wallace, W. (Eds) (1996), *Policy-Making in the European Union*, 3rd edn (Oxford: Oxford University Press).

5   Telò, M. (1995), *L'Italia nel processo di costruzione europea*, in *Storia dell'Italia Repubblicana*, Vol. 3, (Torino: Einaudi).

6   Quermonne, J.-L., (1992), Existe-t-il un modèle politique européen?, in *Revue Française de Science Politiques*, April 1992.

7   Lodge, J. (1995), *Institutions and Policies of the European Community* (London: Frances Pinter).

8   Kohler-Koch, B. (1996), Catching up with change: the transformation of governance in the European Union, *Journal of European Public Policy*, 3(3), September, p. 360.

9   Scharpf, F. (1994), *Community and Autonomy: Multilevel Policy-Making in the European Union*, EUI Working papers of the Robert Schuman Center, RSC 94/1.

10   Andersen, S. and Eliassen, K. (Eds) (1996), *The European Union. How Democratic is it?* (London: SAGE).

11   Marks, G., Hooghe, L. and Blank, K. (1995), *European Integration and the State*, EUI Working papers of the Robert Schuman Center, RSC 1995/7.

12   Wessels, W. and Maurer, A. (2001), *The Evolution of the EU system: Offers and Demands for National Actors*, paper for ECSA Conference, Madison, June, p. 5.

13   Alesina, A. *et al.* (2001), *Institutional Rules for Federations*, mimeo, Harvard University and European Central Bank.

governance to the 'American model'. Endogenous growth literature has highlighted the role of institutional and policy variables' influences, and the steady-state equilibrium of economic expansion, with an emphasis on the consequences of an income distribution process (Bertola, 1993; Alesina and Perotti, 1993; Rodrick, 1999). Public choice literature and labour economics have mainly investigated whether and how different governance structures and wage-bargaining systems affect macroeconomic performance. Some political science models have introduced the role of government partnership and unionisation to extend the analysis of corporatism beyond distributive aspects, to include other policy dimensions of economic institutions (Traxler *et al.*, 1997).

The accessing process of the CEECs (Central and East European Countries) opens in the first part of the 1990s with the 'European Agreements' (so-called Association agreements of the 'second generation'). These treaties define new relationships between the European Union and each member of the CEECs (Central and East European Countries). Initially the process was aimed at creating a free trade area, but the final purpose was the accession of former socialist countries to the Union. In 1993, during the Copenhagen European Council, the entrance criteria were fixed and negotiations were started with four CEECs (Poland, the Czech Republic, Hungary and Slovakia). Between 1994 and 1997 the agreements were extended to most of the CEECs. Negotiations for accession started in 1998 for Estonia, Poland, the Czech Republic, Slovenia, Hungary and Cyprus and, in 1999, were extended to Bulgaria, Latvia, Lithuania, Romania, Slovakia and other non-CEEC countries such as Turkey and Malta. On 1 May 2004, ten new countries entered the European Union, and Romania and Bulgaria became members on 1 January 2007. However, the current political turmoil and the EU's slow economic growth have cast some doubts on whether the EU will be ready to accept new members after 2007 (Croatia, Macedonia and Turkey are official candidate countries; Serbia and Montenegro, Albania, Bosnia and Herzegovina are potential candidate countries).

Alesina *et al.* (2001) have formalised a model in which the issue of Union enlargement is examined by looking at those factors that allow the admittance of a new member by majority rule. The authors maintain that 'only those countries with positive externalities with UE nations, would be admitted as members the Union so that the new entrance doesn't change the median, otherwise at least 50 per cent of the members would object to that' (Alesina et al., 2001, p. 22). They also point out that members of a union tend to favour the entry of new countries only if they have similar preferences to their own.

As the new EU members are much poorer than the current ones, the prospect of further enlargement of the EU gives an emphasis to the issue of regional gaps within the Union. The ongoing process implies several questions about the effects of economic integration on growth and convergence and on optimal policy design.

The enlargement could produce a widening of regional gaps within Europe, which calls for a careful analysis of the cohesion policy models adopted by the EU policy makers. A rethinking has already started in the direction of supply-side interventions stimulating the entrepreneurial environment and promoting competitiveness of local system by capital inflows (Kostoris *et al.*, 2002).

Strong economic arguments in favour of a strengthening of regional policy in an economic union stem from the less-optimistic conclusions on the distribution of gains from integration, reached by theoretical and empirical economic geography (Krugman, 1991; Krugman and Venables, 1995) and endogenous growth literature (Romer, 1986) in which increasing returns and local externalities dominate.

A cohesion policy has become one of the pillars of Europe (e.g. in building the Maastricht Treaty); however, the Agenda 2000 negotiations have pointed out the need for reform in light of enlargement. The following problems have also been stressed: a more rigid budget constraint for regional policy, due also to the burden of pre-accession transfers; a reduction in the number of subsidized areas; and a restriction of the focus of interventions on fewer objectives. In addition, the need to simplify the complex apparatus associated with the allocation of structural funds, and for better coordination among different levels of governance (regions, nations and community), becomes more important as the political and institutional diversity of the members increases (Nizzo, 2001). Nizzo argues that looking for a new cohesion policy goes along with a better consideration of two complementary policies – national development policies (both members and candidate) and EU competition policy (discipline of government aids to the firms and regions). Nizzo (2001) sketches two different reform options. One is based on a differentiation of the policy between previous members and new members –the former would be allocated funds with the old system, and the latter would receive transfers at national level – to avoid competition between regions of current members and regions of new members. The other reform would be based on the subsidiarity principle: the management of the regional development policy would be left to the national level, with a financial contribution from the Union according to the GDP level. The Union competence would be restricted to some specific actions, such as cross-border programmes, transnational cooperations, strategic innovation policy.

Therefore, reform of regional policy includes the fundamental issue of institutional and devolution policies. The decentralisation process is fundamental for regional development, as defining the appropriate level of intervention allows policies to be modulated in relation to the need of the intervention area (bottom-up approach). A decision on the shape of regional policy should be made by local authorities (Maggioni and Bramanti, 2001).

The aspect of the allocation of economic competencies represents one important aspect of the European constitutional debate. Following the normative view of fiscal federalism, there are no reasons for supranational competence in the area of regional policy as it would imply a negligence of individual preferences. The only cases in which this theory admits a central intervention by the member states or by a supranational competence are those where external spillovers arise (interregional externalities) in neighbouring regions belonging to the same country or belonging to different countries (border regions). However, in this case it is also not necessarily an allocation of regional policy competence to the supranational level as transborder extenalities may be internalized by fixing bilateral rules (the Coase Theorem) (Stehn, 2002).

Another question is whether there should be a unique European Social Welfare State (ESWS) model. In addition, if this unique model is to exist, the main problem is then to define the desired level of the ESWS; shall all countries converge toward a minimum common welfare level or to a higher level similar to that of the North European Countries?

To date, the EU policy is quite vague; in fact, whereas there is an explicit common target in terms of financial indicators (defined within the Maastricht Treaty in 1992) there is no target in terms of social protection policies.

In addition, another debated issue is how to proceed with respect to social policy matters.

Notwithstanding commitments to guarantee adequate levels of protection, as advocated and renewed in Article 2 of the Maastricht Treaty, the problems of financing such programmes pose alarming prospects for the implementation of the various protection policies in the member countries.

Hence, one possible consequence of this forced integration is the dismantling of the European social protection systems. As Sinn (1998) stresses, the increasing competitive pressures on national fiscal systems may generate a race-to-the-bottom in terms of social welfare provision. The tighter restrictions thereby imposed upon national budgets to meet economic parameters of entry into the EU have played an important role in conditioning programs that have attempted to improve the social protection system.

The need to bring together social intervention policies at the EU level is stressed by Bertola *et al.* (1999) who argue that 'the failure to provide guidance on the challenges facing social provision at the country level, in light of the removal of economic borders across the Union, exposes European policies to the twin risk of inertia on the one hand, and uncoordinated and unsustainable reforms on the other'.

In order to explore the possibility of a single European Constitution it is of great help to review the state of the art in the field of governance. Within the European countries, a double dichotomy result is pretty evident. At first glance, the Anglo-American corporate system seems to be characterized by dispersed ownership and by a market-based financial system. On the other hand, continental Europe is characterized by concentrated ownership and a bank-based financial system. These aspects are not disjoint, but they can be seen as two sides of the same coin. It is a mixture of economic, political and cultural factors that has been determining the current shape of the European corporate and financial system. Decisions that have once been made and pursued, have led to path-dependent developments and will not be easily overturned – as long as other new forces are not strong enough to bring about a change. Theories that attempt to explain the prevalence of one form of ownership structure in a given country are equally valid in explaining why that particular form of financial market prevailed.

Theories attempting to explain the lack of ownership diffusion in continental Europe can ideally be divided into two broad categories: technical and socio-political. The accounting system, institutional structure and differences in law protecting minority stockholdings, are the most popular technical explanations. In the second group we find the cultural and the social democracy theories. The theory based on the accounting system postulates that ownership does not diffuse where full disclosures are unavailable, since small investors are reluctant to invest in firms because these investors cannot be sure of the actual economic and financial situation.

Regulatory rule from another jurisdiction will not guarantee a similar outcome. Instead, the likely impact of a proposed rule must be examined in terms of the institutional context into which it is being placed.

In this context, it would be interesting to analyse the regulatory reform programmes covering telecommunications, energy (electricity and gas), transport (urban, air and rail) and water, fostered by the European Union since 2000. The extent to which network industries have already been liberalized in the Euro area differs significantly between the various sectors and countries. The telecommunications and electricity sectors are currently attracting the most attention, while the opening up of the gas sector only began very recently. From a theoretical point of view, the fundamental regulatory problem is the goal of stimulating private investment for public utility infrastructure. In particular, one of the possible interpretations of this problem is one that treats regulation as a contracting problem between government and the provider, for which the political and social institutions of a nation must provide sufficient credibility in order to mitigate the threat of expropriation and thereby encourage private investment.

The regulation problem can even be seen in the perspective of the interest group theory, employing a model in which two opposing interest groups seek to influence the decision of a standing regulation. In this way it is possible to examine the impact of exogenous changes in economic conditions and the effects of such changes on the marginal cost of exerting pressure for favourable regulatory decisions. Such policy changes may be spurred by shifting economic conditions. Interesting work in this sense has recently been done, for instance, by David Coen and Adrienne Heritier,[14] and Giandomenico Majone's work on regulatory and deregulatory policies in the EU.

However, recent events – the substantial failure of the so-called Lisbon Strategy, the vote in the European Parliament on the directive on services, the reticence of member States against liberalisation of services (especially the Suez–GdF case), not to mention the French and Dutch votes against the Constitutional treaty – clearly show how the future status of the European Union, therefore, continues to be the subject of political controversy, with widely differing views between Member States.

Major issues currently facing the European Union include, among others, the adoption, abandonment or adjustment of the Constitutional Treaty, the future budget and the Union's enlargement. The accession of Turkey is a major issue of contention among EU member states. Turkey's ambitions date back to the 1963 Ankara Agreements. Preliminary negotiations for membership between Turkey and the EU began on 3 October 2005. Since it has been granted official candidate status, Turkey has enacted many legal reforms to meet the EU's entry requirements. However, due to its religious and cultural differences, Turkey's membership of the EU faces strong opposition from governments of some Member States, which repudiate the possible economic, immigration and cultural implications that it may bring. Analysts believe 2015 is the earliest date the country can join the Union.

---

14 Coen, D. and Héritier, A. (Eds) (2005), *Refining Regulatory Regimes: Utilities in Europe* (Cheltenham: Edward Elgar).

As far as the budget is concerned, after the failure of the negotiations of the 16–17 June 2005 European Council in Brussels, where the EU member States' leaders failed to agree on the common budget,[15] the EU member States, at the December 2005 European Council, finally adopted a decision about the EU budget for the seven years 2007–2013. However, many commentators have envisaged that these debates will yield a major split between governments who call for a broader budget and a more federal union, and governments who demand a slimmer budget.

In short, tension continues to exist within the European Union between the supporters of the intergovernmental method on one side and of the Community method on the other.

---

15 The more controversial issues were the British rebate, negotiated by Margaret Thatcher in 1984, and France's benefits from the Common Agricultural Policy.

Chapter 2

Towards a European Constitution: Fiscal Federalism and the Allocation of Economic Competencies

Jürgen Stehn

The Problem

At its meeting in Laeken in December 2001, the European Council convened a convention on the future of the European Union. The task of the convention is to pave the way for the next Intergovernmental Conference as broadly and openly as possible. It will consider key issues affecting the Union's future development; for example, what do European citizens expect from the Union? How is the division of competencies between the Union and the member states to be organized? And, within the Union, how is the division of competencies between the institutions to be organized? This constitutional debate is timely, because more and more European citizens are looking with suspicion at the growing economic importance of EU institutions and, therefore, demand sound economic reasons for a further centralization of competencies.

The objective of this chapter is to provide an economic rationale for further discussions in the European Convention. The following section will build up a reference system – based on the theory of fiscal federalism – for an economically optimal allocation of competencies within a supranational body like the EU. On basis of the theoretical analysis, the third section proposes an allocation of economic competencies that can serve as an overall guideline for the discussion on establishing an European constitution. The fourth section draws conclusions.

Fiscal Federalism and the Optimal Degree of Economic Integration

The process of European integration has reached a formerly unknown speed. The completion of the Internal Market has led to mutual recognition or harmonization of divergent standards, norms, and regulations among EU member countries. Moreover, the treaty of Maastricht widened the competencies of the EU in various areas of economic policy. At the same time, the former EFTA-members Sweden, Finland, and Austria joined the European Union; the Central and Eastern European reform countries are determined to follow as soon as possible. Above all, the knocking-on-the-door of the young market-economies in Eastern Europe has raised the question of whether a widening of the integration area with countries that are lagging behind with regard to their economic development is in contradiction to a deepening of the European Union, especially with a view to the increasing centralization of economic competencies on the supranational level.

From a normative economic viewpoint, there is almost no contradiction between deepening and widening of an integration area. For economists, 'deepening' means – above all – the implementation of the 'four freedoms' in economic relations among member countries: the freedom of trade in goods, the freedom of trade in services as well as the free movement of capital and people across borders. Thus, a main instrument for the deepening of an integration area is the introduction of the country of origin principle.

An introduction of the country of origin principle in transborder trade between EU member countries means that all goods and services that are produced according to the norms, standards, and regulations of the exporting country can freely be shipped to any other member countries of the EU. The resulting competition of locations consequently leads to a gradual 'market-driven' harmonisation of differing norms, standards, and regulations between member states. In a similar vein, an introduction of the country of origin principle would result in a mutual recognition of workers' qualifications.

In addition, the deepening of integration goes hand in hand with a transfer of certain economic competencies from the national to the supranational level. It is important, however, that the resulting distribution of competencies is based on the strong economic principle of subsidiarity. The main message of this principle is that a transfer of competencies from a minor to a major political level always leads to a negligence of individual preferences. If all public services are supplied by a central government body, the level of supply always reflects a compromise between varying needs of different groups of consumers. Thus, as a consequence of a transfer of competencies in favour of the EU Commission, some groups of consumers become 'forced riders', i.e. they are forced to consume a higher quantity of public goods and services than they prefer, while other groups of consumers will suffer from welfare losses because of an undersupply with public goods and services.

A simple graph can illustrate the welfare losses due to a centralization of competencies (Figure 2.1). For simplification, this graph is based upon the assumption that a nation state can be divided in two regions. Within each region, consumers' preferences with respect to the supply of public goods and services are homogeneous. Thus, the curves D_1 and D_2 illustrate the demand for public goods in region 1 and 2, respectively. A central supply of public goods and services requires a political compromise between the demand of region 1, which amounts to x_1, and region 2, which is given by x_2. In the case that x_3 is the compromise solution, the triangle ABC indicates the welfare losses per head in region 1. In this region, consumers are forced to buy more public goods and services than they wish to. The welfare losses per head in region 2 are given by the triangle CDE that mirrors the decrease in consumer rents due to an undersupply with public goods. This part illustrates the well-known Oates effect (Oates, 1972).

In addition to the Oates effect, there is another effect that leads to additional welfare losses in the case of a centralisation of competencies. It can be realistically

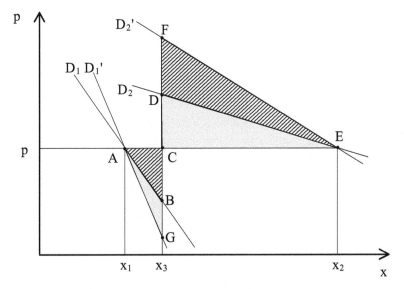

Figure 2.1   Welfare losses due to a centralisation of economic competencies

assumed that the elasticity of demand will decrease after a centralisation of competencies on a higher government entity, because the costs that consumers have to bear for gathering information on the true price (i.e. the tax burden) of a specific public good rise sharply if a central government entity takes over a huge bundle of different public tasks. This case is illustrated by the demand curves D'_1 and D'_2. The elasticity effect increases the welfare losses compared with the Oates effect on AGC in region 1 and CEF in region 2.

As a general rule, the strong economic principle of subsidiarity recommends that economic competencies should be transferred to the lowest possible government body. Only if a transfer of competencies to the supranational level leads to efficiency gains that exceed the welfare losses due to a centralization, should national and regional responsibility be replaced by supranational competencies (Figure 2.1).

Above all, a centralization of tasks within the EU promises to generate welfare gains if the public services and goods supplied by one member country have the characteristics of supranational (international) public goods or lead to positive or negative transborder externalities. In these cases, there would be no incentives for a sufficient decentralized supply. There are also sound economic reasons for a centralization of competencies if centralized production leads to economies of scale and the gains from scale economies compensate for the decrease of consumer rents due to a negligence of individual preferences.

In a similar vein, Alesina *et al.* (2001a, b) formally address the trade-off between the internalization of externalities and the costs of heterogeneity. In their models, unions like the EU are collectives of countries that decide together on the provision of certain supranational 'goods' affecting all members of the Union. 'Goods' in this context include traditional public goods (e.g. defence) as well as policies such as legal or regulatory frameworks. In a multi-country union, some competencies are subtracted from national control and allocated at the union level. If the latter centralizes too many competencies, several countries may not join because they are too distant from the 'median' union member, given that the chosen policy is close to the median preference. On the other hand, if the union centralizes too little, it does not fully benefit from economy of scales and from externalities, which motivate the creation of a union in the first place.

In other words, for a given distribution of preferences by potential union members and over a diverse range of policies, in equilibrium one should observe either small unions that centralize many competencies, or large unions in which few competencies are delegated above national governments. This trade-off is particularly important when the union is considering enlargement. According to this reasoning, enlargement of the union and a deepening of the coordination of policies are contradictory if the new members and the incumbents are heterogeneous. How the union would choose along this trade-off depends on the voting rules within the union.

This is why the discussion about what a union should do is deeply linked to the constitutional issues concerning 'who decides what and how'. Alesina *et al.* (2001c) discuss the possibility of a centralization bias in the unions. If the centralization of tasks in the union is not defined ex ante by constitutional design, the members close to the 'median' have an incentive to increase centralization and harmonization. Anticipating this tendency, potential members will stay out to begin with, leasing to unions that are 'too small'. A union where competencies are fixed ex ante leads to superior outcomes.

The Allocation of Economic Competencies in a European Constitution: Some Overall Guidelines

The process of European integration has gone hand in hand with a shift of economic competencies from the national to the supranational level since the ratification of the Treaty of Rome. Currently the following tasks are mainly allocated to the supranational level:

(1) the common trade policy vis-à-vis third countries and the liberalization of intra-community trade (trade policy);
(2) the supervision of cartels, mergers and acquisitions as well as sectoral and regional subsidies of the member states (competition policy);
(3) the allocation of regional subsidies to backward regions as a main task of the European Structural Funds (regional policy);
(4) the Common Agriculture Policy (CAP);
(5) the promotion of basic and applied research (research policy);
(6) the establishment of common norms for the protection of the environment (environmental policy).

It is obvious that the EU has taken over a broad range of responsibilities in economic policy that are by no means the result of ex ante considerations of the pros and cons of a centralization of economic competencies. Thus, in the course of a formulation of a

European Constitution, it is high time to base the allocation of economic competencies on sound economic theories such as the theory of fiscal federalism. What does this theory recommend with regard to the current supranational competencies of the EU?

Trade Policy

The economic theory of fiscal federalism only recommends a centralization of public tasks in the case of transborder externalities, supranational public goods or scale economies resulting from centralized production. From the perspective of traditional trade theories, trade policy that aims at opening up and liberalizing national markets is neither a supranational public good nor does it cause non-pecuniary transborder externalities because the advantages of a unilateral liberalization of market access can be fully internalized by the acting country. However, the actors in commercial policy obviously do not behave as welfare theory predicts. A striking example is the high subsidies to shrinking sectors in the member states of the EU. In many industries there is even a strong subsidy competition among member states, and some countries in the EU are seeking shelters from intra-community competition by extensively using the exemption rules of Art. 115 EC-Treaty which provide a significant leeway for protectionist purposes. Obviously, politicians in the member states are driven by a neo-mercantilistic perspective of transborder trade that views a liberalization of markets as causing costs rather than causing gains.

A positive explanation for this neo-mercantilist perspective is provided by the new economic theory of politics, which assumes that politicians – like other economic actors – are striving for the maximization of their own utility. From the perspective of individual utility maximization, it can be rational to erect trade barriers or grant subsidies in order to gain votes from influential interest groups. This is especially the case if the search costs that consumers and taxpayers have to bear during their attempt to get information about the effects of public protection measures are higher than the utility arising from additional information. Under these conditions, political decision-maker are more or less free to gain votes from influential interest groups without losing support from consumers and taxpayers.

To be sure, countries that make excessive use of subsidies and protection measures will generally lose international competitiveness in the medium term and politicians will be pushed back on to the liberalization path when a potential decrease of real income makes it profitable for consumers and taxpayers to bear the high information and lobbying costs. However, these market forces are more or less toothless if member countries build up a protection or subsidy cartel by harmonizing their defensive trade and competition strategies. In this case, only an outsider, who is ready to leave the cartel and to serve as some sort of 'lender of last market' by unilaterally liberalizing his/her own home markets, is in a position to break the cartel. However, such an outsider strategy bears high risks since the short time gains from liberalization are generally relatively low, whereas the material losses of interest groups induced by a liberalization of markets are relatively high in the short run. Thus, only countries that have a long tradition of successfully liberalizing markets and that are economically strong with regard to growth and innovation will take the risk to refrain from common protection strategies. For example, the US took over a leading role as an outsider in the multilateral trade negotiations within the GATT until the early 1980s. This was because the US were economically strong enough to keep special domestic interests under control and was, therefore, in a position to make the first step to a new round of worldwide negotiations by offering multilateral concessions that brought all parties back to the table.

Thus, if there is no member state within the EU that is willing to take the leading role in liberalizing markets, the utility maximization of national politicians results in strong negative transborder externalities. In this case, only binding supranational rules that prevent an EU-wide subsidy and protection cartel will bring a supranational community back on the liberalization path. Thus, it is not the opening of markets but the utility maximization of politicians that demands a centralization of trade policy competencies on the supranational level.

Competition Policy

With reference to the economic theory of fiscal federalism, there are sound reasons for a centralization of merger and cartel control at the supranational level. As a matter of fact, national merger and cartel authorities are only in a position to supervise national mergers and cartels, because they simply lack legal authority in third countries. Governments that are striving to attract additional firms from abroad are therefore tempted to loosen their competition rules in order to gain advantages in the international competition for footloose industries. Under these conditions, national competencies for merger and cartel control lead to strong negative transborder externalities. Thus, the formulation and enforcement of basic European guidelines for merger and cartel control is an important supranational task. National governments that aim at establishing stronger competition rules would be free to move ahead of the basic European guidelines.

With regard to the supervision of sectoral and regional subsidies, the reasoning is not as straightforward as with merger and cartel control. Since the main objective of subsidy supervision is to guarantee the functioning of the European Internal Market by preventing competition distortions, the arguments for and against a centralization of competencies in this field are similar to those presented with regard to trade policy. From the strong normative viewpoint of fiscal federalism, there is no reason for supranational competencies, because any single nation state would be better off if political decision-makers refrained from sectoral and regional subsidies that are not oriented at compensating market failure. However, as pointed out above, political actors obviously do not behave as welfare theory predicts. Thus, taking political economy effects into account, a supranational subsidy supervision would help to minimize negative transborder externalities stemming from the utility maximization of politicians.

However, this is not to say that the current subsidy supervision ('aid supervision', as the EU-Commission puts it) should stay unchanged.[1] The current supervision

---

1   See Stehn (2000) for an evaluation of multilateral regulation for the granting of subsidies.

system leaves a broad leeway for discretion by the EU-Commission, because it lacks binding, transparent, and enforceable rules for the granting of national subsidies. Any supranational subsidy scheme has to take into account that some public subsidies are granted to improve the efficiency of national economies by internalizing non-pecuniary externalities. There is no doubt that the funding of universities, public research institutes, and public infrastructure in a broad sense belongs to this group of subsidies. These activities should, therefore, be excluded from a supranational supervision system.

All subsidies that are categorized as non-efficient should be ranked according to their potential competition (trade) distortion effects. It can be realistically assumed that the competition effects of subsidies are the higher, the closer the respective subsidy base is to the end of the value-added chain of a firm. For example, an export subsidy, i.e. a subsidy for the sale of a product, might result in stronger competition effects than a subsidy to basic R&D. Hence, all non-efficient subsidies should be grouped in one of the following seven categories: (1) subsidies to basic R&D; (2) subsidies to applied R&D; (3) subsidies for the adaptation to new environmental standards; (4) investment subsidies (including regional subsidies); (5) production subsidies; (6) sales subsidies (export subsidies, import substitution subsidies); and, as a special case, (7) subsidies for promoting the general operation of firms or industries (subsidies covering the losses of firms, debt forgiveness, etc).

For each category, quantitative thresholds should be set that limit the provision of subsidies to a certain fraction of the respective subsidy base. The thresholds should roughly reflect the potential competition distortion effects of the different kinds of subsidies. One proposal would be to set thresholds of 30 percent for subsidies to basic R&D, 15 percent for subsidies to applied R&D, 10 percent for environmental subsidies, 10 and 5 percent for investment subsidies in backward and 'normal' regions respectively, 5 percent for production subsidies, and 0 percent for sale subsidies and subsidies promoting the general operation of firms. In order to prevent specific firms from gaining disproportionately from certain kinds of subsidies and to facilitate the calculation of the actual subsidization rates, the thresholds should be defined on a firm-specific basis.

Regional Policy

The regional policy of the EU is an integral part of the so-called EU Structural Funds. The main focus of the Funds is on the promotion of backward regions. Almost 70 percent of the total budget is granted for promoting the development and structural adjustment of backward regions, which are defined as regions with a per capita GDP of less than 75 percent of the EU average. Currently, eligible are – above all – the whole territory of Greece, Portugal, and Ireland, about 70 percent of the Spanish regions, the Mezzogiorno, the overseas departments of France, Corsica, Northern Ireland, and Eastern Germany.

From the normative perspective of fiscal federalism, there are almost no reasons for supranational competencies in the area of regional policy. Externalities arising from a subsidization of local enterprises and local infrastructure projects are generally confined to the subsidized region itself. At most, externalities may arise in

Table 2.1   Distribution of structural funds among EU Member States 1994–1999

	Per capita transfers (in €)	Share of GDP (%)
Austria	40	0.23
Belgium	31	0.17
Denmark	25	0.14
Finland	67	0.47
France	37	0.21
Germany	42	0.25
Greece	279	2.79
Ireland	334	2.60
Italy	60	0.37
Luxembourg	37	0.15
Netherlands	23	0.14
Portugal	298	2.73
Spain	171	1.39
Sweden	32	0.21
UK	29	0.19

Source: Stehn (2000).

neighbour regions and – therefore – can generally be internalized within the borders of member states. Only in the rare case of external spillovers between border regions do interregional externalities demand an intervention of more than one member state. However, such an intervention can be confined to the establishment of bilateral rules for the internalization of transborder externalities (the Coase Theorem) and does not necessarily imply an allocation of regional policy competencies to the supranational level.

To be sure, the EU regional policy has strong redistributive effects with regard to per capita income differences among member states. Table 2.1 indicates that per capita transfers out of the Structural Funds increase as per capita GDP declines. The same holds true for the share of transfers in national GDP. Thus, the Structural Funds do not only aim at promoting backward regions but also at redistributing funds from richer to poorer member states. With regard to the allocation of competencies, there is no doubt that a redistribution of funds among member states requires a supranational body that is responsible for the formulation and enforcement of the redistribution scheme. In the case of a decentralized redistribution scheme, member states would have an incentive to act as a free rider and would consequently produce negative external effects for member states acting according to the rules.

However, it makes little economic sense to base a supranational redistribution scheme on the promotion of backward regions, because decisions on the shaping of regional policies should be made by local authorities. Thus, an effective redistribution scheme should be based on unconditional transfers to poorer member states. Moreover, access to structural funds should be restricted to those member states with per capita GDP below the EU average. As a consequence, in an enlarged Union, only Ireland, Spain, Portugal, Greece, and the new Eastern European members would be eligible to redistributive transfers. The size of the transfers should vary according to per capita GDP and should decrease steadily in line with growing income level in these countries. In order to compensate partially for the lost access to the funds on the part of the richer member states, the total budget should be fixed at the current level so that national contributions to the EU budget can be reduced as the poorer member states catch up with their richer partners.

Common Agriculture Policy (CAP)

The objective of the Common Agricultural Policy (CAP) of the EU is to secure the income of European farmers by establishing a network of fixed, guaranteed producer prices for agricultural products, offering direct compensation payments to farmers and erecting high trade barriers for third country producers. From the normative perspective of fiscal federalism there is no reason for a centralization of agriculture support policy on the supranational level. If transborder externalities arose from a national subsidization of farmers, it would be sufficient to integrate agricultural subsidies into the general subsidy supervision of the EU (see above). Thus, responsibility for agriculture policy should be gradually shifted to the national level. A gradual reform strategy should at least include two key elements. First, CAP support prices must be reduced so that export subsidies – a necessary pre-condition for selling high-priced European products on world markets – can be eliminated. Second, direct compensation payments to farmers must be decoupled from production. Only by bringing down CAP support prices to the world market level can the requirement for export subsidies be eliminated. At the same time, it is the only policy that will allow Europe's farmers to participate in the future growth of world markets for agriculture products. As long as there is a requirement for export subsidies, the volume of European agricultural exports will be constrained by commitments to the World Trade Organization (WTO). Once export subsidies have been abolished, these commitments will no longer determine the volume of exports and, above all, Central and Eastern European producers will be in a position to become competitive suppliers on world markets. The requirement for decoupling compensation payments from production also increases with eastward enlargement. It is widely agreed that farmers in the accession countries should not receive such payments because they were not affected by reductions of CAP support prices, the original reason for the introduction of these payments. If, however, no compensation payments are made in one part of the enlarged EU, severe distortions of competition can only be avoided by a decoupling of these payments from production in other parts of the EU.

Research Policy

In the area of research and development policy, the transfer of well-defined competencies might be in accordance with the strong economic principle of subsidiarity that builds the cornerstone of the theory of fiscal federalism. As empirical research indicates, basic research and development, especially with respect to high-technology R&D, can be expected to generate considerable transborder spillover effects giving rise to an almost free dissemination of basic knowledge, because basic knowledge is hard to codify and thus cannot be patented. In this case, transborder externalities can lead to an underinvestment in basic research activities, which can only be prevented by a transfer of responsibilities from the national to the supranational level. However, in order to internalize transborder externalities it is sufficient to make the supranational level responsible for raising and allocating financial funds for research and development. Decisions on the special characteristics of research projects should be made on the national or regional level, because preferences might differ among member states or regions.

Moreover, there are complaints that some countries are hindering the free dissemination of basic R&D findings. Since basic knowledge is a prerequisite for successful applied research, this collusion behaviour might give the participating firms a competitive edge on future product markets. As a matter of fact, there is an obvious contradiction between the empirical finding that basic R&D generates transborder spillover effects and the proposition that some countries are hiding away basic research findings from competitors abroad. However, the general finding of an observable transborder dissemination of basic knowledge does not mean that a formation of successful research cartels is impossible at all. If cartels are in a position to bind their researchers to the cartel on cultural, moral, or contractual grounds, it may be possible to hinder the free dissemination of basic knowledge, at least for some time. Hence, there are some good reasons for a supranational subsidy supervision in the area of research and development policy.

However, there are no economic reasons for a supranational promotion of applied research, because gains from the invention of codifiable and tradable products and production processes can generally be internalized by the inventor.

Environmental Policy

There is no doubt that environmental pollution causes negative external effects; in the case of air and water pollution these external effects often even spill over national boarders. Thus, a centralization of environmental policy competencies in the area of transborder pollution is welfare enhancing. However, this does not hold for environmental pollutions that are confined to single regions or member states. In these cases, the externalities can be internalized on a regional or national level.

Moreover, most current environmental subsidies are granted to facilitate the adaptation of enterprises to new environmental standards that have been set by legal rules. In other words, governments are striving to lower the costs that enterprises have to bear due to the setting of new environmental standards. This is by no means an efficient policy, even from a purely domestic perspective, because it only aims at improving the competitiveness of domestic firms at the expense of competitors abroad. A first-best policy would be to define prices for environmental resources by taxing the source of environmental pollution. Thus, there are sound economic reasons for a supranational supervision of environmental subsidies that prevents an abuse of environmental policy for protectionist purposes.

Conclusions

In this paper, a theoretical reference system was developed that allows assessment of the effectiveness of EU policies with regard to an efficient allocation of economic competencies between the EU and the member states. The reference system is mainly based on the theory of fiscal federalism. Its main message is that a transfer of economic competencies from a minor to a major political level always leads to a negligence of individual preferences and, therefore, can only be economically justified if national policies lead to strong transborder externalities. It was demonstrated that the deepening of the integration process involves significant jurisdictional shifts from member states to the EU that are not justified on economic efficiency grounds. In many areas the strong economic principle of subsidiarity is violated by an increasing tendency of the EU to rely on market intervention. Thus, a European constitution should aim at strengthening the trade and competition policy as well as the subsidy supervision of the EU and at reducing direct market interventions resulting from active industrial policies.

References

Alesina, A., Angeloni, I. and Etro, F. (2001a) *The Political Economy of International Unions* (Cambridge: NBER Working Paper 8645).

Alesina, A., Angeloni, I. and Etro, F. (2001b) *Institutional Rules for Federations*. (Cambridge: NBER Working Paper 8646).

Alesina, A., Angeloni, I. and Schuknech, L. (2001c) *What Does the European Union Do?* (Cambridge: NBER Working Paper 8641).

Laaser, C.-F. and Stehn, J. (1996) Marktwirtschaft und Subsidiarität: Die föderative Arbeitsteilung auf dem Rrüfstand, *Zeitschrift für Wirtschaftspolitik*, 45, pp. 58–91.

Niskanen, K. (1971) *Bureaucracy and Representative Government* (New York: Aldine),

Oates, W. (1972) *Fiscal Federalism* (New York: Atherton).

Stehn, J. (2000) Economic Effects of EU-Enlargement, in: A. Bryson (ed.), *Enlargement of the European Union*, pp. 100–104 (Harcourt Brace Jovanovich).

Chapter 3

Maastricht's Fiscal Rules at Ten: An Assessment

Marco Buti and Gabriele Giudice

Introduction

The Maastricht Treaty is over ten years old. It was negotiated in 1990–91 and signed on 7 February 1992. Among the most relevant and best known provisions of the Treaty are the numerical criteria on budget deficit and debt for joining the euro area. These 3–60 percent targets were complemented in 1997 by the Stability and Growth Pact (SGP), which aims at making budgetary prudence a permanent feature of the new currency region.

The rationale of European Union (EU)'s fiscal rules can be found in the fiscal policy failures in Europe during the 1970s and 1980s (Buti, 2001): high and persistent budget deficits feeding a rising stock of public debt; a tendency to run a pro-cyclical policy which, instead of smoothing the business cycle, contributed to accentuating its swings; and finally, a high share of public sector in the economy going hand in hand with a rising tax burden, which hampered efficiency and job creation.

In the run up to EMU, the Maastricht-*cum*-SGP framework has been widely debated. Some, especially in the academic community, have pointed to its excessive rigidity: as euro area members lose national monetary independence, it may hamper cyclical stabilisation. On the opposite side of the spectrum, others have pointed to the weakness of sanctions in the event of budgetary misbehaviour, which may eventually undermine fiscal discipline and bring Europe back to its pre-Maastricht years.

While EMU is still in its infancy and some of its institutional features are not yet fully consolidated, a number of lessons can nonetheless be drawn on the design and implementation of its budgetary rules. The aim of this paper is to review EMU's fiscal policy framework with a view to identifying its strengths and weaknesses.

The paper is organised as follows. After a brief overview on the debate on fiscal rules, the third section focuses on the rules enshrined in the Maastricht Treaty. The fourth section assesses the budgetary consolidation in Europe during the 1990s in terms of both size and composition in order to ascertain the success of the Maastricht convergence process. The subsequent section reviews the main features of the SGP, by focusing on its preventive and dissuasive aspects. The economics of national fiscal policy under the Treaty and the SGP is analysed in the sixth section by means of a simple model of an optimising government subject to a deficit constraint. The seventh section attempts to identify the key determinants of the Maastricht 'success' and assesses the strengths and weaknesses of the SGP. The final section concludes.

Maastricht's Fiscal Rules

Why Fiscal Rules in EMU?

EMU was built on strong macroeconomic stability requirements. The Treaty of Maastricht contains a clear mandate for an independent monetary authority – the European Central Bank (ECB) – to preserve price stability. It also lays out specific rules ensuring budgetary prudence as a condition to join the euro-area.

In principle, fiscal rules can be justified either to internalise spillovers or by national interest. Both arguments played a role in the design of EMU's budgetary architecture.

The spillovers argument is particularly relevant in a currency area formed of independent countries. Spillovers occur either directly between fiscal authorities or indirectly via the impact of national fiscal policies on the single monetary authority.[1] The perception of a lower steepness of the interest rates schedule in EMU may lead to an overly expansionary fiscal policy and an excessive accumulation of public debt. While the commitment of the central bank to price stability is crucial in preventing such outcome, such commitment is itself a function of budgetary behaviour. The clearest (and somewhat extreme) example of such relationship is given by the so-called Fiscal Theory of the Price Level, which concludes that if the government solvency is not guaranteed then monetary authorities will not be able to control the price level. Hence, fiscal rules are needed to protect the 'functional' independence of the central bank.

Insulating the newly-created central bank from possible pressures of EMU's undisciplined members was a particular concern of traditionally fiscally prudent countries, especially Germany. The EMU framework was seen as a screening device to ensure that only countries with a sufficiently good track-record of fiscal discipline could enter EMU.

Rules justified by national interest are intended to tie governments' hands in a binding supra-national agreement. In such a case, budgetary rules help to counter the factors that have determined fiscal profligacy and resulted in a deficit bias in the domestic political game. This external constraint has been useful in the run-up to EMU. In spite of the favourable period of high growth enjoyed during second half of the 1980s, several EU member states were, in the early 1990s, still confronted with serious fiscal imbalances. Given the relentless increase in the stock of debt, the need to regain sustainable fiscal positions was increasingly recognised even in countries traditionally characterised by weak budgetary discipline. The argument of having to make painful budgetary retrenchments for the 'sake of Europe' was used to win the support of reluctant public opinions (McKinnon, 1997; Buti and Sapir, 1998).

---

1   For a review of the literature on the rationale for fiscal rules and interplay between monetary and fiscal authorities in a monetary union, see Beetsma (2001), Buti *et al.* (2001), Canzoneri and Diba (2001), and Dixit (2000).

In order to achieve and sustain fiscal prudence, two kinds of fiscal rules can be envisaged:[2]

(a) numerical targets, i.e. a constraint on domestic fiscal policy in terms of an indicator of the overall fiscal performance (spending, borrowing, debt);
(b) procedural reforms of budgetary institutions conducive to a responsible fiscal behaviour.

Numerical targets impose a permanent constraint on budgetary policy by establishing a requirement to meet specific targets or by imposing an upper ceiling on given budgetary variables. Their severity depends on the degree of coverage of the government sector, on the budgetary indicator chosen, and on the threshold being targeted. Rigid balanced-budget rules covering both the current and capital balances of general government are an example of highly binding rules, while contingent rules, allowing for tax-smoothing or with escape clauses, are less stringent. The downside of very tight rules is their lack of flexibility in the face of changing economic circumstances.

Procedural reforms impose changes on the procedures according to which government budgets are presented, adopted and executed. 'Hierarchical' procedures are more conducive to fiscal discipline than 'collegial' procedures. At the national level, hierarchical rules attribute strong power to the treasury minister to overrule spending ministers during the intra-governmental preparation of the budget and limit the ability of the parliament to amend the government's budget proposals. At supra-national level, such rules attribute the power to a supra-national body to assess and sanction the budgetary behaviour of national governments.

Numerical and procedural rules have proven effective to achieve and sustain fiscal discipline. Eichengreen (1993) finds that the statutory and constitutional deficit restrictions in US states exert a significant restraining influence on the budgetary behaviour of state governments, and that the more stringent the restrictions the more conducive they are towards the targeted position of a balanced budget. Looking at European experience, Von Hagen (1992) and von Hagen and Harden (1994) also provide empirical evidence which suggests that hierarchical rules helped to avoid excessive government spending and deficits.[3]

A drawback of numerical targets is the incentives they introduce for one-off or accounting measures in an attempt to satisfy the criteria at any cost. This entails a loss of information about the government's true budgetary situation and, as a result, negatively affects the credibility of the government's commitment to fiscal discipline. Empirical evidence for US states shows, however, that even though accounting devices make up a non-negligible part of the fiscal adjustment to numerical targets

---

2   For a discussion of the main characteristics as well as the advantages and disadvantages of numerical targets and procedural rules, see, for example, Alesina and Perotti (1996a, 1996b) Buti and Sapir (1998) and Corsetti and Roubini (1992).

3   The lower government deficits that follow from the imposition of numerical budget targets in US states are mainly obtained in the short run via lower levels of government spending, and not via increased taxation (Bayoumi and Eichengreen, 1995; Poterba, 1996). Over longer time horizons, however, both taxes and spending tend to adjust.

in the short run, they do not appear to be the primary source of deficit reduction in the longer run (Poterba, 1996). To prevent their circumvention and in order to reduce monitoring problems, these targets and, more broadly, the overall accounting framework, need to be simple and transparent.

The choice between numerical and procedural rules depends on several factors. Von Hagen and Harden (1994) find a clear correlation between the size of a country and the nature of its commitment to fiscal discipline: the larger EU member states, such as Germany and France, which were relatively successful in maintaining fiscal discipline during the 1980s relied on procedural rules, while the smaller countries opted for numerical targets.[4]

While numerical targets and procedural reforms are often seen as alternative options to guarantee budgetary prudence, they are not mutually exclusive in practice, and are frequently implemented in parallel. As we will see below, in the case in EMU, while numerical targets had a clear primacy, procedural rules were also called upon to ensure compliance with the budget constraints. An assessment of the characteristics of EMU's fiscal rules against ideal rules standards is provided in the seventh section.

Maastricht's Rules on Budget Deficit and Debt

The Treaty (Article 121) requires a high degree of sustainable convergence for admitting a Member State to monetary union. Compliance with such requirement is assessed by looking at the degree of price stability; the sustainability of the government financial position; the fluctuations in the exchange rate; and the durability of convergence reflected in the convergence of long-term interest rates.[5]

More specifically, concerning budgetary issues, the Treaty states that, once part of the monetary union, 'Member States shall avoid excessive government deficits' (Article 104). Compliance with budgetary discipline is assessed on the basis of two criteria. First, whether the government deficit is below the reference value of 3 percent of GDP, or, if not, whether 'the excess over the reference value is only exceptional and temporary and the ratio remains close to the reference value.'. As to the government debt, the second criterion, it should not exceed the reference value of 60 percent of GDP or, in case of a higher debt ratio, it should be on a decreasing trend and approach the reference value at a satisfactory pace. In addition to setting specific numerical ceilings for government deficit and debt levels, the Treaty rules out monetary financing and privileged access to credit by public authorities.

---

4   According to these authors, in view of their more complex administration and the heterogeneity of interests, the larger countries apparently need more flexible and discretionary rules, while the smaller countries find it easier to unite behind a single budgetary target. Thus, the main determining factor appears to be more the state organisation and institutional complexity of a country rather than simply its size.

5   It should be recalled here that these convergence criteria are still to be applied, as a condition of joining the euro-area, to the three countries that are currently members of the Union but which have not adopted the euro (Denmark, Sweden, the United Kingdom). They will also apply to accession countries.

In assessing the existence of an excessive deficit, the European Commission, which is entrusted with the task of budgetary surveillance in conjunction with the Council, should also take into account whether the government deficit exceeds public investment, and consider all other relevant factors including the medium-term economic and budgetary position of the country.

When a country is subject to a Council decision on the existence of an excessive deficit, a procedure aimed at correcting this situation is initiated. This procedure includes several steps designed to increase pressure on the Member State to take effective measures to curb the deficit. If such corrective measures are not implemented, sanctions may be applied to countries participating in the euro-area. Amongst the sanctions foreseen by the Treaty are non-interest bearing deposits and fines. The Treaty, however, leaves a certain discretion to the Council on the application and the content of these sanctions and does not set time limits on the various steps of the procedure.

Numerical targets have been complemented by a common accounting framework (ESA-95). By increasing the transparency and comparability of budget figures, accounting rules restrain the temptation of policy makers to obtain a strategic advantage by creating confusion concerning the government's underlying budgetary situation (Alesina and Perotti, 1996a, 1996b). They also increase the feasibility of expenditure control.

While the importance of effective national budgetary procedures is recognised in the Treaty, their design and application is left to the realm of subsidiarity. Article 3 of Protocol n. 5 on the Excessive Deficit Procedure specifies that 'Member States shall ensure that national procedures in the budgetary area enable them to meet their obligations in this area deriving from this Treaty'. In a number of countries, the combination of a harmonised accounting framework with the need to meet the numerical targets has led to significant reforms in domestic procedures conducive to budgetary discipline.[6]

Have the Maastricht Rules been Effective?

As referred to above, international experience shows that both numerical and procedural rules can be effective in curbing governments' bias towards deficits. Furthermore, we have argued that the sharp dichotomy between the two types of rules often found in the literature is somewhat misleading in the case of the Maastricht Treaty.

The bottom line of this debate, however, is the effectiveness of the Maastricht process in achieving and sustaining fiscal rectitude. The main questions therefore are: have the rules introduced by the Maastricht Treaty helped consolidate public finances? Have they allowed EU countries to escape from the trap of unsustainable deficits and growing debt in which they seemed to be stuck in the past two decades? Does the current budgetary consolidation represent a genuine regime-shift in running budgetary policy?

---

6   See European Commission (2001a), Fischer (2001) and Fischer and Giudice (2001).

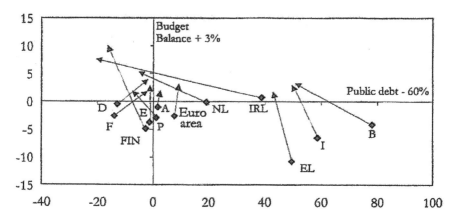

Figure 3.1   Public finance convergence in the euro area: 1993–2000

Note: Countries in the top left quadrant have a budget deficit below 3% of GDP and a public debt ratio below 60% of GDP. Belgium, Italy and Greece respect the debt criterion because their debt ratio, while being above the reference value, is considered to decrease at sufficient speed.
Source: Commission Services.

Size of the Budgetary Retrenchment

Undeniably, the imposition of the Maastricht budgetary targets set off a genuine consolidation process in euro-area member states. As can be seen in Figure 3.1, in practically all member states budget deficits declined substantially since 1993, the year that marked the entry into force of the Maastricht Treaty and in which the euro-area registered the historically high deficit ratio of 5.5 percent of GDP.[7] However, in some countries, public debt started to decrease only in the second half of the period – when primary surpluses became high enough to compensate the for snowball effect – and in Germany and France it actually increased, although starting from a level below the 60 percent of GDP reference value.

Faced with the need to put public finances on a sounder footing and, in some cases, to come to grips with a looming unsustainability problem, policy-makers enacted a strong adjustment as of 1993. Under pressure from the calendar for joining EMU, fiscal consolidation continued through 1996 and 1997 aided by lower interest rates thanks to reduced risk premia. Between 1993 and 1997, the actual deficit fell by 3.5 percentage points in the euro area, and was brought back below the 3 percent of GDP threshold in all Member States, except for Greece which did so in 1999. Since

---

7   In interpreting the graph, it has to be considered that, while for the majority of EU countries the chosen periods correspond to the start of large-scale budgetary consolidation, a number of countries (for example, Ireland) had carried out the bulk of the budgetary retrenchment during previous years, thereby enjoying the fruit of their efforts – in terms of a declining debt ratio – during the subsequent period. Therefore, in these countries, only relatively minor adjustments were required in the 1990s. See European Commission (2000).

then, deficits continued to fall towards balance at the end of the decade. However, the pace of consolidation has slowed down considerably and structural balances stopped improving as of 1999 in several Member States. Public debt also declined in most countries, but in some of them very slowly.

At national level, some spectacular turnarounds in fiscal performance occurred. Italy and Greece managed to reduce their budget deficits by 7 and 10 percentage points of GDP respectively, between 1993 and 2000. Finland quickly regained control of its public finances after the recession of the early 1990s. In contrast, countries such as Germany and France, traditional bastions of fiscal prudence, have struggled to keep control of budget deficits and debt, which were fuelled, respectively, by the costs of unification and subdued economic performance in the first part of the period.

In a recent study, von Hagen *et al.* (2001) examined whether this consolidation resulted from a specific Maastricht effect, i.e. whether the convergence process created its own political dynamic helping the governments achieve fiscal adjustments. Analysing the probabilities of starting fiscal consolidation, the authors find that most of the consolidations that began before 1995 in the euro area are not predicted by a model of budgetary behaviour estimated over past data. This suggests that the Maastricht process did create some political pressure of its own on the governments to undertake fiscal consolidations, and this pressure was effective mainly in the first half of the 1990s.

The sheer size of the budgetary adjustment may have induced favourable non-Keynesian effects in some countries, thereby helping to sustain the retrenchment efforts. As argued first by Giavazzi and Pagano (1990), there is a non-linearity between budgetary adjustment and economic activity: while, in the event of small cuts, traditional Keynesian effects dominate, confidence and crowding-in effects may help in offsetting the direct reduction in demand in response to larger adjustment packages.[8]

The fiscal retrenchment of the 1990s cannot be assessed without considering the broader picture of nominal convergence. This requires bringing monetary policy into the picture. As reported by the European Commission (2000), while basically cautious because of the need to bring down inflation, monetary policy on average played a supportive role in the public finance consolidation of the 1990s.[9] Monetary policy seems to have facilitated fiscal adjustment, although this was not true for all countries. In particular, this may not have been the case in countries combining strong consolidation needs on the fiscal side and high inflation, such as Italy (European Commission, 1999).

---

8 European Commission (1999) finds evidence of non-Keynesian effects in the case of Italy in the 1990's consolidation.

9 Evidence of a coordinated behaviour of monetary and fiscal authorities is also found in other studies. Wyplosz (1999) finds that the policy-mix in EU countries since 1980 has tended to be of the 'substitutability' type: fiscal relaxation is accompanied by monetary tightening and vice-versa. These results correspond closely to those obtained by Mélitz (1997, 2002).

Composition

The composition of budgetary consolidation appears to play an important role in determining its success. There is increasing evidence in the literature that deficit reductions that take place through expenditure cuts, rather than tax increases, have a much higher probability of reducing the stock of debt and permanently reduce the deficit.[10]

In order to capture, in a synthetic manner, the composition of the budgetary adjustment over the period 1993–2000, Figure 3.2 decomposes the discretionary policy changes for individual EU countries over the period 1993–2000 into changes in total revenue and in primary expenditure. The diagonal from top right to bottom left indicates the direction of the budgetary adjustment: the area above it marks a deterioration in the cyclically-adjusted primary balance, while the area indicates a structural consolidation. The diagonal from top left to bottom right marks the composition of the adjustment: the combinations where revenue changes or expenditure changes dominate are shown in the figure.

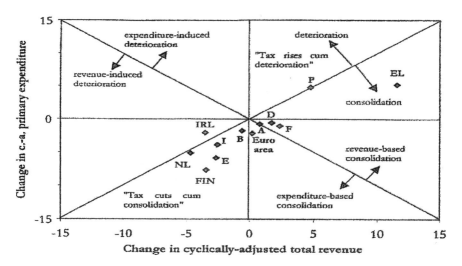

Figure 3.2 Composition of the fiscal adjustment, 1993–2000, in points of GDP

Source: Commission Services.

As shown in Figure 3.2, practically all countries lie below the top right–bottom left diagonal, meaning that their cyclically-adjusted primary balance improved during the period. As to composition, only Portugal and Greece – the two countries starting from a low level of total revenue – pursued a revenue-based retrenchment and several countries combined discretionary cuts in spending with a reduction in tax revenue, thus reducing the overall size of the public sector.

---

10 See, for example, Alesina and Perotti (1996a, 1996b), Perotti (1996, 1999).

In sum, one may conclude that the fiscal adjustment appeared to be of good quality. This conclusion is strengthened by the observation that, during the consolidation process, the composition of the adjustment tended to improve as, in a number of countries where initially the adjustment was revenue-based, it later became expenditure-based.[11]

Beyond Maastricht: the Stability and Growth Pact

While the Maastricht Treaty establishes the entry conditions for Member States to join the single currency, the SGP aims at making budgetary discipline a permanent feature of EMU. After the initial proposal by the German Government in November 1995, negotiations on the Pact were conducted during 1996 and the first half of 1997. The most difficult political issues were settled at the European Council in Dublin in December 1996 and the final package was adopted by the European Council in Amsterdam in June 1997.[12]

The SGP consists of a preventive arm, Regulation (EC) No 1466/97, which aims to strengthen the surveillance of budgetary positions and the surveillance and co-ordination of economic policies, and a dissuasive arm, Regulation (EC) No 1467/97, which aims to accelerate and clarify the excessive deficit procedure of the Treaty. It also includes a Resolution of the European Council of 17 June 1997, which issues firm political guidelines in order to implement the SGP in a strict and timely manner, spelling out the responsibilities of the institutional actors involved (the Council, the Commission and the Member States).[13]

Prevention

While the Treaty strongly emphasised the punishment in the case of failure to respect the criteria, the Pact elaborated mechanisms to prevent the occurrence of excessive deficits in order to avoid having to use such sanctions.

The most important innovation of the Pact is that it states that the medium-term budgetary position must be 'close to balance or in surplus': this would allow the full operation of automatic stabilisers in recessions without exceeding the 3 percent of GDP reference value for the deficit. This is an important novelty because it clearly establishes the 3 percent of GDP deficit not as a target, but as a ceiling.[14]

---

11 The European Commission (2000) suggests that a sort of switching strategy occurred in these countries. Von Hagen *et al.* (2001) conclude that this was not a deliberate strategy as countries were forced to move to an expenditure-based retrenchment by the failure to reduce substantially the fiscal imbalances in the early phase of revenue-based retrenchment.

12 For a historical perspective in the negotiations leading to the SGP, see Costello (2001) and Stark (2001).

13 For a detailed account of the legal aspects of the SGP, see Cabral (2001). For a thorough review of the debate on the SGP, see various chapters in Brunila *et al.* (2001).

14 Although the Treaty is clear in setting the 3 percent of GDP deficit as an upper threshold, before the Pact it was considered by most commentators as a target. Such interpretation is consistent with the observation that such value corresponded to the average level of public

To facilitate the monitoring of national budgetary developments and to make possible an early identification and assessment of risks, Member States having adopted the single currency submit 'stability programmes' while Member States not having adopted the single currency submit 'convergence programmes'. Programmes, which are made public, include the indication of the medium-term objective for the budgetary balance, the adjustment path and the budgetary and other economic policy measures to attain it. This information covers the current and preceding year and at least the following three years. In the latest updates, long-term sustainability issues are also covered. The Council is committed to carry out the examination and may deliver an opinion on the programmes and their updates – on a recommendation from the Commission – within at most two months of their submission.

These programmes represent the key element of the enhanced surveillance procedure introduced with the Pact (Fischer and Giudice, 2001). They provide a transparent frame of reference for fiscal monitoring at EU level – in the peer review setting of the ECOFIN Council – and as such allow for a consistent cross-country assessment of budgetary developments and policies. In this context, particular attention is given to possible 'significant divergences' of budgetary positions from the medium-term budgetary objectives. Should significant slippage from the targets set in the programmes be identified, the Council can issue an 'early warning' recommendation under Article 99(4) of the Treaty urging the Member State concerned to take adjustment measures. When monitoring the programmes, the Council should take into account the relevant cyclical and structural characteristics of the economy of each Member State.

Dissuasion

Regulation 1467/97 sets out the provisions to speed up and clarify the excessive deficit procedure of the Treaty, having as its objective to deter excessive general government deficits and, if they occur, to further their prompt correction. Above all, it specifies when a deficit above 3 percent of GDP is not considered excessive and the extent of the sanctions in case of persistent excessive deficits.

As recalled above, according to the Treaty, a deficit is excessive if it is higher than the reference value of 3 percent of GDP 'unless the excess over the reference value is only exceptional and temporary and the ratio remains close to the reference value.' The SGP clarifies the concepts of exceptional and temporary situations. The *exceptionality* clause can be called upon when the excess of the deficit over the reference value results from:

- An unusual event outside the control of the Member State in question and which has a major impact on the financial position of the general government.
- A severe economic downturn. As a rule, a downturn is considered exceptional only if there is an annual fall of real GDP of at least 2 percent. An annual fall of

---

investment over the previous two decades in the EU. It underlined also the internal consistency between the deficit and the debt reference values under the assumption of a 5 percent rate of growth of nominal GDP (see Gros and Thygesen, 1998).

GDP of less than 2 percent could nevertheless be considered exceptional in the light of further supporting evidence, such as the abruptness of the downturn or the accumulated loss of output relative to past trends. In its Resolution on the Pact, the European Council however agreed that, in any event, in evaluating whether the economic downturn is severe, the Member States will, as a rule, take an annual fall in real GDP of at least 0.75 percent as a reference point and that Member States committed themselves not to invoke the benefit of this clause unless they are in severe recession.

An excess of the deficit over 3 percent of GDP is considered *temporary* if budgetary forecasts as provided by the Commission indicate that the deficit will fall below the reference value following the end of the unusual event or the severe economic downturn. This means that this clause applies only insofar as the 'exceptional' conditions mentioned above persist.

The *closeness* to the 3 percent of GDP threshold has not been defined in the SGP, the reason being that, presumably, no Member State wanted to pre-judge at the time the level of the deficit that would be acceptable for qualifying for euro area membership.

Regulation 1467/97 also sets up a tight timetable for the Excessive Deficit Procedure so as to arrive at a speedy decision on the existence of an excessive deficit. Finally, the SGP spells out the type and scale of sanctions in the event of persistent excessive deficit of euro-area members.[15] So far, the implementation of the Pact has never arrived at the sanctions stage.

Combining Discipline and Flexibility: a Simple Model of National Fiscal Policy under the SGP

The SGP aims at maintaining fiscal discipline while creating the necessary room for manoeuvre to allow fiscal policy to pursue cyclical stabilisation – a role that has become more prominent as countries in EMU have lost national monetary independence. Indeed, some have interpreted the Pact as a commitment technology to free national fiscal policies from the burden of high deficits and debt which hampered their use for stabilisation purposes (Buti *et al.*, 1998).

We pointed out in the previous section that a novelty of the SGP is the introduction of an objective of medium-term budgetary position of 'close-to-balance or in surplus' which clearly establishes the 3 percent of GDP deficit not as a target but as a hard

---

15 In the first year of application of the sanctions, the country in question is required to make a non-interest bearing deposit composed of a fixed component equal to 0.2 percent of GDP and a variable component equal to one tenth of the difference between the deficit and the 3 percent of GDP reference value. A ceiling of 0.5 percent of GDP is set. The fixed component aims at providing an incentive not to incur an excessive deficit, while the variable component represents an incentive to limit the excess over the 3 percent of GDP threshold. In each subsequent year, until the excessive deficit decision is abrogated, only the variable component will be applied. As a rule, a deposit is to be converted into a fine after two years if the excessive deficit persists.

ceiling. In order to illustrate how fiscal policy can achieve these goals under the Pact, this section lays out a simple model of an economy where output is subject to transitory shocks and can deviate temporarily from a fixed potential level, and the government cares about both output and deficit stabilisation.[16]

Aggregate demand and supply respectively are written as follows:

$$y = \phi_1 d - \phi_2 (i - \pi^e) + \varepsilon \qquad (1)$$

$$\pi = \pi^e + \omega y \qquad (2)$$

where y is output, d is the budget deficit (percentage of GDP), i is the interest rate, π is inflation, π^e is expected inflation and ε is a transitory demand shock. The suffix 'e' indicates expected value. All variables are expressed as changes from baseline.

The budget deficit is split into a structural component, d_s, and a cyclical component that depends on y and a parameter α capturing the automatic stabilisers:

$$d = d_s - \alpha y \qquad (3)$$

We replace equation (3) in equation (1) to find:

$$y = \frac{1}{1 + \alpha \phi_1} \left[\phi_1 d_s - \phi_2 (i - \pi^e) + \varepsilon \right] \qquad (4)$$

The next step is to describe the policy behaviour. Since we are interested in fiscal policy, we choose the simplest possible behavioural rule for the central bank. It is assumed that monetary authorities set the interest rate so as to ensure price stability in the medium-run, i.e. in the absence of shocks. By setting $\varepsilon = 0$, under π^e, a level of output equal to potential (that is $y = 0$ in equation 2) is consistent with price stability. Hence, in equilibrium, the value of the interest rate is simply:

$$i = \frac{\phi_1}{\phi_2} d_s \qquad (5)$$

This implies that, in the medium-run, monetary policy will offset any effect of fiscal policy on output and prices via an appropriate level of the interest rate, but, in the short run, the central bank does not react to shocks. This may be rationalised by positing high interest rate smoothing by the central bank.

Our assumption on fiscal policy attempts to proxy the basic features of EMU's budgetary constraints on the behaviour of individual countries. It is assumed that the government cares about deficit as well as output stabilisation.[17] In order to examine the largest possible spectrum of policy options, we write a fairly general expression of the loss function of fiscal authorities:

---

16 For the sake of simplicity, foreign trade is disregarded. We also ignore supply shocks. The model is a modified version of that of by Buti *et al.* (2001) who analyse a more complex set of interactions between demand and supply, and monetary and fiscal behaviour.

17 In this simple framework, since we disregard supply shocks, stabilising output is tantamount to stabilising inflation. Hence adding an inflation term in the loss function would not change the results.

$$L = \frac{1}{2}\left[\bar{d}^2 + \lambda(y - y^*)^2\right] \tag{6}$$

where $\bar{d} = d_s - \eta \alpha y$ is the weighted average of structural and nominal deficit with the coefficient η varying between 0 (fiscal authorities focus on the structural deficit) and 1 (fiscal authorities care about nominal deficits). λ captures the relative preference for deficit and output stabilisation. If the government wants to stabilise output around its potential level, then $y^* = 0$. However, if for electoral or other political economy reasons, it attempts to push output beyond its potential, then $y^* = 0$.

This expression of the fiscal authorities' loss function allows us to rationalise, in a very simple setting, the current debate on fiscal behaviour in EMU. First of all, there is still a discussion in Europe of whether governments should be concerned with actual or structural (that is cyclically-adjusted) budget balances. The SGP states that the budgets should be close to balance or in surplus 'over the cycle'. This would imply considering the medium term budgetary targets in structural terms (hence in our model $\eta = 0$). However, given the legacy of the convergence process where it was necessary to satisfy the deficit criterion in actual terms, there may still be a tendency to focus on actual balances. This may be even more the case in the early years of EMU when the deficit may still be relatively close to the 3 percent of GDP ceiling. If so, η may be set at or close to 1.

Second, one can imagine different scenarios on the government's preference for output stabilisation. In what can be dubbed the 'true spirit' of the SGP, countries keep a structural budget position at around close to balance and simply let automatic stabilisers work freely.[18] In our model, this boils down to setting $\eta = \lambda = 0$. The economic philosophy behind this prescription is tax-smoothing (Barro, 1979). It also reflects a mistrust of fiscal fine tuning, a view that is largely consensual in the economic literature (European Commission, 2001a). Alternatively, one can envisage a more active government which, having lost national monetary independence, may feel that the shock-absorption ensured by automatic stabilisers is not sufficient. Then the weight of output in the loss function, λ, can be positive. Finally, as argued by Buti and Sapir (2002a), the SGP, by widening the budgetary room for manoeuvre, may also re-create the incentives for 'politically-motivated' fiscal policy. In this case, we would have $\lambda > 0$ and $y^* > 0$. By minimising equation (6) with respect to d_s after substituting from previous equations, we find:[19]

$$d_s = \frac{\lambda \phi_1}{1 + \alpha \phi_1(1-\eta)} y^* + \frac{\eta \alpha [1 + \alpha \phi_1(1-\eta)] - \lambda \phi_1}{[1 + \alpha \phi_1(1-\eta)]^2 + \lambda \phi_1^2} \varepsilon$$

18 Analyses show that the working of automatic stabilisers provide a cushion of some 20 to 30 percent in large euro-area countries in the event of demand shocks (European Commission, 2001a).

19 We assume that the operational variable of fiscal policy is the interest-inclusive structural deficit. Given our monetary rule (that keeps interest rates unchanged in the short run) choosing the primary balance would have not changed the qualitative conclusions.

Interestingly, as already shown in Buti *et al.* (2001), if the government attempts to push output beyond potential (i.e. $y^* > 0$), it ends up with a deficit bias in equilibrium (i.e. when $\varepsilon = 0$). Fiscal authorities stimulate the economy and will do so until a further increase in the deficit away from the preferred level will be too costly. However, in equilibrium they will always be frustrated as the output will be equal to potential. In addition, this will imply a sub-optimal policy-mix with higher interest rates and deficit levels.[20]

As expected, the larger the preference for output stabilisation (that is, the larger λ), the higher the deficit bias. On the contrary, larger automatic stabilisers imply a lower inflation bias. Less evidently, the larger a weight given to the stabilisation of actual deficit compared to the structural deficit (which implies a larger η), the larger the deficit bias. The reason for this result is that a government that cares mainly about the stabilisation of actual deficit is helped by the feedback effect arising from the automatic stabilisers which, following a fiscal stimulus, maintain the deficit closer to target. This effect provides a further incentive for the government to keep stimulating the economy and hence results, in equilibrium, into a larger deficit bias.

The degree of 'policy activism' of the government, which is captured by the coefficient of ε in equation (7), is influenced by the preference for output stabilisation, λ. As expected, under $\eta = 0$ and $\lambda = 0$, there is a counter-cyclical reaction to shocks that is larger the higher the preference for output stabilisation, λ. By contrast, $\eta > 0$ combined with a relatively low λ, gives rise to a pro-cyclical discretionary reaction to shocks.[21]

In order to obtain the degree of output stabilisation, we replace equation (7) into equation (4) and, taking into account equation (5), we obtain:

$$y = \frac{1 + \alpha\phi_1(1-\eta)}{\left[1 + \alpha\phi_1(1-\eta)\right]^2 + \lambda\phi_1^2} \varepsilon \qquad (8)$$

Under $\lambda = 0$, we find maximum stabilisation if $\eta = 0$, that is when the government keeps an unchanged structural balance and simply lets automatic stabilisers play freely. It is easy to show that for reasonable values of λ, the result that the highest stabilisation is attained when $\eta = 0$ is confirmed.[22]

---

20 This is the equivalent of the Barro–Gordon inflation bias in monetary policy (Barro and Gordon, 1983). In this model, the only way to have supply higher than potential is to generate an inflation surprise. While this is engineered by the central bank in the Barro–Gordon model, it is fiscal policy that does this in our model. However, while in Barro–Gordon it is inflation expectations that adjust upwards in equilibrium, in our model economic agents anticipate the reaction of the central bank, which will raise interest rates to bring inflation back under control. Hence, we do not end up with an inflation bias, but with both higher deficits and interest rates, a sub-optimal combination which in the long run will affect negatively the rate of potential growth.

21 Clearly, if $\eta=1$ and $\lambda=0$, a pro-cyclical response occurs systematically because the policy-maker that cares about stabilising the actual deficit, always compensates the cyclical effect of the shock. If $\eta=1$ but $\lambda>0$ we have a pro-cyclical policy if $\alpha/\phi_1 < \lambda$. It can be shown that, for most values of λ, this result still holds.

22 For instance, this holds if output and deficit stabilisation have the same weight in the government preferences (i.e. $\lambda=1$).

In order to withstand 'bad' shocks without exceeding a given deficit ceiling, the government has to select an appropriate baseline structural budget balance. This can be defined as follows:

$$\hat{d}_s \leq \hat{d} - d(\hat{\varepsilon}) \tag{9}$$

where d is the deficit ceiling and ε is a large, negative shock. Equation (9) indicates that if fiscal authorities set a budgetary objective equal to in 'normal' times, then, under the current structural features of the economy and policy preferences, only for negative shocks larger than $\hat{\varepsilon}$ will the deficit exceed its upper ceiling.[23]

By replacing equations (7) and (8) in equation (9), under the assumption of 'well behaved' government (i.e. $y^*=0$), we obtain:

$$\hat{d}_s \leq \hat{d} + \frac{\{\alpha[1+\alpha\phi_1(1-\eta)](1-\eta)+\lambda\phi_1\}\hat{\varepsilon}}{[1+\alpha\phi_1(1-\eta)]^2 + \lambda\phi_1^2} \tag{10}$$

It is easy to show that, under normal values of the parameters, a lower η implies a lower $\hat{d}_s$: since the government pays less attention to the actual balance and is ready to accept larger fluctuations in the deficit, a more ambitious target is required in normal times in order to respect the deficit ceiling during recessions. In addition a rise in the preference for output stabilisation, λ, entails larger fluctuations in the actual deficit, thereby entailing a lower $\hat{d}_s$. In other words, EMU countries with a preference for active fiscal management must create a larger safety margin under the deficit.

The impact of a rise in the size of automatic stabilisers α, depends on the value of η. Under $\eta = 0$, as the larger smoothing impact ensured by a higher α leads to a lower change in discretionary policy, the net effect is uncertain. Under $\eta = 1$, since the authorities do not distinguish between discretionary and cyclical changes in the budget, the value of η has no effect on the actual deficit and, hence, on .

The main results for output and deficit stabilisation in the event are depicted in Figure 3.3 which illustrates the case of a negative shock.

The upward sloping line illustrates the relationship between budget deficit and output in the demand function. In equilibrium, the system stands at the origin. A negative shock shifts that schedule downwards. If the government keeps the structural deficit unchanged and lets the automatic stabilisers work (which corresponds to , $\lambda=0$ $\lambda=\eta=0$ implying that the loss function is aligned onto the y-axis), the new equilibrium is point A on the y-axis. As shown in equation (4), the increase in the actual deficit provides a certain degree of cyclical smoothing. The new level of the actual deficit, d^A depends on α, which is the slope of the dotted line going through the origin.

---

23 Under the assumptions $\lambda=\eta=0$, $\hat{d}_s$ corresponds to the so-called 'minimal benchmarks'. These are budget balance positions that would allow us to accommodate 'normal' cyclical fluctuations without breaching the 3 percent ceiling. They are computed on the basis of the past business cycle experience of EU countries. For detailed explanation and a critical assessment, see European Commission (2000) and Artis and Buti (2000).

If the government has a preference for output stabilisation ($\lambda > 0$ but still $\eta = 0$), it will choose a point like C, which implies a larger output stabilisation (with output returning to E) and some deterioration in the structural deficit (now at d_s^C)

If, on the contrary, the government is mainly concerned with the stabilisation of the actual, rather than the structural, deficit, it may try to offset the impact of

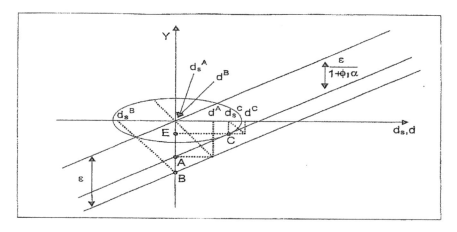

Figure 3.3   Stabilising output and deficit under different preferences

automatic stabilisers on the actual deficit. Point B in Figure 3.3 shows the limit case of perfect offsetting: here, the authorities enact a pro-cyclical fiscal tightening that compensates fully the effect of automatic stabilisers (d_s^B is reduced in order to keep d^B unchanged), thereby entailing a fall in output by the full extent of the shock ε (zero smoothing).

Given the simplicity of our analytical framework, these results should obviously not be overstated. Nevertheless, a powerful policy message underpinning the SGP framework, emerges from the above analysis: if fiscal authorities want to achieve high output stabilisation while maintaining fiscal discipline, they have to focus on structural rather than actual deficits and avoid using fiscal policy artificially to boost output beyond potential.

Maastricht Worked. Will the SGP?

We have shown that the Maastricht Treaty was successful in forcing countries to consolidate their public finances and that the SGP complemented the Treaty with new rules to ensure that fiscal discipline be maintained in EMU while creating room for the work of automatic stabilisers. We argued in the previous section that this is indeed a reachable objective if governments focus on the stabilisation of structural balances. However, while Maastricht has worked in the run up to EMU, the question is still whether the SGP will also work. In order to provide an answer, in this section we first look at how the EMU framework fares with respect to ideal rules standards, then at the political economy underpinning it. We will conclude with a discussion of a number of open issues that will need to be tackled to ensure the success of the Pact.

Maastricht and SGP: Rating against Desirable Rules Standards

Are the fiscal rules of EMU 'good' rules? Kopits and Symansky (1998) identify a number of desirable features against which the quality of fiscal rules should be assessed.[24] In Table 3.1 we provide a subjective judgement of the Maastricht convergence criteria and the SGP against the Kopits–Symansky *desiderata*.

The first column lists the ideal standards to be met by a fiscal rule and in the second and third column we separate between the Treaty provisions and the 'full' EMU rules made of the Treaty requirements and the SGP.

A *well-defined* fiscal rule is paramount to allow effective enforcement. The Treaty criteria is well-defined as to the indicators to be constrained and the institutional coverage. Additionally, the SGP specifies the escape clauses and the type of penalties to be applied in case of persistent excessive deficits. On *transparency*, the Treaty and the SGP obviously use the same accounting conventions, but the institutional

Table 3.1   EMU's fiscal rules against ideal rules standards

Ideal fiscal rule	Treaty	Treaty + SGP
Well-defined	++	+++
Transparent	++	+++
Simple	+++	++
Flexibility	++	++
Adequate relative to final goal	++	+++
Enforceable	+	++
Consistent with other policies	+	++
Underpinned by public finances reforms	+	++

arrangements of the SGP (especially its preventive harm) appear superior. Compared to the Treaty, *simplicity* has been reduced by the more developed mechanisms and procedures of the SGP. However, compared to other fiscal rules, those of EMU remain simple, even in the SGP version.[25] As to *flexibility*, while the main rules are unchanged, the SGP includes a tighter specification of the escape clauses, thereby reducing the discretion of the Council. At the same time, by putting more emphasis

---

24 See also Kopits (2001).

25 Actually, erring on the side of simplicity is typical of fiscal rules which are to be applied in a multi-country context and monitored centrally. For instance, as argued by Balassone and Franco (2001b), given the uncertainty on the definition of public investment and the related moral hazard problems, application of the 'golden rule' of deficit financing, which may be desirable at the national level, would have been highly problematic in the EU.

on medium-term targets and by highlighting the implications of cyclical fluctuations, it reduces the pro-cyclical bias inherent in nominal targets. As to *adequacy* vis-à-vis the final goal – i.e. avoiding excessive deficits, and ensuring an appropriate fiscal policy framework in EMU – complying with the close-to-balance rule and letting automatic stabilisers work is preferable to a simple deficit ceiling. The specification of the sanctions and the timetable of the Excessive Deficit Procedure are set to improve *enforceability*. The overall framework of the Pact also appears more suitable to ensure *consistency* of policies (e.g. by moving towards the integration of fiscal surveillance and broader economic policy coordination under the Broad Economic Policy Guidelines of article 99). Finally, given the increasing attention to composition and long term sustainability in the stability programmes, the implementation of the SGP is more likely to be underpinned by *tax and spending reforms* necessary to buttress fiscal prudence.

In sum, the SGP put flesh to the bones of the Treaty, leading to better rules and procedures, although at the cost of somewhat more complexity and lower flexibility. It remains, however, to be seen whether the SGP will prove as successful as Maastricht undoubtedly was. A political economy perspective helps elucidate this issue.

Maastricht versus SGP: the Political Economy of Fiscal Rules

As argued earlier, Maastricht set off a genuine budgetary retrenchment which brought back public finances in the EU from the brink of unsustainability to more manageable conditions. Although the fiscal adjustment cannot be attributed exclusively to the Maastricht rules, the latter undoubtedly played a major role in the fiscal turnaround in the 1990s and they came to be regarded as a binding constraint in the public opinion in many EU countries.

While a full interpretation of the success of Maastricht is beyond the scope of the present paper, a number of key factors that have characterised this process can be identified. In our view, the main ingredients of Maastricht's success were the following:

- *Public visibility*. The objective of meeting the Maastricht convergence criteria became the centrepiece of government strategies in many EU countries. Public visibility was greatly facilitated by the simplicity of the 3 percent of GDP deficit criterion which provided a clear signpost for economic policies regardless of the government political colour, especially in countries that entered the 1990s with very high deficits and looming unsustainability threats. High visibility, together with easy monitoring, was also one of the reasons for preferring numerical targets over national procedural rules.[26]
- *Clear structure of incentives*. Reward and penalty, linked with the Maastricht

---

26 This marks a difference between the fiscal and the monetary rules of the Treaty, because in the monetary domain, the mandate, institutional organisation and procedures of the European and national central banks are spelled out in detail. It thus appears that numerical targets have been preferred in the fiscal domain, while in the monetary domain procedural rules have been imposed (Eichengreen, 1996).

public finance requirements, were very clearly laid out. Politically, meeting the convergence criteria would allow budgetary laggards to join the virtuous countries in the new policy regime. Conversely, failing to comply with the Maastricht public finance criteria carried the penalty of exclusion from the euro area. This was considered too hard a political sanction especially for countries traditionally at the forefront of the process of European integration. Market incentives were also crucial, notably because countries with high deficits and debt levels adopting a credible adjustment programme could enjoy – at a less costly and more rapid pace – a reduction of risk-premium in interest rates, which would help lower public finance imbalances.

- *Political ownership.* The whole debate on fiscal requirements of EMU reflected Germany's concern with fiscal discipline: the public finance criteria of Maastricht, first, and the SGP, later, clearly bear Germany's fingerprints. The German priority of preserving price stability within overall macroeconomic stability led to the adoption of tight fiscal rules. Strong macroeconomic stability came to be regarded as an essential pre-condition for Germany to accept merging monetary sovereignty into a single currency.
- *Constraining calendar.* The Treaty sets very clear deadlines for moving to the final stage of EMU. Launching the single currency in 1997 required a majority of countries meeting the convergence criteria. In any event, whatever the number of participating countries, a single currency area would be established at the latest in 1999. Once the issue of postponement faded, countries willing to join with the first wave, had no choice but to make the required consolidation effort to meet the convergence requirements.
- *Effective monitoring.* The simplicity and the (largely) unambiguous definition of the fiscal requirements – especially that concerning the budget deficit – allowed an effective monitoring on the part of the European Commission, which played the role of an external agent commonly entrusted with the correct interpretation and implementation of the Treaty criteria.
- *Collegial culture.* The process of convergence allowed a collegial culture of stability and a confidence climate to be progressively built through personal contact amongst policy-makers and national and EU officials. This new climate facilitated peer pressure between national authorities and enhanced the role and authority of the European institutions.

If our interpretation of the political economy of Maastricht is correct, one may ask how the SGP fares in relation with the above factors: to what extent have the ingredients that determined Maastricht's success been transferred to the SGP?

The elements that come out clearly strengthened in the Pact are the monitoring of budgetary policies and the collegial culture within the multilateral surveillance of economic policies. As to the other factors, some have changed nature and others are clearly less prominent under the SGP. The political ownership of the SGP seems to be shifting towards smaller countries with structural surpluses which, although numerous, have a relatively small weight in the euro area. Relative to a simple deficit ceiling, the close-to-balance rule enjoys lower political visibility. Similarly, and probably more importantly, the structure of incentives has changed with the move to a single currency: the market incentives have been reduced with the convergence of interest rates and the carrot of entry has been eaten while the stick of exclusion has been replaced by the threat of uncertain and delayed pecuniary sanctions.

While the jury is still out on the effectiveness of the Pact in securing fiscal discipline in EMU, the gloomy predictions that the consolidation of the 1990s was simply an opportunistic move to be admitted to the euro club have not materialised. The challenge for the SGP now is to govern fiscal policy in a currency union – necessarily a complex task in a regime of decentralised fiscal responsibility. The outcome will depend on how a number of open issues in the implementation of the Pact will be tackled.

Open Issues in the Implementation of the SGP

The experience of the early years of EMU points to a number of issues that will need to be addressed to enhance the effectiveness of the current set of rules.[27]

First, a major issue is related to the definition of a medium term position of 'close to balance or in surplus'. According to the logic of the Pact, this should be interpreted in cyclically-adjusted terms. As we argued before, this would provide a higher degree of output stabilisation while safeguarding the 3 percent of GDP deficit ceiling. However, focusing primarily on structural balances is difficult because measures of underlying budgetary positions depend on the method used in estimating budgetary elasticities to the cycle and, especially, output gaps. Since the calculations are model-dependent, it may be politically difficult to point the finger at a country on this basis (Ross and Ubide, 2001). A key step in overcoming these difficulties lies in the agreement between the SGP actors on a common methodology for calculating output gap and structural balances.[28]

Second, a criticism frequently levied against the SGP is its *asymmetric working*: while an excess over the 3 percent of GDP deficit ceiling is sanctioned, there is no apparent reward for appropriate budgetary behaviour in good times. In other words, as pointed out by Bean (1998) the Pact is 'all sticks and no carrots'. The asymmetric nature of the SGP was apparent in 2000 when the buoyant economic conditions were not exploited to accelerate the fiscal consolidation, especially in Germany, France and Italy, which actually fell short of the planned fiscal efforts (Buti and Sapir, 2002a). A proposal that could be explored in this context is that of giving the possibility to euro area members of establishing, on a voluntary basis, buffer funds (as in some US States and Canadian provinces) which would be used in times of recession and replenished in upturns. The setting up of these funds is currently discouraged by the accounting rules (ESA 95) which imply that any transfer to the fund would not reduce the surplus in good times but lead to a higher deficit in bad times. According to these proposals, a more flexible interpretation of national accounts should ensure

---

27 The discussion in this section is based on Buti and Martinot (2000), Fischer and Giudice (2001) and Brunila *et al.* (2001). See also the chapters on fiscal policy in Buti *et al.* (2002a) and Buti and Sapir (2002b).

28 Major progress has been accomplished in such a direction during the course of 2001 and 2002.

that a transfer of resources to the fund reduces the surplus and withdrawals from the fund are deficit-neutral. This would provide a clear incentive for governments not to 'waste' the surpluses in good times while increasing the room for manoeuvre in bad times (the safety margin between close-to-balance and 3 percent ceiling plus the resources drawn from the fund).

Third, if countries abide by the SGP's fiscal philosophy, they will choose a broadly balanced budget in structural terms and let automatic stabilisers play freely over the cycle. Given the heterogeneous features of tax and welfare systems in the euro-area, countries will extract *different degrees of cyclical stabilisation.*[29] While a different size of automatic stabilisers may reflect heterogeneous social preferences on stabilisation in relation to other policy objectives, that degree of stabilisation may be considered too low in some countries given the loss of monetary independence. In order to attain an adequate degree of stabilisation, alternative options include a more active use of discretionary fiscal policy or public finance reforms that aim at increasing the smoothing power of automatic stabilisers. In both cases, a possible trade-off between stabilisation and efficiency arises.[30] It remains to be seen how the current framework of the SGP would accommodate such developments. Recently, a number of authors (Wren-Lewis, 2000, 2002, and Wyplosz, 2001), proposed to 'externalise' the discretionary stabilisation function by separating it from the allocation and redistribution functions. Responsibility of implementing temporary changes in key tax rates falls to a committee of independent experts similar in spirit to institutions in the monetary area (such as the Monetary Policy Committee of the Bank of England). According to the proponents, this would avoid some of the typical pitfalls of active fiscal management, namely the implementation lags and the irreversibility of fiscal measures.[31] It goes without saying that such a proposal – while intellectually seductive – would have major institutional implications for domestic budgetary arrangements. In any event, unless the current accounting rules are reformed, the room for manoeuvre for the discretionary stimulus would have to be created in order not to breach the 3 percent of GDP deficit ceiling when an active fiscal policy is enacted on top of the automatic stabilisers. For a number of countries, this would imply going beyond the close-to-balance rule of the Pact.

Fourth, the Treaty and the Pact leave to the Member States the internal organisation for the respect of the targets.[32] However, the financial relevance of

---

29 See European Commission (2001a) and Brunila, Buti and in't Veld (2002) for simulations of the smoothing effectiveness of automatic stabilisers with the Commission model QUEST and comparisons with similar exercises in the recent literature.

30 For an extension of the model in section 5 to encompass the choice of an optimum *a* under $\eta=0$, see Brunila *et al.* (2002). In a similar setting, Buti *et al.* (2002) show that the trade-off between stabilisation and efficiency may be more apparent than real in countries characterised by high and distortionary taxes, which affect the elasticity of output supply.

31 A milder version of this proposal has been retained by the report of the Swedish Committee on stabilisation policy in case Sweden joins the EMU.

32 The Maastricht Treaty (in art. 3 of the Protocol on the Excessive Deficit Procedure) includes a specific provision requiring the governments of Member States to ensure that their national budgetary procedures and institutions enable them to fulfil their obligation to maintain sound and sustainable public finances.

regional governments and other sub-sectors of the government in the budget process in federal states (Germany, Spain, Belgium, Austria) and strongly regionalised states (Italy) has highlighted the necessity for Member States to find solutions to secure sustained discipline at all levels of government (Fischer and Giudice, 2001). To solve this co-ordination problem, several Member States have already adopted special arrangements among government levels. The most evident example, as it is directly linked to the SGP process, is the introduction of *internal stability pacts* by several Member States. A common characteristic of these pacts is the effort to clarify and share the responsibility for budget discipline among the different levels of government.[33] However, the jury is still out on the effectiveness and sustainability of these new institutional arrangements.

Finally, while the Pact has focused so far mainly on creating a sufficient safety margin under the 3 percent of GDP deficit ceiling, *other priorities* are coming to the fore. Incorporating long-run sustainability concerns, especially in view of the expected budgetary implications of ageing populations, and improving the quality of public finances (reducing the tax burden, restructuring public spending) will be the next frontier in the implementation of the SGP. Kopits (1997) remarked that mere respect of the Maastricht guidelines did not necessarily ensure the long run sustainability of pension systems. A specific concern has been raised in relation to the close-to-balance rule: on the one hand, maintaining a broadly balanced budget may deter the adoption of fundamental pension reforms (such as a greater role of funding) which enhance discipline in the longer run, but are costly in the short run; on the other hand, there are good arguments to move into surplus in the coming years so as to have more room for manoeuvre to accommodate the budgetary impact of ageing (see Buti and Martinot, 2000). As for composition, it is important to make sure that the balanced budget requirement does not result in a sub-optimal level of public investment which may be unduly squeezed under the current rules.[34] This question is crucial, especially in the perspective of enlargement of the EU, since the new members – most of which are still in a catching up phase – will have public investment needs difficult to square with the close-to-balance rule of the Pact.

Conclusions

This paper has analysed the design and rationale of EMU's fiscal rules, their implementation over the last ten years and likely future success. Our main conclusions are the following.

(a) While a stark opposition between numerical and procedural rules is unwarranted, numerical targets appear more adequate to jump-start the

---

33 See Balassone and Franco (2001a) and Balassone *et al.* (2002).

34 Balassone and Franco (2001b, p. 376) notice that 'the problems involved in the transition from deficit to tax financing of public investment are similar to those involved in the transition from pay-as-you-go to a funded pension scheme. In both cases the burden on current generations depends on the speed of transition and the stock of debt.'

process of budgetary retrenchment.

(b) The Maastricht convergence criteria allowed one to achieve a genuine budgetary consolidation which, given its size and composition, is unlikely to be reversed in future years.

(c) A number of political economy ingredients (public visibility, clear incentive structure, political ownership, constraining calendar, central monitoring, collegial culture) have played a key role in the Maastricht success.

(d) Several open issues need to be addressed if the Pact is to become an effective framework for conducting fiscal policy in EMU: correct its asymmetric working, better define the medium term targets; foster coherent institutional reforms at the national level; factor in quality and sustainability of public finances in the multilateral surveillance.

References

Alesina, A. and Perotti, R. (1996a) *Budget Deficits and Budget Institutions* (IMF Working Paper, 52).

Alesina, A. and Perotti, R. (1996b) Fiscal discipline and the budget process, in: *American Economic Review*, (AEA Papers and Proceedings), 86: 401–407.

Artis, M.J. and Buti, M. (2000) 'Close to balance or in surplus' – a policy maker's guide to the implementation of the stability and growth pact, *Journal of Common Market Studies*, 38(4): 563–92.

Balassone, F. and Franco, D. (2001a) Fiscal federalism and the stability and growth pact: a difficult union, in *Fiscal Rules* (Banca d'Italia workshop on public finance).

Balassone, F. and Franco, D. (2001b) The SGP and the 'Golden Rule', in: A. Brunila, M. Buti and D. Franco (Eds) *The Stability and Growth Pact – The Architecture of Fiscal Policy in EMU* (Basingstoke, UK: Palgrave).

Balassone, F., Franco, D. and Zotteri, S. (2002) Fiscal Rules for sub-national governments: what lessons from EMU countries. Conference on *Rules-Based Macroeconomic Policies in Emerging Market Economies*, Oaxaca, Mexico, February (World Bank and IMF).

Barro, R.J. (1979) On the determination of public debt, *Journal of Political Economy*, 87: 940–71.

Barro, R.J. and Gordon, D.B. (1983) Rules, discretion and reputation in a model of monetary policy, *Journal of Monetary Economics*, 12: 101–121.

Bayoumi, T. and Eichengreen, B. (1995) Restraining yourself: the implications of fiscal rules for economic stabilisation, *IMF Staff Papers*, 42: 32–48.

Bean, C.R. (1998) Discussion, *Economic Policy*, 26: 104–107.

Beetsma, R. (2001) *Does EMU Need a Stability Pact?* In: A. Brunila, M. Buti and D. Franco (Eds) *The Stability and Growth Pact – The Architecture of Fiscal Policy in EMU* (Basingstoke, UK: Palgrave).

Brunila, A., Buti, M. and Franco, D. (Eds) (2001) *The Stability and Growth Pact – The Architecture of Fiscal Policy in EMU* (Basingstoke, UK: Palgrave).

Brunila, A., Buti, M. and in't Veld, J. (2002) *Cyclical Stabilisation under the Stability and Growth Path: How Effective Are Automatic Stabilisers?* (Banca d'Italia workshop on public finance, March).

Buti, M. (2001) The stability and growth pact three years on: an assessment, in: *Fiscal Policy in EMU* (Stockholm: Seminar, May).

Buti, M. and Giudice, G. (2002) EMU's fiscal rules: what can and cannot be exported, in: IMF, World Bank Conference, *Rules-Based Macroeconomic Policies in Emerging Market Economies*, Oaxaca, Mexico, February 14–16.

Buti, M. and Martinot, B. (2000) Open issues in the implementation of the stability and growth pact, *National Institute Economic Review*, 174: 92–104.

Buti, M. and Sapir, A. (Eds) (1998) *Economic Policy in EMU – A Study by the European Commission Services* (Oxford: University Press).

Buti, M. and Sapir, A. (2002a) EMU in the early years: differences and credibility, in: M. Buti and A. Sapir (Eds) *EMU and Economic Policy in Europe – Challenges of the Early Years* (Edward Elgar).

Buti, M. and Sapir, A. (Eds) (2002b) *EMU and Economic Policy in Europe – Challenges of the Early Years* (Edward Elgar).

Buti, M., Franco, D. and Ongena, H. (1998) Fiscal discipline and flexibility in EMU: the implementation of the stability and growth pact, *Oxford Review of Economic Policy*, 14(3): 81–97.

Buti, M., Roeger, W. and in't Veld, J. (2001) Stabilising output and inflation: policy conflicts and coordination under a stability pact, *Journal of Common Market Studies*, 39: 801–28.

Buti, M., von Hagen, J. and Martinez-Mongay, C. (Eds) (2002a) *The Behaviour of Fiscal Authorities – Stabilisation, Growth and Institutions* (Palgrave).

Buti, M., Martinez-Mongay, C., van den Noord, P. and Sekkat, K. (2002b) Automatic stabilisers and market flexibility in EMU: is there a trade-off? In *The Interactions between Fiscal and Monetary Policies in EMU*, (Brussels: European Commission, 8 March).

Cabral, A.J. (2001) Main aspects of the working of the SGP, in: A. Brunila, M. Buti and D. Franco (Eds) *The Stability and Growth Pact – The Architecture of Fiscal Policy in EMU* (Basingstoke, UK: Palgrave).

Canzoneri, M.B. and Diba, B.T. (2001) The stability and growth pact: a delicate balance or an albatross? In: A. Brunila, M. Buti and D. Franco (Eds) *The Stability and Growth Pact – The Architecture of Fiscal Policy in EMU* (Basingstoke, UK: Palgrave).

Corsetti, G. and Roubini, N. (1992) *Tax Smoothing Discretion versus Balanced Budget Rules in the Presence of Politically Motivated Fiscal Deficits: The Design of Optimal Fiscal Rules for Europe after 1992* (CEPR Discussion Paper, 682).

Costello, D. (2001) The SGP: how did we get there? In: A. Brunila, M. Buti and D. Franco (Eds) (2001) *The Stability and Growth Pact – The Architecture of Fiscal Policy in EMU* (Basingstoke, UK: Palgrave).

Dixit, A. (2000) *Games of Monetary and Fiscal Interactions in the EMU* (Working Paper, Princeton, August).

Eichengreen, B. (1993) Fiscal policy and EMU, in: B. Eichengreen and J. Frieden (Eds) *The Political Economy of European Monetary Integration* (Colorado: Westview Press).

Eichengreen, B. (1996) Saving Europe's automatic stabilisers, *National Institute Economic Review*, 159: 92–98.

European Commission (1999) Italy's slow growth in the 1990s: facts, explanations and prospects, *European Economy, Reports and Studies*, 5.

European Commission (2000) Public finances in EMU – 2000, *European Economy, Reports and Studies*, 3.

European Commission (2001a) Public finances in EMU – 2001, *European Economy, Reports and Studies*, 3.

European Commission (2001b) Autumn 2001 forecasts, *European Economy, Supplement A*, 10.

European Commission (2002) Evaluation of the 2001 pre-accession economic programmes of candidates countries, *European Economy, Enlargement, Papers*, 7.

Fischer, J. (2001) National and EU budgetary rules and procedures: an evolving interaction, *Fiscal Rules* (Banca d'Italia workshop on public finance, 1–3 February).

Fischer, J. and Giudice, G. (2001) The stability and convergence programmes, in: A. Brunila, M. Buti and D. Franco (Eds) *The Stability and Growth Pact – The Architecture of Fiscal Policy in EMU* (Basingstoke, UK: Palgrave).

Giavazzi, F. and Pagano, M. (1990) Can severe fiscal adjustment be expansionary? In: *NBER Macroeconomics Annuals* (Cambridge: MIT Press).

Gros, D. and Thygesen, N. (1998) *European Monetary Integration* (Longman: Harlow).

Kopits, G. (1997) Are social security finances compatible with EMU? In: *Financial Crisis: A Never-Ending Story*, pp. 35–45 (Vienna: Osterreichische Nationalbank).

Kopits, G. (2001) *Fiscal Rules: Useful Policy Framework or Unnecessary Ornament?* (IMF Working Paper, 145).

Kopits, G. and Symansky, S. (1998) *Fiscal Policy Rules* (IMF, Paper, 162).

McKinnon, R.I. (1997) EMU as a device for collective fiscal retrenchment, in: *American Economic Review* (AEA Papers), 87: 211–13.

Mélitz, J. (1997) *Some Cross-country Evidence about Debt, Deficits, and the Behaviour of Monetary and Fiscal Authorities* (CEPR, Paper, 1653).

Mélitz, J. (2002) Some cross-country evidence about fiscal policy behaviour and consequences for EMU, in: M. Buti, M., J. von Hagen and C. Martinez-Mongay (Eds) *The Behaviour of Fiscal Authorities – Stabilisation, Growth and Institutions* (Palgrave).

Perotti, R. (1996) Fiscal consolidation in Europe: composition matters, *American Economic Review* (AEA Papers), 86: 105–110.

Perotti, R. (1999) Fiscal policy in good times and bad, *Quarterly Journal of Economics*, 114: 1399–436.

Poterba, J.M. (1996) Budget institutions and fiscal policy in the U.S. States, *American Economic Review* (AEA Papers), 86: 395–400.

Ross, K. and A. Ubide A. (2001) *Mind the Gap: What is the Best Measure of Slack in the Euro Area* (IMF, Working Paper 203).

Stark, J. (2001) Genesis of a pact, in: A. Brunila, M. Buti and D. Franco (Eds) *The Stability and Growth Pact – The Architecture of Fiscal Policy in EMU* (Basingstoke, UK: Palgrave).

von Hagen, J. (1992) Budgeting procedures and fiscal performance in the EC, *European Economy* (Papers), 96.

von Hagen, J. and Harden, I. (1994) National budget processes and fiscal performance, *European Economy, Reports and Studies*, 3: 311–418.

von Hagen, J., Hallett, H.A. and Strauch, R. (2001) Budgetary consolidation in EMU, *European Economy* (Papers), 148.

Wren-Lewis, S. (2000) The limits to discretionary fiscal stabilisation policy, *Oxford Review of Economic Policy*, 16: 92–105.

Wren-Lewis, S. (2002) Fiscal policy, inflation and stabilisation in EMU, in: Workshop *The Interactions between Fiscal and Monetary Policies in EMU*, Bruxelles, 8 March.

Wyplosz, C. (1999) *Economic Policy Coordination in EMU: Strategies and Institutions* (ZEI, Policy Paper, B11).

Wyplosz, C. (2001) *Fiscal Policy: Institutions vs. Rules*, Report Swedish Government's Committee on Stabilisation Policy in EMU (December).

Chapter 4

Productive Efficiency and Corporatist Institutions

Ernesto Felli and Fabio Padovano

Introduction

The economic performance of the OECD countries varied substantially over the 1970s, the 1980s and the first half of the 1990s, both in the performance's time series and the cross-sectional dimension. Considering unemployment and total factor productivity in the industrial sector, the variation in countries' performances has been much greater since the first oil price shock in 1973 than before (OECD, 1997). The traditional explanations based on business cycle models seem insufficient to explain such a variation. A strand of literature has developed that seeks to investigate whether differences in institutional settings account for the causes of inter- and within-country variation in economic performance. In particular, much interest has focused on the potential importance of collective wage bargaining systems.

The literature distinguishes four levels at which wage bargaining may take place, each denoting a higher degree of market power in the labor market:

- *Firm level*: firms and employees negotiate over wages and working conditions at the level of the individual enterprise;
- *Industry level*: the confederation of employers of that industry bargain with the unions of that sector or of the crafts employed in that sector;
- *Economy level*: national unions and employers' associations negotiate for the whole economy;
- *National level*: negotiations between national unions and confederations of industries are 'coordinated' by the government, which enters as a third party in the process. The latter type of governance has often been referred to as 'corporatist' (Tarantelli, 1986; Calmfors, 1993).

OECD countries occupy quite different positions on this scale. For example, the Nordic countries have traditionally been characterized by centralized bargaining systems, whereas the United States and Canada stand at the more decentralized extreme. In between, there are countries such as Belgium, Germany and the Netherlands characterized by intermediate bargaining systems. Furthermore, the 1990s especially have seen countries changing their wage setting systems, be it centralized or decentralized, for essentially the same reason, namely, to increase the productive efficiency of the economy (Pekkarinen *et al.*, 1992). Examples of 'corporatism' – i.e. centralization of wage bargaining, long believed to be highly successful – such as Sweden (Marshall, 1996) and Australia (Dowrick, 1993), collapsed for allegedly having reduced productivity growth. At the same time, countries that built their postwar development on decentralized bargaining, like Italy, drifted increasingly towards corporatism to deal with structural problems of the economy that were inhibiting its further expansion (Bonatti, 1994; Ciampi, 1996), such as distortive wage indexation, generous pension systems and the like.

Hypotheses about the possible impact of institutional arrangements on labor market performance may be described by two extremes. On one hand, the 'eurosclerosis' view implies that non-market institutions and regulations are rigidities that hurt economic performance.[1] On the other hand, the 'corporatist' view argues that institutional arrangements exist to overcome various market failures and may therefore improve economic performance. Both hypotheses assume a linear relationship between economic performance and the degree of centralization of the wage setting system. This viewpoint was challenged first by Calmfors and Driffill (1988) and then by Dowrick and Spencer (1994), Alesina and Perotti (1997) and others who argue that the relationship is nonlinear; either centralized or decentralized bargaining systems are likely to outperform the intermediate forms of bargaining. The relation between bargaining institutions and the employment rate (as well as, as we shall see, with other indicators of economic performance) is said to be 'hump-shaped': unemployment rates, as well as other static indicators of poor economic performance, are lower in both centralized and decentralized systems. Of course, whenever indicators of good economic performance are used, the relationship becomes U-shaped. This nonlinear hypothesis applies to the setting of wage bargaining systems in the more general intuition of Olson (1982) that the formation of distributional coalitions or interest groups, such as trade unions and employer associations, leads to an increase of market power that induces wasteful rent-seeking behavior and hinders the efficient allocation of resources. These inefficiencies will be lowest when the scope of the interests of the single union/confederation of employers is at the extremes. When their interests are all encompassing, unions and confederations of employers internalize the social effects of their activities, by adopting centralized governance systems.[2] At the opposite extreme, when the influence of special interest groups is negligible, the decentralized systems can attain the efficient allocation of resources that neoclassical microeconomic theory postulates. In between, special interest groups' activities jeopardize productive efficiency the most. Yet, Olson argues that corporatism is a second best solution with respect to the decentralized system. Corporatism involves

---

1   A variant of this interpretation is Blanchard (1997, 1998) and Blanchard and Wolfers (1999), which identify a mix of shocks and institutions at work in explaining the eurosclerosis. See also Caballero and Hammour (2000), who analyze the effect of institutional environment on macroeconomic restructuring in Europe. For a survey, see Flanagan (1999).

2   As Olson (1982, p. 48) puts it: '...The incentives facing an encompassing special-interest organization are dramatically different from those facing an organization that represents only a narrow segment of society. [...] The members of the highly encompassing organization own so much of the society that they have an important incentive to be actively concerned about how productive it is; they are in the same position as a partner in a firm that has only a few partners'.

higher transaction costs and free riding problems within the interest groups that are absent when governance is decentralized.[3]

These theoretical intuitions have been tested, with mixed results, on a wide array of indicators of static and dynamic economic performance, such as employment and wage levels, strike activity, Okun's and other misery indices, inflation, output levels, earnings inequality, per capita income growth, growth of real earnings (OECD, 1997; Calmfors, 1993). What has been left out of this set of dependent variables is the one that the logic of these theories most directly refers to: productive efficiency. The motivation and main task of this paper is to fill this lacuna.

We proxy the efficiency variable by total factor productivity (TFP), based on the Divisia (Tornqvist–Theil) index number methodology. In an economy without distortions, the Solow residual measures aggregate technology change – productivity and technology coincide.[4] But productivity and technology may differ because of distortions such as imperfect competition, indivisibilities, fixed inputs and slow adjustment. As these situations may very across the economy, we consider total factor productivity both at the aggregate level of the macroeconomy, and for the manufacturing sector only. Furthermore, Hulten (2000) provides a convincing defense of the use of TFP in empirical analysis, and Basu and Fernald (2001) show that, even with distortions such as imperfect competition (when productivity and technology differ), it remains an excellent index of welfare change.[5]

The paper is organized as follows. The next section reviews the theoretical and empirical literature. The section after provides a simple theoretical model, and its econometric counterpart, which reassumes the main hypotheses formulated in the literature on how wage-setting institutions affect total factor productivity (and growth thereof), conditional on different degrees of labor and credit market power and on other institutional arrangements. The fourth section describes the coding methods for the characteristics of the wage-setting institutions in the OECD countries. The fifth section illustrates the specification of the econometric model and the main features of the dataset. In the sixth section, we present and discuss the results of the estimates of the model of the fifth section. Finally, the seventh section sums up the main findings of the analysis.

---

3   Keynes (1927) is an early formulation of this idea.

4   The assumptions made by Solow (1957) are: perfect competition in both the markets of product and labor, constant return to scale, zero transaction costs, full utilization of all inputs and their instantaneous adjustment to the desired demand levels. Under these hypotheses, the Solow residual measures technology change (i.e. productivity and technology coincide).

5   Nadiri and Prucha (1999) review the arguments against the traditional method and present the complementary approach to productivity analysis based on the dynamic factor demand model. As they note, the former approach is appealing for its simplicity, 'in that it can easily implemented'.

Literature Review

Theoretical Contributions

Economic models of the relation between wage setting institutions and economic performance revolve around the following basic intuitions. If a trade union and an individual employer bargain, the employment/productive efficiency effect of wage increases depends strongly on the price elasticities of demand for the firm's product. A monopoly firm, for example, facing price inelastic demand can simply translate wage increases onto its customers without losing sales. As the number of competitors increases, or as the products that they supply become closer substitutes for the firms' own output, the price elasticity of demand that the firm faces will rise. In a perfectly competitive market, firms face an infinitely elastic demand curve, so that any price rise resulting from higher wages will reduce the demand for the specific firm's output towards zero. In such markets, the trade-off between wage increases and employment at the firm level is large and will be recognized as such by enterprise-based unions (Mitchell, 1994). Unions that bargain at the industry level may exploit their market power to secure higher wages for that industry's worker (Booth, 1995; Calmfors, 1993). The resulting higher prices for that industry's output will not reduce demand by as much as in the competitive case, since there are unlikely to be many closed substitutes at the industry level. Hence, productive inefficiencies deriving from wage rises or rigidities in employment conditions will affect employment in the industry less. Consumers pay the price for the higher wage. As above, the strength of the wage–employment relationship depends on the number and the closeness of the substitute products. The general conclusion is that more decentralized bargaining brings greater discipline in unions' demands of wage levels and employment conditions through the elasticity of demand in the product market. Therefore, economies with more decentralized wage bargaining systems will exhibit lower real wages, higher productive efficiency and higher levels of employment.

A second relationship between wage setting institutions and economic performance focuses on the presence of negative externalities to the economy from higher wages in certain sectors. Consumer price externalities are the first example: higher wages for some workers lead to higher prices for all consumers and this to lower real disposable income for those who do not benefit from the bargained higher wages. Input price externalities are a second case in point: higher wages here cause higher input prices and therefore lower output and employment in the sectors using these inputs. The key issue is to what extent these externalities are taken into account in the bargaining process. If workers are not altruistic, none of these externalities will be internalized under decentralized bargaining, because those who receive the benefit are only a very small percentage of those who are harmed by higher bargained wages. Under centralized wage bargaining there is coincidence between the group that benefits and the one that is harmed by the higher wages. As a consequence, more centralized unions and employers' associations will internalize to a much greater extent the macroeconomic consequences of their actions and will agree to reduce real wage levels, since there are no large outside groups that could be negatively affected by such measures.

In this centralized wage bargaining system, the role of the government deserves special attention. In most collective bargaining systems unions tend to determine wage level and employment conditions, while employers set the employment level as a residual. Hence a certain number of outsiders may still exist, which generates the classic conflict between insiders and outsiders in the labor market. Since government is relatively more responsive to outsiders' concerns than unions and confederations of employers, its participation in highly centralized wage bargaining processes may further reduce the unemployment levels reached without its intervention (Bruno and Sachs, 1985).

Alesina and Perotti (1997) analyze the fiscal implications of the economic performance-wage setting institutions relationship in a context where income redistribution and openness to foreign markets is explicitly accounted for. There are three sorts of agents in their model: firms, unions (workers' agents) and a group of non-working individuals, who live off income redistribution and can be thought of as pensioners and/or unemployed workers. The basic idea is that an increase in labor taxation, used to finance income redistribution to pensioners and/or unemployed workers, pushes labor unions to increase wage pressure, which in turns induces higher labor costs and a loss of competitiveness (measured as the ratio of domestic to foreign total unit labor costs). As a consequence, the demand for exports and employment falls. Most importantly, the distortions caused by fiscal policy depend on the institutional features of the labor market. Distortions are low when labor markets are close to being perfectly competitive and increase with the average size of the unions. However, at very high levels of centralization of the labor market, when wage negotiations take place at the national level, the mechanism by which labor taxation is transmitted to labor costs changes. In economy-wide bargaining, the unions are able to internalize the positive link between higher taxation and welfare benefits, especially if the government too is involved in the negotiations. This induces the union to moderate its wage claims. In very centralized labor markets the distortionary effects of fiscal policy are likely to be lower than in countries with an intermediate level of centralization. The relationship between changes in labor taxation and changes in competitiveness is hump-shaped; a given increase in taxation induces a larger increase in relative unit labor costs in countries with intermediate levels of centralization and smaller increases in countries with highly centralized and highly decentralized labor markets.

While most of the theories have little to say about rates of productivity growth, Dowrick and Spencer (1994) draw some interesting implication in this dynamic setting. The key elements of the Calmfors and Driffill's (1988) analysis can be seen at work with respect to unions and productivity changes. Their argument suggests that unions are likely to oppose technological changes that increase productivity, whether they are introduced through new capital equipment or through changes in working practices, in situations where labor demand is inelastic. The reason is that firms will 'cash in' the productivity increase without proportionally augmenting employment. Similarly, unions are likely to favor productivity increasing changes when labor demand is elastic. Institutional reforms that decrease the elasticity of labor demand and therefore increase wage pressure, such as a move towards industry level wage negotiation from very decentralized and/or very centralized settings, will make it more likely that unions oppose labor saving innovations. The logic of their argument is straightforward: productivity growth implies that jobs have to be cast off from the industry as a whole. At the firm level, however, an enterprise union will account only for the employment prospects of its own members. By agreeing to productivity increases, the enterprise union can make their employing firm more competitive within the industry. This may increase employment within that firm, even though industry employment in the aggregate is falling. Thus, it is job competition between enterprise unions that is likely to make them open to changes in technologies and working practices. It can also be argued that centralization will determine productivity growth via its effect on price. Technological progress reduces the relative price of a product and increases the purchasing power of the wage. While this effect is negligible for workers in an individual firm or industry, a centralized union will recognize that real wage increases must ultimately come from real productivity growth. This line of argument eventually suggests that there is a U-shaped relationship between dynamic economic performance and the degree of centralization of the wage setting systems.

This literature concurs in viewing corporatism, or centralized wage bargaining, as an institutional response to moderate anti-productive practices of pervasive unions. Corporatism allows co-opting union leadership into the formal structure of government and so reducing the anti-growth effects of union activities. Alvarez *et al.* (1991) sum up the contributions of a wide political science literature on the matter by theorizing that governments, be they leftist or rightist, adapt to control the aims of labor, and resort to corporatist governance whenever the power of trade unions is too high for decentralized decision-making to attain the most efficient solutions. When, instead, union influence is low, decentralized decision-making appears the first-best governance system.

Richard Freeman (2000a, 2000b) agrees with this relativistic belief: capitalist countries differ markedly in their market institutions, but these differences may have large effects on income distribution rather than on productive efficiency. He concludes that the case for a 'single peaked capitalism', i.e. one aiming at maximizing only efficiency in production (the 'standard' being represented by the US economy), is not well placed. Edmund Phelps (1999a, 1999b) instead sees corporatism – a system where central government seeks to coordinate and reconcile private interests – as opposed to regulated capitalism and concludes that it is the crisis of corporatism responsible for the structural slump of some European countries and of Japan. Thus, it is the case for creating the institutions for capitalism in countries like Italy (Phelps, 1999c).

Empirical Contributions

The empirical literature on this topic is relatively sparse and inconclusive.[6] Some analyses found a positive relationship between a country's economic performance

---

6   With the exception of the relationships between centralized wage-setting arrangements and wage dispersion, which is empirically well established. See Freeman (1998), Davis and Henrekson (2000) and Johanson and Groth (2001).

and the degree of corporatism (Bruno and Sachs, 1985; Crouch, 1985; Tarantelli, 1986). More corporatist economies exhibited better economic performance, typically measured by some composite 'misery index', such as the sum of the inflation and unemployment rates. Calmfors and Driffill (1988) challenged this finding. They reported some evidence of a U-shaped relationship between economic performance and centralization; in the 1974–1985 period, intermediate countries exhibited, on average, worse economic performance than either centralized or decentralized systems.

Outside this line of discussion, Phelps (1994) finds evidence that the countries with very centralized wage-bargaining or corporatist institutions (measured by the Tarantelli's index) are the least sensitive to shocks.

More recent empirical work, using a variety of countries, time periods and performance indicators, has produced a mixed set of findings. This new research deals with two types of indicators of economic performance; one strand focuses on static indicators, such as unemployment, inflation and wage levels, Okun index, earning dispersion. The second concentrates on indicators of dynamic performance, like per capita output growth and productivity growth. Within the first group Bleaney (1996) provides mixed results, as unemployment and inflation appear negatively and linearly related with corporatism; but this relationship tends to become hump-shaped in later years. Rowthorn (1992) also finds that the nonlinear relationship emerges in the 1980s. Soskice (1991), instead, finds a constant positive linear relationship between coordination and various measures of economic performance; Traxler *et al.* (1997), as well as Johanson and Groth (2001), report a negative linear relationship between coordination and unemployment, a U-shaped relationship between coordination and employment and mixed results for various misery indices, with little time series variation. Freeman (1998) show similar patterns between wage dispersion and indices of corporatism. Alesina and Perotti's (1997) analysis is strongly supportive of a nonlinear relationship between union centralization and average labor costs, once the wage effects of labor taxation are accounted for. Finally, OECD (1994) provides a fairly exhaustive review of this empirical literature and offers mixed results for a variety of proxies for institutional differences in wage bargaining systems and static economic performance indicators. With the exception of Layard *et al.* (1991) and Johanson and Groth (2001), who estimate a structural model of the wage and price determination process, these empirical contributions rely heavily on single-equation specifications.

No clearer picture can be gained from the studies on the effect of centralization and dynamic economic performance. Heitger (1987) is the pioneer work; he adduces positive support for a hump-shaped hypothesis using total factor productivity growth as the regressand. However, he supplies no testing of the econometric specification such as the sensitivity of their results to outliers and to the ranking criteria. Additionally, while he controls for differences in investment across countries and for technological catch-up, he does not control for variations in employment, so his estimates really refer to capital productivity growth rather than to total factor productivity growth. He uses a time-invariant index of corporatism, derived from Bruno and Sachs (1985), ignoring any institutional change that occurred over the sample period. Dowrick (1993), Grier (1997) and Galli and Padovano (1999) improve on many of these dimensions, although in the context of an output growth model, rather than a factor productivity model. Grier's (1997) and Galli and Padovano's (1998) researches lend most support to Olson's (1982) hypothesis, namely, that centralization is a second best and intermediate cases a third best solution with respect to decentralization. It thus seems that the hump-shaped hypothesis captures only part of the relationship between economic performance and wage bargaining institutions.

That aside, another heterogeneous group of papers analyzes, under different hypotheses and models, the relationship between the institutions of the financial markets, the wage-setting process and the economic performance (Cukierman and Lippi, 1999; La Porta *et al.*, 2000; Di Nardo and Hallock, 2000).

There are four main suggestions that emerge from this review of the literature:

- While the theoretical models focus on the effects on productive efficiency of the different wage bargaining settings and institutions, no satisfactory empirical analysis has been carried out that uses the closest proxy to productive efficiency, namely, total factor productivity (level or growth).
- Both the theoretical and the empirical literature show that wage bargaining institutions have several dimensions that impact on productive efficiency: centralization, coordination, unionization, and government intervention. Collapsing all of them into one single index (being it quantitative or qualitative) is likely to cause a loss of explanatory power of the model.
- Recent empirical works point out the need to control the relationship between wage bargaining institutions and productive efficiency for other conditioning phenomena, chiefly wage compression and the efficiency of the credit market.
- Most empirical analyses are not explicitly derived from a theoretical model; they are fairly casual tests of theories described in the literature review. This approach may only point out robust partial correlations among the data. A theoretical model is required to allow structural interpretations of the estimated coefficients.

Theory

We consider an economy made of a continuum of countries $j \in [0,J)$ and sectors $s \in [0,S)$. A large number of competitive firms $i \in [0,n)$ populates the economy; they are identical in all respects except for the attributes of their employees. Employment L is made of two kinds of workers: those who belong to a perfectly competitive labor market, N, and unionized workers, U. Labor issues of the N-type workers tend to be negotiated at a decentralized, firm level; those of the U-type workers, instead, tend to be conducted by unions and a confederation of employers, with the possible participation of the government. Workers may differ for their skill, incentives, effort and like; however, to keep the analysis as simple as possible, we consider only the differences in productivity that may arise from belonging to a union or not. In each period t, the single firm of country j and sector s produces some amount of output, Y_{ijst}, according to a constant-returns-to-scale technology:

$$Y_{jist} = K_{jist}^{1-\alpha} (N_{jist} + \Gamma U_{jist})^{\alpha} Z_{jist}, \qquad 0 < \alpha < 1, \Gamma \begin{Bmatrix} < 1 \\ = 1 \\ > 1 \end{Bmatrix} \tag{1}$$

where K is the stock of physical capital, U are the unionized workers and N are the non-unionized workers employed by the firm at time t. α indicates factor shares. The relative productivity of unionized workers with respect to non-unionized ones may be higher, equal or lower, depending on the effects of wage-setting institutions. When $\Gamma=1$, there are no differences in productivity between the two kinds of workers; alternatively, unionized workers may be more productive, $\Gamma>1$, or less productive, $\Gamma<1$, than non-unionized ones. Since n is the total mass of firms in the economy, aggregate output at country level is given by $Y_{jt} = \int_0^n Y_{it}$ in each period t.

Z is a vector of variables and shocks affecting output in some way. We assume that Z is made of two sets of factors:

- A component φ which may be either a random variable $E(\varphi_{jsi}\varepsilon_t)=0$, or a fixed constant taking a value in t which is specific to the j and/or s locations (country and sectors), $\varphi_{jist}=\varphi_{jis}$;
- A set $\mathbf{X}$ of variables affecting directly or indirectly TFP.

In other words $Z = \varphi_{jit} + \boldsymbol{\mu}_n \mathbf{X}'_{jit}$, where n is the dimension of $\mathbf{X}$ (the number of variables in $\mathbf{X}$).

The stock of capital is subject to the usual law of motion, $K_{jist+1} = (1 - \delta) K_{jist} + I_{jist}$, where δ is the depreciation rate[7] and I is gross investment.

Each firm obtains real net profits according to:

$$\pi_{jist} = Y_{jist} - \bar{v}N_{jist} - v(\Gamma) U_{jist} - (I_{jist} + \delta K_{jist}) \tag{2}$$

where v and $\bar{v} \neq \alpha$ are the collective real wage and the competitive real wage, respectively. Non-unionized workers receive their product (real) wage, but this compensation depends on their relative productivity with respect to the productivity of workers with monopoly power.

If wage differentials are absent, firm i maximizes the Hamiltonian:

$$\underset{K_{jit} I_{jit} \lambda}{\text{Max}} \sum_{t=0}^{\infty} \Psi_t \left[\pi(K_{jsit}, v_t) - (I_{jsit} + \delta K_{jsit}) + \lambda_{jsit}(I_{jsit} + (1-\delta)K_{jsit} - K_{jsit+1}) \right]$$

where

$$\Psi_t = \prod_{i=0}^{t}(1+r_i)^{-1} \text{ is the discount rate and if } r_t = r \forall t, \text{ then} \Psi_t = (1+r_t)^{-t}$$

Eliminating the multiplier λ_t, we obtain the condition that has to be satisfied (together with the transversality condition) along the optimal path:

---

7   Assuming perfect capital mobility across countries and sectors and homogeneous amortization rules, we can treat δ as independent by location.

$$\frac{\partial \pi(K_{jsit+1}, V_{t+1})}{\partial K_{jsit+1}} = \delta + r_{t+1} \tag{3}$$

In a partial equilibrium framework, the optimal choices of the single firm may be determined as a static maximization sequence: at the time t, each firm maximizes equation (2) subject to equation (1), taking v and $\bar{v}$ as given. Solving this sequence gives the same optimal condition (3).

In order to assess and test the relationship between the characteristics of bargaining institutions and productivity, we reformulate equation (1) in intensive form. Substituting for N, dividing by L and taking logs, we obtain:

$$\frac{y_{jsit}}{l_{jsit}} = \frac{z_{jsit}}{l_{jsit}} + (1-\alpha)\frac{k_{jsit}}{l_{jsit}} + \alpha + \alpha(\Gamma-1)\frac{u_{jsit}}{l_{jsit}} \tag{4}$$

where small letters mean natural logs.

To express equation (4) in terms of total factor productivity (TFP), we subtract $(1-\alpha)(k/l)$ from both sides of equation (4) and rearrange, obtaining the following equation, which measures the effects of market power in the labor market and wage setting institutions together with the other institutional factors on TFP:

$$TFP_{jsit} = z_{jsit} + \alpha(\Gamma-1)u_{jsit}$$
$$\text{where } TFP_{jsit} = y_{jsit} - (1-\alpha)k_{jsit} - \alpha l_{jsit} \tag{5}$$

In order to disentangle the productivity differential to be attributed to market power in the labor market from the productivity differential due to the institutions created to manage that market power we postulate a multiplicative process for the market power parameter. Thus we put:

$$\Gamma = \eta \chi$$

If $\eta > 1$, then market power can be interpreted as increasing TFP through equation (5); if $\eta < 1$ market power in the labor market decreases it; if $\eta = 1$ market power is neutral with respect to TFP. Similarly, if $\chi > 1$ there is evidence that wage setting institutions increase TFP through equation (5); if $\chi < 1$ these institutions reduce total factor productivity; if $\chi = 1$ they have no effect on it. Through this we control for both capital per worker and the type of labor (with or without market power). Thus, in the estimation procedure starting from an equation like (5) we were able, after controlling for the percentage of the labor force that belongs to a labor sector with market power, to retrieve these two components from the estimated coefficients.

Empirical Analysis

Characteristics and Measures of Wage Setting Institutions

To obtain from equation (5) a testable empirical model we have to resolve two kinds of problems. The first group of problems involves the empirical counterparts of the variables appearing in equation (5). The second group is related to the functional form and to the dynamic specification of the TFP equation. These issues are tied together, as in the empirical analysis we use pooled time-series cross-section data.

Empirical analyses depend crucially on the classification of the collective bargaining characteristics of the various countries; in terms of our model, on the way we code the η and χ parameters. The literature has highlighted two qualitative characteristics of wage bargaining systems, 'centralization' and 'coordination', and two cardinal measures, trade union density and the rate of coverage of collective bargaining. The first two refer to wage setting institutions; they thus are dimensions of the χ parameter. The latter two are indexes of labor market power and can thus be considered as measures of the η parameter.

Measures of the χ Parameter

Whereas it is relatively straightforward to measure union density and collective bargaining coverage, the degree of the so-called corporatism that characterizes a country is more difficult to use in applied work. This is because:

- there is no standard definition of corporatism;
- the institutional features behind corporatism are difficult to quantify;
- several different aspects of the economic and political system have to be combined into one measure.

Lehmbruch (1984) identifies three standard features of corporatism:

- The existence of strong centralized organizations of employers and worker representatives with an exclusive right of representation;
- The privileged access of such centralized organizations to government;
- Social partnership between labor and capital to regulate conflict over interests and coordination with government.

Other authors insist on the presence of centralized, monopolistic union federations and employer associations, as well as centralized collective bargaining arrangements (Schmitter, 1981) and, in general, on the capacity of organizations to regulate their members (Crouch, 1985).

All these definitions lead to a specification of the variable 'corporatism', which bundles together various characteristics of this wage setting system. Recently, researchers have preferred to disentangle two features of corporatism in separate variables; one referring to the notion of *centralization* (Calmfors and Driffill, 1988), the other to *coordination* (Soskice, 1991) that characterizes the country's wage setting system.

Centralization describes the *locus* of the formal structure of wage bargaining. Typically four broad levels are distinguished:

- Government intervention into the negotiations between peak organizations;
- The national, or central bargaining negotiated between peak organizations, which may cover the whole economy (centralized bargaining);
- Negotiations between unions and employer associations regarding wages and conditions of work for particular industries or crafts (intermediate bargaining);
- Firm level bargaining between unions and management (decentralized bargaining).

We thus construct a proxy, termed CENT, for centralization. It takes the value of 1 when bargaining is decentralized, i.e. it takes place at the firm level; 2 for industry, sectoral and craft-level bargaining; 3 for centralized bargaining between peak organizations without the participation of the government; 4 when the government intervenes in the bargaining process between national unions and confederation of industries.

Analyses of coordination, instead, focus on the *degree of consensus* between the collective bargaining partners. Peak organizations often cater for several and possibly conflicting interests. The organization's ability to harmonize these interests and to solve internal free riding problems increases its internal coordination and improves the ability to attain its goals. Bargaining may well be coordinated even when it is decentralized, as in the case of 'pattern bargaining' or 'covered coordination'. Soskice (1991) insists on this point, which leads him to re-evaluate Calmfors and Driffill's classification, arguing that bargaining systems in Japan and Switzerland are centralized due to the existence of coordinated employers associations and networks in both countries.

In this chapter we follow this approach, which has become general in the literature (OECD, 1997), and distinguish information about coordination and centralization of the collective bargaining. Thus, the characteristics of the degree of *coordination* (variable COOR) have been assigned a value of: 1 for uncoordinated bargaining; 2 for when unions (and federation of employers) are coordinated at the industry, sectoral or craft-level; or 3 when coordination of unions and federation of employers takes the form of peak organizations, e.g. nationwide unions.

Measures of the η Parameter

The analysis of the relationship between the wage bargaining system and the economic performance needs to incorporate the extent of the bargaining systems, over and beyond the level at which it takes place and the degree of coordination. Even relatively centralized bargaining will have little effect if few workers are covered. This paper captures the latitude of collective bargaining by looking at the percentage of the labor force that is unionized (UD) and to the coverage of collective bargaining (COV).

Union density UD is the standard variable used in the literature and is the most direct proxy to the U variable in the theoretical model. Data for UD refers to the percentage of the non-agricultural labor force that pays a regular contribution to a trade union and derives from *Europa Yearbook* (various years).

UD alone, however, is not a good proxy for the degree of unionization. It does not take into account the free riding problems and the union's actual ability to impose its decisions to the labor force. In most countries, the percentage of workers who are covered by collective agreements is higher than the percentage belonging to trade unions (OECD, 1997). France is the extreme case, combining the lowest unionization rate and one of the highest coverage rates. There are two reasons for the higher collective bargaining rate: (a) employers may extend collective agreements to non-union workers; (b) collective bargaining agreements may be extended by statute to third parties. The coverage rate will thus depend at least as much on the share of employers belonging to the employers' association and the government's use of statutory extensions as on trade union density itself. We thus use COV, the percentage of labor force whose wages and conditions of work are set by a contract negotiated between the unions and the firm or confederation, alongside UD.

Other Conditioning Variables

In specifying the empirical counterparts of variables in Z, we leave to the empirical testing the selection of the form of the country/sector specific component of Z. As for the components of Z that have a direct effect on TFP, credit market imperfections and wage dispersion were the ones that turned out significant in most of our estimates. We have also considered openness to international trade and measures of mark-up in the output markets. They never turned out significant and were then omitted from the regression results.

The inclusion of an index for credit market imperfections is a way to control for what possibility the financial sector gives to firms to substitute capital for labor as a response to high labor costs engendered by unions' demands. The idea is that firms surrounded by well-developed financial markets may yield more easily to union demands that raise unit labor cost because the lower cost of debit makes it easier to substitute capital for labor (Cukierman and Lippi, 1999). We used as a proxy for these characteristics the ratio of the lending rate to the deposit rate (MR). The spread between these rates is a measure of inefficiency in the credit markets. The more inefficient this market, the more difficult is for firms to substitute capital for labor whose costs are higher than its productivity. A negative sign on this variable is expected.

There are many proofs and persuasive arguments that 'corporatist' institutions generate smaller wage differentials than a decentralized system. Wage dispersion is negatively correlated with the centralization of collective bargaining across countries, although the relationship is weakened somewhat by the 1990s (OECD, 1997, Flanagan, 1999). A smaller variance across the mean wage reduces the possibility to reward labor according to its productivity and hence workers' incentive to exert effort. Thus, the omission of a measure of these wage differentials might pollute the relationship between total factor productivity and the various dimensions of the wage bargaining structure. Our measure of wage dispersion takes this argument into account. Calculations were drawn from the ISDB data set.

Finally, since the dependent variable TFP is expressed as an index, as we shall see in the next section, we have indexed the regressors as well, by normalizing each of them by the lowest value they assume in the data set.

Specification and Data Description

As we have seen in the preceding sections, the related literature has stressed a nonlinear-form relationship between productivity and wage bargaining systems. Thus, the empirical analysis is carried out estimating an equation of the following general form

$$TFP_{jit} = \hat{\beta}_1 WB_{jit} + \hat{\beta}_2 (WB_{jit})^2 + \hat{\mu}_1 MR_{jit} + \hat{\mu}_1 WD_{jit} + \hat{\varphi}_{jit} + \hat{\varepsilon}_{it} \qquad (6)$$

where WB summarizes the measures for the characteristics of the wage bargaining system described in the preceding section, MR is the proxy for the credit market imperfections, WD is the wage dispersion index and $\beta_n = \alpha\,(\mu - 1)(\chi - 1)$.

The inclusion of the quadratic term allows a nonlinear effect of wage setting institutions on TFP. In particular, if $\beta_1 < 0$ and $\beta_2 > 0$, the relationship may be U-shaped.

We estimated equation (6) using annual data for the aggregate of total industries (labeled TIN) and for the manufacturing sector (labeled MAN) for a panel of some OECD countries: Australia, Belgium, Canada, Denmark, Finland, France, Germany, Italy, Japan, the Netherlands, Norway, the United Kingdom, and the United States.

In our estimates we maintained the definition of total factor productivity given by OECD (1998). In calculating TFP indices, OECD uses a standardized weighting method across the countries of the sample. In practice, the weights attached to labor inputs were set to 70 percent for all sector and countries, with the exception of 'electricity, gas and water', 'mining', 'finance, insurance, real state and business service', where a labor weight of 33 percent was employed. Total factor productivity indices were calculated using the following formula:

$$TFP = \frac{\dfrac{VA}{ET^{w_i} \cdot GCS^{1-w_i}}}{TFP_0}$$

where *VA* is gross value added, *ET* total employment, *GCS* gross capital stock, *w* standardized labor share weights, and *TFP*$_0$ is the 1990 value of total factor productivity.[8]

The main features of the data in the panel we employed are partially summarized in Table 4.A1 in the Appendix. Data are from OECD (1994, 1997, 1998) and supplemented with data from *IMF, Europa and World Yearbook* (various years),

---

8   For the details see *ISDB User's guide* (OECD, 1998, pp. 50–52).

Galli and Padovano (1999) and Pekkarinen *et al.* (1992), Visser (1990) and Calmfors and Driffill (1988).

For all countries in the sample, total factor productivity in the private sector (*TIN*) shows a clear upward trend. In fact, all *TIN* are I(1) processes, at least at the 5 percent level of an ADF test. At the same time, *TIN* series show some deviations from this trend, and when this happens the deviations seem to follow a cyclical pattern, as is shown in Figures 4.A1 and 4.A2 in the Appendix. In the econometric estimates we cope with this problem.

The data on bargaining systems show considerable time series and cross-country variation, especially during the 1980s and the 1990s, which also followed different patterns for the various characteristics of wage negotiation systems. In Europe, trade union density ranged from 9 percent in France (the lowest recorded in the OECD area) to 93 percent in Sweden. Between the early 1980s and the 1990s it roughly halved in France, and fell by a quarter in Australia, Japan, The Netherlands, the United Kingdom and the US. On the other hand, countries such as Finland and Sweden showed increases in trade union density since the 1980s.

Other countries, instead, were characterized by more stable conditions. The coverage rate has shown only a moderate reduction in the 1980s, in contrast with the sharper contraction in union density. Only Japan, the UK and the USA have experienced a noticeable reduction in collective bargaining coverage.

Countries characterized to have consistently centralized bargaining systems include Australia, and Finland. At the other end of the range Canada, Japan, and the USA are characterized by enterprise level bargaining and thus have the lowest values for the centralization measures. Finally, sector level bargaining is predominant in continental Europe. However, the degree of centralization and coordination has changed considerably in a number of countries over the past 20 years. For example, in Sweden, centralized bargaining weakened and eventually disappeared, a change that was followed, although to a lesser extent, in a few other Nordic countries (Visser, 1996, Wallerstein and Golden, 1997). Noticeable decentralization has also taken place in Australia (Dowrick, 1993) and in the UK (Millward *et al.*, 1992). Yet, there has been no unitary trend across the OECD countries towards more decentralized bargaining. Italy, Norway and Portugal saw a move towards more centralized and/ or coordinated bargaining (through tripartite agreements, social pacts and the like) while in others the degree of centralization and coordination did not change.

The existence of wage drift shows that centralization measures do not reveal the whole picture: centralized bargaining may turn out uncoordinated if lower level negotiations undermine its intentions. Nor is centralization a necessary condition for cooperation in bargaining. Coordination among dominant employers and unions in a decentralized or industry bargaining setting and pattern bargaining, where certain dominant employers and unions act as *de facto* leaders, may be an alternative to centralization and can result in economy-wide coordinated outcomes. For example, Germany has traditionally coordinated bargaining, as shown by its high scores on coordination measures, despite separate negotiations taking place for each industry. Despite the preponderance of enterprise bargaining in Japan, unions and, in particular, employers associations often coordinate bargaining strategies among individual members (Sako, 1997).

Table 4.1　　TFP and corporatist institutions: the U-shaped curve (1971–1995)

	Total Industries (TIN)			Manufacturing (MAN)		
UD	-0.03	-0.02	-0.03	-0.09	-0.10	-0.10
	(-3.80)	(-3.17)	(-4.61)	(-3.61)	(-4.55)	(-7.03)
UD^2	0.02	0.01	0.01	0.04	0.05	0.05
	(4.2)	(3.74)	(5.69)	(4.13)	(5.61)	(6.78)
COOR+COV	-0.33	-0.26	-0.27	-0.61	-.53	-0.53
	(-6.48)	(-4.67)	(-10.0)	(-3.70)	(5.61)	(-5.86)
(COOR+COV)^2	0.08	0.07	0.08	0.19	0.18	0.17
	(4.79)	(3.80)	(8.50)	(3.66)	(5.00)	(5.55)
CENT	-0.07	-0.04	-0.05	-0.12	-0.07	-0.07
	(-3.90)	(-2.94)	(-5.59)	(-1.25)	(1.76)	(-2.37)
CENT^2	0.04	0.02	0.02	0.03	-0.01	0.0006
	(3.04)	(1.07)	(2.65)	(0.42)	(-0.23)	(0.024)
MR	-0.06	-0.02	-0.09	-0.08	-0.03	0.01
	(-4.50)	(-1.16)	(-1.18)	(2.0)	(-0.09)	(0.37)
WD	0.06	0.04	0.04	0.09	0.07	0.07
	(9.71)	(4.47)	(12.79)	(4.80)	(4.52)	(7.61)
TFP(-1)	Yes	Yes	Yes	Yes	Yes	Yes
CYCLE		0.63	0.64		0.91	0.79
		(23.2)	(59.0)		(15.13)	(21.17)
FIXED EFFECTS	yes	Yes	Yes	Yes	Yes	Yes
GLS	Yes	Yes		Yes	Yes	
SUR			Yes			Yes
$\bar{R}^2$	0.98	0.99	0.99	0.96	0.98	0.98
DW	1.8	1.4	1.35	1.89	1.65	1.56
N. obs.	350	336	336	350	336	336

Note: Dependent variable is log(TFP$_{jt}$). All the variables are in logs, except MR.
White Heteroskedasticity-Consistent Standard Errors and Covariance. T-statistics in parentheses. Cycle is the log-differenced ratio of the observed real GDP to potential output; this latter is obtained using the Hodrey–Prescott Filter.

Estimation Results

Table 4.1 shows the results we obtained using several variants of the basic specification (equation (6)). All these estimates are based on a fixed effects model (different intercepts for each pool member), augmented for cross-section specific coefficients of the lagged endogenous variable (TFP_{t-1}). The variants of the basic specification are obtained when we add a term for the business cycle and when we employ two different estimation techniques, so that the weighting of observations takes into account the presence of cross-section heteroskedasticity (GLS) or both cross-section heteroskedasticity and contemporaneous correlation (SUR).

The hypothesis of a U-shaped relationship between TFP and the wage bargaining system seems strongly supported by our estimates. The coefficient on the linear variables UD, (COOR+COV) and CENT is negative, while the coefficient on the squared is positive. These results lead us to interpret 'corporatism' as a series of institutional responses to the negative spillovers that intermediate, industry level bargaining engenders. Interestingly, the U-shaped relationship on union density suggests that unions tend to moderate their demands when their influence is either minimal or, at the opposite extreme, nationwide. Coverage is significant only if considered with coordination, a sign that only well-coordinated peak confederations of unions and of employers are able to increase the applicability of their agreements through legislation. As long as the aggregate of total industries (TIN) is considered, all the coefficients relative to the labor market characteristics are of the expected sign and statistically significant; they also show a remarkable robustness throughout the different specifications. In the estimates related to the manufacturing sector alone, the CENT variable is not always significant. This is all the more likely since government intervention in the bargaining process between unions and the confederation of employers usually takes place at a level above that of a single sector.

Our estimates also point out that the credit market imperfections negatively affect productivity, even if this result is less robust and more sensible to the different specifications and aggregations we adopted. The role of wage differentials in enhancing total factor productivity also receives clear support. The results about both control variables are then consistent with theory.

As we have noted, the growth rate of TFP looks fairly constant; when it deviates from the trend, it does so following a cyclical pattern. To control for this effect, in some variants of our estimates we have included among the regressors the variable termed CYCLE. This regressor is specified as the log-differenced ratio of the observed real GDP to the Hodrey–Prescott generated trend. The deviations of GDP from the trend exert a relevant impact on the TFP index; the coefficient on CYCLE is strongly significant. The inclusion of this variable, however, seems to raise some problems of autocorrelation for the TIN aggregate estimates.

The special sensitivity to the cycle term and the related autocorrelation problems that affect these estimates might be the sign of some misspecification of the model. One might argue that the mixed trend-cycle pattern of the TFP growth biases the estimates obtained with the model in log levels. In other words, this model might be capturing the effects of some disproportionate combination of cyclical and structural factors. To tackle these potential problems and to investigate the representation of the cyclical disturbance, we estimate a more parsimonious model, by imposing the following restrictions on the estimated coefficients of the labor market variables: (1) we sum up all the variables representing the wage bargaining system in a single term and impose on them the constraint to exhibit the same coefficient; (2) we difference all the variables of the model, include their lagged levels in the estimated equation, and a quadratic term in levels, only for the labor market variables.

In Table 4.2, we present the results relative to the two main variants that we have chosen. In the first variant, the cycle component is captured by the same variable of Table 4.1, now labeled GAP; in the second, we model the cyclical pattern as a simple

Table 4.2   TFP and corporatist institutions (1971–1995)

	Total Industries (TIN)	
Dln(UD+COOR+COV+CEN)	-0.17	-0.15
	(-3.16)	(-2.46)
ln((UD+COOR+COV+CEN)^2	0.04	0.03
	(3.51)	(2.51)
ln(UD+COOR+COV+CEN)$_{t-1}$	-0.17	-0.14
	(-3.28)	(-2.68)
ln(TFP)$_{t-1}$	-0.03	-0.03
	(-5.87)	(-3.27)
D(MR)	-0.01	-0.05
	(-0.92)	(2.58)
MR$_{t-1}$	-0.06	-0.02
	(-4.50)	(-1.14)
Dln(WD)	0.08	0.009
	(2.01)	(0.45)
WD$_{t-1}$	0.001	0.02
	(2.53)	(2.56)
GAP	0.64	
	(24.3)	-0.17
AR(2)		(-3.01)
FIXED EFFECTS	Yes	Yes
GLS	Yes	Yes
$\bar{R}^2$	0.72	0.16
S.E. of regression	0.0099	0.017
DW	1.23	1.86
N. obs.	336	336

Note: The dependent variable is Dln(TFP$_{jt}$).
White Heteroskedasticity-Consistent Standard Errors and Covariance. T-statistics in parentheses.
D is the first-difference operator and ln is the natural logarithm.

AR(2) process. We do not report the results for the manufacturing sector alone, as they are substantially similar to those of the overall economy.

    While the main results of the previous model are substantially preserved also in this new analysis, we are also able to infer some new insights. First, we observe a negative short-run impact of labor market institutions over the productivity growth, even if the U-shaped relationship seems to conserve its explicative power. Second, when we omit the GAP variable from the estimates, and model the cyclical variations though an AR(2) process, the estimated model does not collapse. Rather, it retains its main properties, even if we observe a dramatic, but not surprising, increase of the standard error of regression.

Conclusion

It is difficult to accurately assess the impact of corporatist institutions (different systems of collective bargaining and financial rules) on measures of productive efficiency, because of the problems to specify their interactions, the difficulties to measure the various aspects of wage bargaining systems and the need to consider additional conditioning factors, which the theory often neglects.

Econometric problems aside, the empirical results presented here depict a reasonably clear picture of a complex setting, once the possible biases coming from disturbing factors are put under control.

In one sense, our results are not in contrast with the claims of the literature following Calmfors and Driffill (1988), especially Dowrick and Spencer (1994); we do find robust evidence of a U-shaped relationship with productive efficiency, and are able to confirm the hypothesis that coordination and coverage are an institutional means to internalize the negative spillovers of highly pervasive unions.

What progress this chapter marks over previous mutually contrasting findings of the empirical literature is due to the choice of (a) a wide array of indicators of characteristics of the wage bargaining processes, rather than collapsing these characteristics into a single index of 'centralization'; and (b) a dependent variable that is both different from those generally used in the literature but at the same time close to the logic of the theoretical literature with respect to the effects of institutions and rules (collective bargaining, financial markets, etc) on the dynamics of productive efficiency.

In addition, we have extended the analysis to the effects of financial imperfections and of wage dispersion, and provided an accurate specification of the cross-section and dynamic properties of the econometric model.

References

Alesina, A. and Perotti, R. (1997) The welfare state and competitiveness, *American Economic Review*, 87(5): 921–39.

Alvarez, R., Garrett, G. and Lange, P. (1991) Government partisanship, labor organization and macroeconomic performance, *American Political Science Review*, 85: 539–56.

Basu, S. and Fernald, J. (2001) Why is productivity procyclical? Why do we care? In: C. Hulten, E. Dean and M. Harper (Eds) *New Developments in Productivity Analysis* (Cambridge, MA: National Bureau of Economic Research).

Blanchard, O.J. (1997) The medium run, *Brooking Papers on Economic Activity*, 2: 89–158.

Blanchard, O.J. (1998) *Revisiting European Unemployment: Unemployment, Capital Accumulation and Factor Prices*, NBER, Working Paper Series, n. 6566.

Blanchard, O.J. and Wolfers, J. (1999) *The Role of Shocks and Institutions in the Rise of European Unemployment: The Aggregate Evidence*, NBER Working Paper Series, n. 7282.

Bleaney, M. (1996) Central bank independence, wage-bargaining structure and macroeconomic performance in OECD countries, *Oxford Economic Papers*, 48: 20–38.

Bonatti, L. (1994) Gradi di Centralizzazione Salariale ed Occupazione. Il Dibattito Teorico e il Caso Italiano, *Lavoro e Relazioni Industriali*, 4: 49–101.

Booth, A. (1995) *The Economics of the Trade Union* (Cambridge: Cambridge University Press).

Bruno, M. and Sachs, G. (1985) *The Economics of Worldwide Stagflation* (Cambridge: Harvard University Press).

Caballero, R.J. and Hammour M.L. (2000) *Institutions, Restructuring, and Macroeconomic Performance*, NBER Working Paper Series, n. 7720.

Calmfors, L. (1993) *Centralization of Wage Bargaining and Economic Performance: A Survey*, OECD Economics Department Working Papers, n. 131.

Calmfors, L. and Driffill, J. (1988) Bargaining structure, corporatism and economic performance, *Economic Policy*, 3: 13–61.

Ciampi, C.A. (1996) *Un metodo per governare* (Bologna: Il Mulino).

Crouch, C. (1985) Conditions for trade union wage restraint, in: L. Lindberg and C. Maier (Eds) *The Politics of Inflation and Economic Stagflation*, pp. 105–139 (Washington, DC: Brookings).

Cukierman, A. and Lippi, F. (1999) Central bank independence, centralization of wage bargaining, inflation and unemployment: theory and some evidence, *European Economic Review*, 43: 1395–434.

Davis, S.J and Henrekson, M. (2000) *Wage Setting Institutions as Industrial Policy*, NBER Working Paper Series, n. 7502.

Di Nardo, J. and Hallock, K.F. (2000) *When Unions 'Mattered': Assessing the Impact of Strikes on Financial Markets: 1925-1937*, NBER Working Paper Series n. 7794.

Dowrick, S. (1993) Wage bargaining systems and productivity growth in OECD countries. Mimeo (Australian National University).

Dowrick, S. and Spencer, B. (1994) Union attitudes to labor saving innovations: when are unions luddites? *Journal of Labor Economics*, 12(2): 316–44.

Flanagan, R.J. (1999) Macroeconomic performance and collective bargaining: an international perspective, *Journal of Economic Literature*, XXXVII: 1150–75.

Freeman, R.B. (1988) Labour market institutions and economic performance, *Economic Policy*, April: 64–80.

Freeman, R.B. (2000a) *Single Peaked vs. Diversified Capitalism: The Relation Between Economic Institutions and Outcomes*, NBER Working Paper Series, n. 7566.

Freeman , R.B. (2000b) *The US Economic Model at Y2k: Lodestar for Advanced Capitalism?*, NBER Working Paper Series, n. 7757.

Galli, E. and Padovano, F. (1999) Corporatist vs. decentralized governance and economic growth, *Journal for Institutional Innovation, Development and Transition*, 3: 31–41.

Grier, K. (1997) Governments, unions and economic growth, in: W. Bergstrom (Ed.) *Governments and Growth* (Oxford: Oxford University Press).

Gwartney, J., Lawson, R. and Block, W. (1996) *Economic Freedom of the World, 1975-1995* (Vancouver: The Fraser Institute).

Heitger, B. (1987) Corporatism, technological gaps and growth in OECD countries, Weltwirtschaftliches Archiv, 123: 463–73.

Hulten, C.R. (2000) *Total Factor Productivity: A Short Biography*, NBER Working Paper Series, n. 7471.

International Monetary Fund (various years) *International Financial Statistics*, (Washington, DC: IMF).

Johanson, A. and Groth, C. (2001) *Essay on Macroeconomic Fluctuations and Nominal Wage Rigidity* (IIES Monograph No. 43).

Keynes, J. (1927) *The End of Laissez-Faire* (London: McMillan).

La Porta, R., Lopez-de-Silanes, F. and Shleifer, A. (2000) *Government Ownership of Banks* (NBER Working Paper Series, n. 7620).

Layard, R., Nickell S.J and Jackman R. (1991) *Unemployment: Macroeconomic Performance and the Labour Market* (Oxford: Oxford University Press).

Lembruch, G. (1984) Concertation and the structure of corporatist networks, in: J.H. Goldthorpe (Ed) *Order and Conflict in Contemporary Capitalism* (Oxford: Clarendon Press).

Marshall, M. (1996) The changing face of Swedish corporatism: the disintegration of consensus, *Journal of Economic Issues*, 30: 843–58.

Millward, N., Stevens, M., Smart, D. and Hawes, W. (1992) *Workplace Industrial Relations in Transition* (Aldershot: Dartmouth).

Mitchell, D. (1994) A decade of concession bargaining, in C. Crouch and C. Kerr (Eds) *Labor Economics ands Industrial Relations: Markets and Institutions* (Cambridge: Harvard University Press).

Nadiri, I and Prucha, I. (1999) *Dynamic Factor Demand Models and Productivity Analysis*, NBER Working Paper n. 7079, April.

OECD (1994) *Employment Outlook* (Paris: OECD).

OECD (1997) *Employment Outlook* (Paris: OECD).

OECD (1998) *ISDB: International Sectoral Data Bank* (Paris: OECD).

Olson, M. (1982) *The Rise and Decline of Nations* (New Haven: Yale University Press).

Pekkarinen, J., Pohjola, M. and Rowthorn, B. (Eds) (1992) *Social Corporatism: A Superior Economic System?* (Oxford, Clarendon Press).

Phelps, E.S. (1994) *Structural Slumps* (Cambridge: Harvard University Press).

Phelps, E.S. (1999a) Lessons from the corporatist crisis in some Asian nations, *Journal of Policy Modeling*, 21(3): 331–39.

Phelps, E.S. (1999b) The global crisis of corporatism, *The Wall Street Journal*, March 25, p. A26.

Phelps, E.S. (1999c) Creating the institutions for capitalism in Italy and wage setting plans for the 'Mezzogiorno', *Fifth Semi-annual Advisor's Report* (CNR Strategic Project, November).

Rowthorn, R.E. (1992) Centralization, employment and wage dispersion, *Economic Journal*, 102: 506–23.

Sako, M. (1997) Shunto: the role of the employer and union coordination at the industry and inter-sectoral levels, in: M. Sako and H. Sato (Eds) *Japanese Labour and Management in Transition* (London: LSE/Routledge).

Salgado, R. (2002) *Impact of Structural Reforms on Productivity Growth in Industrial Countries* (International Monetary Fund, Working Paper, 02-10, January).

Schmitter, P.C. (1981) Interest intermediation and regime governability in contemporary Western Europe and North America, in: S. Berger (Ed.) *Organizing Interests in Western Europe* (Cambridge, UK: Cambridge University Press).

Solow, R.M. (1957) Technological change and the aggregate production function, *Review of Economic and Statistics*, 39: 312–20.

Soskice, D. (1991) Wage determination: the changing role of institutions in advanced industrialized countries, *Oxford Review of Economic Policy*, 6: 36–61.

Tarantelli, E. (1986) The regulation of inflation and unemployment, *Industrial Relations*, 25: 1–25.

Traxler, F., Kittel, B. and Lengauer, S. (1997) Globalization, collective bargaining and performance, *Transfer*, 4: 787–806.

Visser, J. (1990) In search of inclusive unionism, *Bulletin of Comparative Labor Relations*, 18.

Visser, J. (1996) Corporatism beyond repair? Industrial relations in Sweden, in: J. van Ruysseveldt and J. Visser (Eds) *Industrial Relations in Europe* (London: Sage.

Wallerstein, M. and Golden, M. (1997) The fragmentation of the Bargaining Society: Wage setting In the Nordic Countries, 1950–92. Mimeo.

Appendix

Table 4.A1 Descriptive statistics

	TIN	COV	CENT	COOR	WD	MR
Mean	0.893442	3.980170	1.924993	2.062131	29.77784	8.414454
Sum	302.8768	1349.278	652.5725	699.0625	10094.69	2852.500
Median	0.906300	4.569444	2.000000	2.150000	28.09506	10.00000
Maximum	1.109500	5.444444	4.000000	3.000000	83.47878	10.00000
Minimum	0.637900	1.000000	1.000000	1.000000	11.90007	1.000000
Sum Sq. Dev.	273.7122	6015.040	1355.397	1578.260	362622.1	25447.75
Std. Dev.	0.095913	1.381068	0.541749	0.635958	13.54635	2.068014
Skewness	-0.390903	-0.986105	-0.353694	-0.235496	1.251343	-1.062794
Kurtosis	2.290135	2.531694	2.717487	2.060696	4.568519	2.965610
Jarque–Bera	15.75118	58.03848	8.195488	15.59577	123.2221	63.83526
Probability	0.000380	0.000000	0.016610	0.000411	0.000000	0.000000
Observations	339	339	339	339	339	339
Cross sections	14	14	14	14	14	14

Table 4.A2 Total factor productivity correlation matrix – total industries

	TIN AUS	TIN BEL	TIN CAN	TIN DNK	TIN FIN	TIN FRA	TIN GBR
TIN_AUS	1.000000	0.952487	0.813086	0.970066	0.974226	0.968174	0.931298
TIN_BEL	0.952487	1.000000	0.775637	0.984570	0.961176	0.990274	0.939155
TIN_CAN	0.813086	0.775637	1.000000	0.796034	0.779579	0.820179	0.808255
TIN_DNK	0.970066	0.984570	0.796034	1.000000	0.980788	0.992318	0.958246
TIN_FIN	0.974226	0.961176	0.779579	0.980788	1.000000	0.974762	0.955978
TIN_FRA	0.968174	0.990274	0.820179	0.992318	0.974762	1.000000	0.955784
TIN_GBR	0.931298	0.939155	0.808255	0.958246	0.955978	0.955784	1.000000
TIN_GER	0.967080	0.972189	0.819314	0.985425	0.960087	0.988486	0.932792
TIN_ITA	0.973513	0.981452	0.813780	0.980351	0.970875	0.990916	0.935401
TIN_JPN	0.942778	0.969439	0.746836	0.978242	0.967114	0.974599	0.956189
TIN_NLD	0.951088	0.974778	0.848467	0.973046	0.937332	0.982870	0.910139
TIN_NOR	0.977053	0.951388	0.785542	0.977791	0.964458	0.969818	0.899891
TIN_SWE	0.968709	0.968297	0.834893	0.982041	0.980452	0.977700	0.952512
TIN_USA	0.883546	0.829409	0.848187	0.885684	0.894632	0.869606	0.917825

	TIN GER	TIN ITA	TIN JPN	TIN NLD	TIN NOR	TIN SWE	TIN USA
TIN_AUS	0.967080	0.973513	0.942778	0.951088	0.977053	0.968709	0.883546
TIN_BEL	0.972189	0.981452	0.969439	0.974778	0.951388	0.968297	0.829409
TIN_CAN	0.819314	0.813780	0.746836	0.848467	0.785542	0.834893	0.848187
TIN_DNK	0.985425	0.980351	0.978242	0.973046	0.977791	0.982041	0.885684
TIN_FIN	0.960087	0.970875	0.967114	0.937332	0.964458	0.980452	0.894632
TIN_FRA	0.988486	0.990916	0.974599	0.982870	0.969818	0.977700	0.869606
TIN_GBR	0.932792	0.935401	0.956189	0.910139	0.899891	0.952512	0.917825
TIN_GER	1.000000	0.988751	0.962680	0.980775	0.982561	0.957619	0.869309
TIN_ITA	0.988751	1.000000	0.961874	0.977080	0.971622	0.964423	0.845948
TIN_JPN	0.962680	0.961874	1.000000	0.927511	0.944745	0.944344	0.884132
TIN_NLD	0.980775	0.977080	0.927511	1.000000	0.960909	0.956800	0.823180
TIN_NOR	0.982561	0.971622	0.944745	0.960909	1.000000	0.956800	0.868517
TIN_SWE	0.957619	0.964423	0.944344	0.956800	0.956800	1.000000	0.884313
TIN_USA	0.869309	0.845948	0.884132	0.823180	0.868517	0.884313	1.000000

Table 4.A2 (continued)

	TFPMAN_AUS	TFPMAN_BEL	TFPMAN_CAN	TFPMAN_DNK	TFPMAN_FIN	TFPMAN_FRA	TFPMAN_GBR
TFPMAN_AUS	1.000000	0.956434	0.901330	0.854290	0.949754	0.958415	0.886253
TFPMAN_BEL	0.956434	1.000000	0.834045	0.915014	0.895410	0.961426	0.885866
TFPMAN_CAN	0.901330	0.834045	1.000000	0.719566	0.912143	0.891618	0.848600
TFPMAN_DNK	0.854290	0.915014	0.719566	1.000000	0.777355	0.879877	0.677722
TFPMAN_FIN	0.949754	0.895410	0.912143	0.777355	1.000000	0.942512	0.831185
TFPMAN_FRA	0.958415	0.961426	0.891618	0.879877	0.942512	1.000000	0.838849
TFPMAN_GBR	0.886253	0.885866	0.848600	0.677722	0.831185	0.838849	1.000000
TFPMAN_GER	0.931743	0.959780	0.832450	0.892817	0.823885	0.931272	0.866919
TFPMAN_ITA	0.988055	0.982262	0.883406	0.879005	0.932027	0.967492	0.907646
TFPMAN_JPN	0.958384	0.983223	0.826297	0.857898	0.887709	0.951914	0.910913
TFPMAN_NLD	0.964840	0.985739	0.887464	0.920670	0.930865	0.980071	0.861443
TFPMAN_NOR	0.390060	0.403888	0.528550	0.323099	0.383072	0.322385	0.607009
TFPMAN_SWE	0.933250	0.888292	0.925011	0.786616	0.987370	0.923803	0.837841
TFPMAN_USA	0.938141	0.888979	0.955231	0.720762	0.919955	0.909068	0.944689

	TFPMAN_GER	TFPMAN_ITA	TFPMAN_JPN	TFPMAN_NLD	TFPMAN_NOR	TFPMAN_SWE	TFPMAN_USA
TFPMAN_AUS	0.931743	0.988055	0.958384	0.964840	0.390060	0.933250	0.938141
TFPMAN_BEL	0.959780	0.982262	0.983223	0.985739	0.403888	0.888292	0.888979
TFPMAN_CAN	0.832450	0.883406	0.826297	0.887464	0.528550	0.925011	0.955231
TFPMAN_DNK	0.892817	0.879005	0.857898	0.920670	0.323099	0.786616	0.720762
TFPMAN_FIN	0.823885	0.932027	0.887709	0.930865	0.383072	0.987370	0.919955
TFPMAN_FRA	0.931272	0.967492	0.951914	0.980071	0.322385	0.923803	0.909068
TFPMAN_GBR	0.866919	0.907646	0.910913	0.861443	0.607009	0.837841	0.944689
TFPMAN_GER	1.000000	0.961831	0.958245	0.956305	0.402357	0.823841	0.867124
TFPMAN_ITA	0.961831	1.000000	0.981404	0.980917	0.422856	0.920880	0.930117
TFPMAN_JPN	0.958245	0.981404	1.000000	0.963559	0.403200	0.867979	0.902619
TFPMAN_NLD	0.956305	0.980917	0.963559	1.000000	0.406783	0.930006	0.903511
TFPMAN_NOR	0.402357	0.422856	0.403200	0.406783	1.000000	0.481585	0.531368
TFPMAN_SWE	0.823841	0.920880	0.867979	0.930006	0.481585	1.000000	0.917073
TFPMAN_USA	0.867124	0.930117	0.902619	0.903511	0.531368	0.917073	1.000000

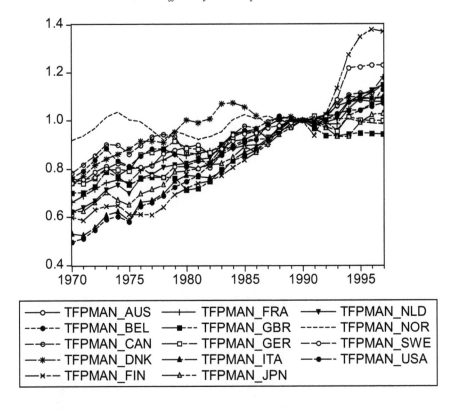

Figure 4.A1   Multifactor productivity in the private sector (TIN)

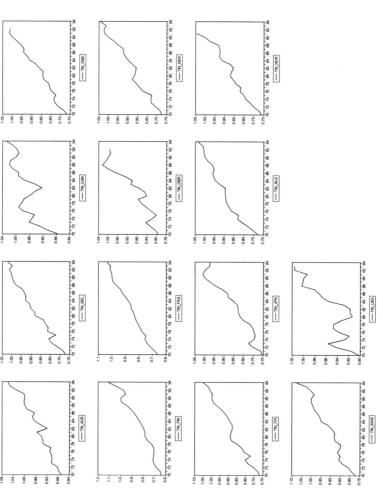

Figure 4.A2 Multifactor productivity in the private sector (TIN): 14 countries*

*TINs are plotted in the following order starting from northwest: Australia, Belgium, Canada, Denmark, Finland, France, United Kingdom, Germany, Italy, Japan, the Netherlands, Norway, Sweden and the US.

Chapter 5

Growth Effects of European Integration: Implications for EU Enlargement

Jesús Crespo-Cuaresma, Maria Antoinette Dimitz and
Doris Ritzberger-Grünwald

Introduction

For the last 50 years there has been widespread discussion about the economic consequences of European integration. The basic questions are: is economic integration growth enhancing? Are the rich getting richer and the poor getting poorer, or will the income levels of the EC/EU member countries converge as a consequence of integration? Furthermore, which countries will profit most from intensified trade among the members?

The theoretical literature on economic growth has gone through several phases, and the answers to the above questions depend on the specification of the respective growth model.

From the late 1950s to the mid-1980s the simple Solow-Swan 'exogenous growth model' dominated the literature (Solow, 1956). According to the neoclassical theory, the economy converges towards a steady state due to diminishing returns to investment in physical capital. Assuming a constant population, the long-run growth rate is solely determined by the rate of technological change, which is assumed to be exogenous. As the growth rate is therefore independent of any economic behaviour, economic policy changes will only have a temporary effect on economic activity.

The same is true for economic integration. Technological change is considered a public good common to all countries, so that they all share the same long-run growth rate determined by technological progress only. Therefore, the integrated economy will expand along this unchanged steady-state growth path in the long run, and the reallocation of resources will only temporarily have an influence on the growth rate. Hence, according to the neoclassical view of growth, European integration should not have a lasting effect on growth rates. However, the income levels should converge perfectly.

In the mid-1980s the so-called 'endogenous growth theory' revolutionized the literature on economic growth (Romer, 1990). Technology that was formerly considered a public good and exogenous now became endogenous and subject to decision-making processes at individual firms. According to this concept, enterprises have an incentive to invest in research, as the development of new technologies assures them of the possession of temporary monopoly power. But the absorption of monopoly rents is limited, as knowledge is only partially excludable. Patent protection is limited in time, and inventions can be used as inputs to further research and new technological innovations. These knowledge spillovers prevent the firms from collecting the full monopoly rent for their new inventions.

The aspect of the new growth theory according to which technological progress depends on the research activities of individual firms, which seek to collect monopoly rents, opens a new view on the issue of economic growth in an integrated region: now an increased scale of the economy will have a lasting positive effect on growth. On the one hand, knowledge spillovers imply increasing returns to scale to capital accumulation. On the other hand, the monopoly rent increases with the number of consumers while the costs for research and development are independent of the size of the economy. The prospect of higher profits increases the incentive for further research and hence spurs economic growth. These two factors together imply that the long-run growth rate increases with the size of the economy.[1]

To sum it up, the consequences of European integration are fundamentally different within the framework of endogenous growth. The more countries join the Economic Union and hence the larger the scale of the integrated economy, the higher is the incentive for research and development and, accordingly, the higher is the growth rate. Enhanced growth is now not only a transitory, but a permanent phenomenon from which all countries profit in the long run.

Most empirical papers on economic growth aim at detecting the main determinants of long-run growth without referring explicitly to regional integration (for European regions see for example Sala-i-Martin, 1996). The first papers dealing with the question of a possible growth bonus associated with European integration were all cross-country studies. Basically, they compare EU members with other countries that have not joined the European Union, mostly countries at a similar stage of development. The basic question is whether there exists a global growth benefit from being an EU member. Most of the studies do not find any such growth bonus (see for example De Melo *et al.*, 1992 or Landau, 1995).

However, panel data regression techniques opened up a new way to deal with the question of possible growth benefits associated with EU membership. This makes it possible to focus exclusively on the current EU Member States. The basic question then can be whether, in retrospect, the current EU members profited from regional integration.

There are two studies that ask questions similar to the ones discussed in our paper, although they look at a wider set of countries and do not exclusively focus on EU members.

Vanhoudt (1999) tests the validity of the neoclassical implication that regional integration has no impact on long-term growth against the alternative model based on endogenous growth theory. He carries out panel data regressions on 23 OECD countries to check whether EU membership had a positive impact on growth

---

1   A countervailing effect of integration, which could work in the opposite direction to the one described in the text, refers to the fact that, in a larger market, competition is more intense and monopoly rents are smaller and more short-lived. However, empirical research on the effect of trade integration on growth suggests a dominant role of the growth enhancing effect. See below for some references.

compared to developed countries that have not joined the European Union. He does not find evidence of a significant long-run growth bonus associated either with EU membership or with membership length. In addition, the results do not support the hypothesis of a scale effect on growth. The author concludes that the neoclassical hypothesis cannot be rejected by the data.

Henrekson *et al.* (1997), who focus on EC as well as on EFTA member countries, find the opposite result: EC/EFTA membership may increase growth rates significantly, by around 0.6 to 0.8 percentage point per year. However, apparently it does not matter whether a country is an EC or an EFTA member. Their results support the hypothesis that regional integration in Europe can have significant growth effects and suggest that further regional integration may be growth enhancing in the long run. However, the results of the paper are not completely robust with respect to changes in the model specification.

Both these studies and the present paper deal with the question of whether European integration had a positive impact on long-term growth in the member countries. Our study, however, deviates from the other two in that it exclusively focuses on the current EU Member States,[2] in that it deals with the issue of convergence within the integrated European economy. Our questions are: have per capita income levels in European countries converged towards each other since the 1960s? And if EU membership had a favourable impact on growth in these countries, can we detect subsets of countries that profited more than average from EU membership? Can we conclude from these asymmetric gains in growth that convergence was also a consequence of intensified economic involvement due to European integration?

Convergence and Growth in the EU – Concepts and First Results

The term *β-convergence* was coined by Barro and Sala-i-Martin (1992) and refers to the negative correlation between initial levels of real GDP per capita and its average yearly growth rate either after conditioning for certain control variables (*conditional β-convergence*) or without conditioning (*unconditional β-convergence*). For a complete survey on the empirical literature dealing with evidence on β-convergence see, for example, Durlauf and Quah (1998).[3] Together with the concept of β-convergence, Barro and Sala-i-Martin (1992) introduce the complementary concept of *σ-convergence*, which refers to the decrease of the dispersion of real GDP per capita across economic units through time. It should be noted that β-convergence is a necessary but not sufficient condition for σ-convergence.

---

2   Another recent contribution to this branch of literature, Badinger (2001), focuses exclusively on European countries using a somehow different approach and finding again no evidence for a growth bonus of EU membership.

3   Notice that this approach is not free from criticism. For a critical view and alternative concepts of convergence based on the time series properties of real GDP per capita, see for example Bernard and Durlauf (1996).

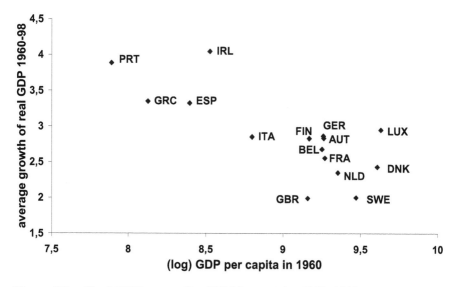

Figure 5.1   Real GDP per capita: EU-15 countries 1960–1998

Figure 5.1 shows the evolution of real GDP per capita between 1960 and 1998 in the 15 current EU Member States to provide a first visual approach to the study of convergence in the EU. Evidence of β-convergence is difficult to extract from the graph, but becomes clearer when we use a scatter relating initial levels of real GDP per capita to average growth.

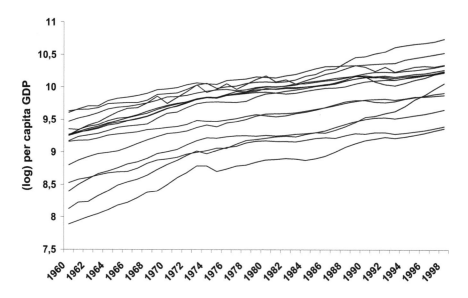

Figure 5.2   GDP per capita in 1960 versus growth: EU-15 countries 1960–1998

Figure 5.2 shows a scatter plot aimed at checking for (unconditional) β-convergence in the European Union for the period 1960–98: on the x-axis, the (log) level of real GDP per capita is represented, while the y-axis shows the average yearly growth of real GDP per capita in the period 1960–98. A visual inspection shows a negative relationship between both variables.

This first indication of convergence is confirmed by dividing the data into four subperiods (1961–70, 1971–80, 1981–90, 1991–98)[4] and estimating the β parameter in the panel regression

$$\left[\ln\left(y_{T t,i}\right)-\ln\left(y_{0 t,i}\right)\right]/n_t - \alpha + \beta \ln\left(y_{0 t,i}\right)+u_{t,i} \qquad (1)$$

where $y_{T t,i}$ refers to the real GDP per capita in the last year of period t (t=1,2,3,4 stands for each of the subperiods described above) for country i, $y_{0 t,i}$ refers to the value of real GDP per capita in the initial year of period t and n_t is the number of years in period t. Equation (1) has been estimated based on different assumptions for the error term, and the results are presented in Table 5.1.[5]
The first column shows the result for the assumption that the error term is independent

Table 5.1   Unconditional β-convergence in the EU

	Common Intercept	Fixed Effects (one way)	Fixed Effects (two way)
β	-1.91*** (0.20)	-3.02*** (0.37)	-4.88*** (1.41)
Obs.	56	56	56
R^2_{adj}	51.3%	62.3%	62.4%

***(**)[*] stands for 1% (5%) [10%] significant.

of the cross-sectional units (countries) and iid normal (that is, the panel is estimated as if it were a cross-country regression). The second column shows the results for the assumption of fixed country effects, that is,

$$u_{t,i=\mu_i} + \varepsilon_t \qquad (2)$$

where μ_i is a country-specific constant and ε_t is white noise. Finally, the third column shows the estimated β under the assumption of fixed country and time effects, that is,

$$u_{t,i} = \mu_i + \lambda_t + \varepsilon_t \qquad (3)$$

---

4   A minimum amount of eight years seems reasonable for studying long-term growth features, because thus business cycle fluctuations are eliminated.

5   Throughout the study, Luxembourg was excluded from the estimations for two reasons: It is typically considered an outlier, and no data on average education years is available for this country in Barro and Lee (2001).

where μ_i and ε_i are defined as above, and λ_i is an exclusively time-dependent constant effect.

All specifications reported in Table 5.1 point at the existence of very significant unconditional β-convergence across the current EU members for the period 1960–98.

Figure 5.3 shows the evolution of the cross-country coefficient of variation of per capita GDP for the period 1960–98. By visual inspection, the trend is clearly decreasing, indicating σ-convergence. Whether the standard deviation in the final period is significantly different from that of the first period can be investigated using the test developed by Carree and Klomp (1997). The result indicates σ-convergence.

Figure 5.3   Real GDP per capita dispersion: EU-15 countries 1960–1998

Growth and EU Membership

The Basic Model and Some Extensions

In order to study explicitly the determinants of long-term growth in Europe in the last four decades, equation (1) will be extended by including an augmented set of explanatory variables. The obvious candidates to form part of the group are those variables that are explicitly implied by economic theory and which have been used in virtually every empirical study on economic growth: the initial (log) level of per capita GDP (evaluated in our case at the first year of each subperiod), the investment

Table 5.2   Growth panel data regressions

Model	1	2	3	4
Initial GDP	-5.60*** (1.44)	-3.80*** (0.53)	-4.73*** (0.73)	-4.74*** (0.76)
Investment Rate	0.13** (0.05)	0.13*** (0.04)	0.17*** (0.04)	0.18*** (0.04)
Years of Education	0.12 (0.10)	0.22 (0.16)	0.34** (0.16)	0.35** (0.16)
Inflation Rate		-0.12*** (0.02)	-0.11*** (0.02)	-0.11*** (0.03)
Government Cons.		-0.06 (0.08)	-0.01 (0.1)	–
Openness		0.06** (0.03)	0.06** (0.03)	0.06** (0.03)
Years in the EU			0.04* (0.02)	0.04** (0.01)
Observations	56	56	56	56
R^2_{adj}	63.8%	76.3%	77.1%	77.7%

All EU countries except Luxembourg included (data for West Germany until 1991, unified Germany afterwards), with data ranging from 1960 to 1998, divided into four periods: 1960–1970, 1971–1980, 1981–1990 and 1991–1998. White heteroskedasticity/serial correlation-corrected standard errors in parenthesis. Fixed effects estimation with period specific time dummies included if jointly significant. ***(**)[*] stands for 1% (5%) [10%] significant.

rate (subperiod average) and some proxy for human capital (average years of education of population over 25, evaluated at the first year of the subperiod).[6]

Together with these basic variables, others that are considered to be relevant to economic growth have been included in the econometric specification. The specification in which all the estimated models presented in Table 5.2 are nested is:

$$\left[\ln\left(y_{Tt,i}\right)-\left(\ln y_{0t,i}\right)\right]/n_t = \beta_1 \ln\left(y_{0t,i}\right)+\beta_2 INV_{t,i}+\beta_3 \cdot$$
$$\beta_4 INF_{t,i}+\beta_5 GOV_{t,i}+\beta_6 OR_{t,i}+\beta_7 YEA_{t,i}+u_{t,i} \tag{4}$$

where $\ln(y_{0t,i})$ is the (log) initial GDP per capita of country i in subperiod t, $INV_{t,i}$ is the investment rate, $ED_{t,i}$ refers to the years of education, $INF_{t,i}$ is the subperiod-average inflation rate, $GOV_{t,i}$ is government consumption over GDP, $OP_{t,i}$ is openness of the economy defined as trade over GDP, and $YEA_{t,i}$ is the average length of EU membership (in years) for country i in subperiod t.[7] The error term $u_{t,i}$ is assumed to be composed by a constant country-specific effect and a common constant time effect, although in the estimation the latter will only be included if found significant.

---

6   Empirical studies dealing with a more heterogeneous set of countries tend to include population growth as an explanatory variable. In our case, the variable appeared insignificant in every specification in which it was included and was therefore not added to the set of explanatory variables. The same occurred when a socio-demographic variable like female participation in the labour market was used. A possible explanation of the lack of significance of labour participation would be the high correlation between this variable and initial GDP.

7   For Germany we use data for West Germany until 1991, and for the unified Germany from 1991 onwards. Initially, an additional dummy variable was included in order to account for the German unification, but it appeared insignificant in all specifications.

Table 5.2 shows the results of the estimation of the different specifications of our growth model.

In a first step, growth is regressed on initial GDP, the investment rate and the years of education. All coefficients in the first column have the expected signs. Growth depends negatively on initial GDP, indicating β-convergence. The investment rate enters positively (see for example Barro, 1991; Levine and Renelt, 1992). Turning to education, most authors find that the overall level of education is growth enhancing (see for example Barro, 1991).[8] Our positive coefficient for the average years of education seems to support this result, although it is not significant at the 10 percent level. A similar result is found for example by Levine and Renelt (1992).

In a second step, the inflation rate, government consumption over GDP and openness of the economy are added to the model as variables. The inclusion of these three variables does not change the signs of the first three factors, as can be seen in the second column. Inflation enters the equation with a negative sign, indicating the growth-hampering effect of high increases in the price level (for a detailed study on this relationship, see Barro, 1995). The minus sign of the coefficient for the government consumption ratio implies a negative relationship between government expenditure and growth. Other empirical studies, for example Barro (1991) and Barro (1997) also found this result. The intuition is that government spending has only a temporary influence on growth while, in the long run, the growth-hampering impact of high debt levels as a consequence of excessive government spending as well as possible allocative inefficiencies predominate. In our case, however, the coefficient is not significant (a result also found by Levine and Renelt, 1992). Finally the coefficient for the openness of the economy is significant and shows the expected positive sign, supporting the view that trade stimulates growth. This result is also found by Harrison (1995), Sachs and Warner (1995).

In the final step, the model is modified by inclusion of the subperiod-average number of years since a country's accession to the European Union. Notice that, having controlled already for openness, the EU membership variable will reflect growth effects of regional integration different from those directly related to trade.[9] The positive and significant coefficient in column 3 indicates that the longer a country has been a member of the EU, the more it profits from membership. The inclusion of this new variable leaves the signs of the other coefficients unchanged. The coefficient for education is still positive, but it is now significant at the 5 percent level. This extended model explains 78 percent of the variation in growth.

To check for robustness the model is also estimated without government consumption, as the coefficient proved insignificant in models 2 and 3. However, the

---

8   There is, however, some indication that primary education has a negative impact on growth, see for example Barro (1997).

9   The fact that our openness variable is defined as trade over GDP implies that trade-related technology absorption is already partly captured by the positive coefficient for $OP_{t,i}$. This is expected actually to reduce our coefficient for the impact of the EU membership variable and reinforces the importance of technological spillovers as a driving force for growth.

other coefficients remain practically unchanged, some of them becoming even more significant. This strengthens the robustness of our previous results.

The effect represented by the coefficient of the variable $YEA_{t,i}$ affects only countries that have been members of the EU for at least one year in a given subperiod. It could be the case, however, that a larger regionally integrated space also has an effect on the growth rates of countries that do not form part of it yet. In order to check for this possibility and to shed a light on whether membership is actually required for gaining growth benefits from regional integration, the model was re-estimated by replacing $YEA_{t,i}$ with a scale variable common to all countries but variable in time, which captures the size of the regionally integrated unit. We used three different specifications of the scale variable (aggregate population, aggregate GDP and aggregate labour force), and the coefficient always appeared positive, but

Table 5.3   Testing for linearity

	Single threshold	Double threshold	
	$\hat{\gamma}$	$\hat{\gamma}_1$	$\hat{\gamma}_2$
Initial GDP per-capita (logged)		9.25	9.80
Bootstrap p-value	0.027	0.169	

Bootstrap p-values based on 1000 replications. Threshold values found by grid search in the central 50% of the distribution of the threshold value.

insignificant. Therefore, the growth benefits associated with regional integration seem to be due to formal participation in the union.

Another objection to our conclusion could be that it is not EU membership itself that enhances growth, but that the accompanying stability measures for nominal macroeconomic variables had a positive impact on growth performance. Partly this was already accounted for by including the inflation rate as an explanatory variable. To check, in addition, for the impact of a potential decrease in the exchange rate volatility caused by EU membership, the standard deviation of the exchange rate against the US dollar for each country was included as an additional independent variable. However, its coefficient appeared insignificant in all specifications. This indicates that exchange rate policy does not explain the existence of a growth bonus associated with EU membership.

To sum up, our model so far explains a considerable part of the variation in growth, and the results strongly support the hypothesis of (conditional) β-convergence: poorer countries have caught up with the richer ones since the 1960s, and the rate of convergence is found to be between approximately 3.5 and 5.5 percent, depending on the specification used.[10] Furthermore, the coefficients support the hypothesis of

---

10 The rate of convergence has been computed as $\lambda = -[1 - \exp{(\beta T)}]/T$, where β is the coefficient corresponding to initial GDP per capita, and T is the subperiod length. The expression for λ results from the log linearisation around the steady state in the classical Solow model.

Table 5.4   Threshold panel data regressions

Model	1T	2T
Initial GDP	-4.09*** (0.68)	-4.47*** (0.65)
Investment Rate	0.14*** (0.04)	0.16*** (0.03)
Years of Education	0.17 (0.14)	0.20 (0.13)
Inflation Rate	-0.13** (0.03)	-0.13*** (0.03)
Government Cons.	-0.05 (0.09)	–
Openness	0.05** (0.02)	0.05** (0.02)
Years in the EU $\times I (y_{0t} \leq \hat{\gamma})$	0.09*** (0.02)	0.09*** (0.02)
Years in the EU $\times I (y_{0t} > \hat{\gamma})$	0.04** (0.01)	0.04*** (0.01)
Observations	56	56
R^2_{adj}	83.2%	83.4%

a positive impact of investment, education and openness on growth, as well as a negative impact of high inflation rates. Finally the results not only point at a growth-enhancing effect of EU membership, but they also show that this effect gained importance over the duration of membership.

Who Profits Most from EU Membership?

One interesting extension to the basic models is to look in more detail at the finding that EU membership is growth enhancing and, furthermore, becomes even more so the longer a country belongs to the grouping. A particularly interesting question is whether a subgroup of countries profited more from EU membership than other countries. The idea is to divide the sample of countries into subsets with respect to one of the other variables and to investigate whether the coefficient for the years of membership differs significantly across subgroups.

One basic way to do that would be to split the sample according to a priori defined rules. For example, one could define poor, medium and rich countries by setting the borderline income levels. The threshold panel data technique, however, offers a more neutral approach. It allows testing of whether such subgroups can be found at all and how many subsets are appropriate. Furthermore, it estimates explicitly the borderline income levels. The main advantage of this approach is that it avoids ad hoc definitions of subgroups, but tests the hypothesis of the existence of subsets against the alternative of no division of the sample.

In our extension of the basic model we test whether countries with a lower initial per capita income level profited more or less from EU membership than more developed countries. If subsamples according to initial income levels can be identified and the coefficient for the years of EU membership is significantly higher for initially poorer countries, this would be an indication of increased economic convergence as a consequence of European integration. If, however, we get the opposite result, this would indicate that the initially richer countries are also the ones that profit most from intensified economic involvement.

Table 5.3 gives the results of the threshold estimation, and Table 5.4 presents the parameter estimates of the threshold model.[11] The estimation procedure identifies exactly one threshold at a level of (log) initial GDP per capita equal to 9.8 (approximately, US$18,000). A 95 percent confidence interval around the threshold estimate computed using the empirical likelihood function is [9.70, 9.81]. The test for linearity rejects the null of no threshold effect at a 5 percent significance level, and the null of one threshold cannot be rejected when tested against the alternative of two thresholds.

Looking at the original data set, we see that at the beginning of our sample, that is in 1960, all countries had an initial income level below the threshold. In 1970, Denmark and Sweden had broken through the threshold. Ten years later, six more countries had followed and only the incomes of Greece, Ireland, Italy, Portugal, Spain and the United Kingdom remained below the threshold. In 1991, finally, the income levels in Italy and the UK exceeded the threshold income level, so that the subgroup of less developed countries was now limited to the classical catching-up countries Greece, Ireland, Portugal and Spain. Towards the very end of our data set, the income level of Ireland, which recently experienced two-digit growth rates, exceeded the threshold level.

The next step is to divide the sample in each period according to this threshold and rerun the panel regressions. The results are shown in Table 5.4, where we now have a separate coefficient for the length of EU membership for each subgroup. The coefficient for the years of EU membership is positive and significant for both subgroups. Furthermore we find that the coefficient differs significantly across groups and is significantly higher for the countries with lower initial income levels. All the other coefficients show the expected signs. The new model, which splits the countries into two subgroups according to their initial income levels, explains around 83 percent of the variation in growth.[12]

Hence, while countries with a higher level of development grew faster the longer they were members of the EU, this effect is even more pronounced when it comes to the subgroup of less advanced countries.[13] This finding can be interpreted as another indication for a catching-up process of poorer towards richer countries in Europe in the sense that with two countries entering the EU at the same point in time the growth bonus is larger for the less advanced country.[14] Not only do our results show that

---

11 For literature on the threshold panel data estimation see, for example, Baltagi (1995), Hansen (1996, 1999) and Andrews and Ploberger (1994).

12 To check for robustness the model was re-estimated using Switzerland as an external control country. The coefficients remained similar in terms of sign, range and significance. The goodness of fit, furthermore, improved considerably. The results are not reported in the tables and are available upon request from the authors.

13 The exercise was repeated using the relative level of GDP per capita with respect to the average of current Member States as a threshold variable. However, the test for linearity could not reject the null of linearity at any reasonable significance level. This suggests that it is the absolute level of development of the country that determines the asymmetric effect of EU membership on long term growth.

14 This, however, does not imply that this growth bonus has actually led to absolute convergence of the EU member states. The different entry dates and the cumulative nature of

countries with lower initial incomes grew faster than the more advanced countries' β-convergence, the estimates also imply that countries that exhibit per capita income levels below the threshold profit more from long-term EU membership than richer countries.[15]

Conclusions and Prospects for Further Research

The empirical study performed in this paper shows that EU membership has had a positive and asymmetric effect on long-term economic growth. As the model specification uses openness as a control variable, the growth effect picked up by the regional integration variable differs from that resulting from intensified trade and would relate to the improvements in the transmission of technological knowledge among the EU Member States. The results may be seen as constituting new empirical support for endogenous growth theory and would imply that it is the relatively less developed countries that profit most from access to the broader technological framework offered by the regionally integrated unit.

However, one could argue that technology is not the only factor explaining the growth bonus associated with EU membership. One argument that may as well be used to interpret the results relies upon the assumption that financial help from the EU to relatively poorer members actually does have an effect on long-term growth. In fact, the EU budget generated major net financial transfers to the four cohesion countries – Greece, Portugal, Ireland and Spain.[16] In 2000, these net transfers accounted for 3.6 percent of Greek GNP, 1.9 percent of Portuguese GNP, 1.8 percent of Irish GNP and 0.9 percent of Spanish GNP. To a lesser extent, Finland, Denmark and Italy also showed positive net balances (see European Commission, 2001).

Have these transfers been successful? To answer this question, the European Commission runs several macroeconomic models (for an overview see the *Sixth Periodic Report* – European Commission, 1999). The *Beutel* model, for instance, is used to investigate how much of the economic growth in the Member States covered can be attributed to EU co-funded programmes and EU grants. According to the model, EU transfers during the two programming periods (1989 to 1993 and 1994 to 1999) are found to have increased GDP growth in the four cohesion countries by an average of 0.5 percentage points in the first period and 0.7 percentage points in the second period.

---

the growth bonus have led to several more advanced economies profiting relatively more from integration.

15   In order to check whether the effect – or absence of the effect – of government consumption on growth differs depending on the absolute level of government consumption in a country, we checked the results for the inclusion of an extra threshold effect on the parameter of government consumption, with the level of government consumption itself as a threshold variable. The test, however, was not able to reject the null of linearity at any sensible significance level.

16   The cohesion fund was established in 1993, after the Mediterranean countries Greece (1981) and Spain and Portugal (1986) had joined the European Union. Cohesion countries are EU member countries whose GDP per capita is lower than 90 percent of the EU average.

As a result, income disparities have been reduced, and the gap in GDP per capita between the four cohesion countries and the rest of the European Union has narrowed (the average GDP per capita in the four cohesion countries went up from 65 percent of the EU average in 1986 to 78 percent in 1999). The overall result of a number of macroeconomic models is that one third of the reduction in disparities is due to the Structural Funds (Moucque, 2000). Therefore, EU transfers should be taken into account when analysing the process of convergence. However, the non-availability of proper time series has prevented an implementation of such a variable into our model so far.

Fölster and Henrekson (2001) find a robust and negative relationship between government size and economic growth. This could provide another possible explanation for our result that EU membership had a positive impact on growth, as due to liberalization measures inherent to the integration process the size of the government in EU Member States has decreased rapidly in the last decades. Possible other sources of the growth bonus could be the stabilization of expectations in the context of the European Exchange Rate Mechanism or the preparations for monetary union. The dollar exchange rate, which was implemented into our model without any significant result, can be seen as only a first step to cover this exchange rate effect.

Another possible source of the growth bonus is the changes in the institutional framework due to European integration. Whereas the completion of the internal market or, in other words, the openness of the countries is covered more or less by the trade variable, there are other developments that could also play a role. Examples are the legal and the institutional framework of the financial sector, the scale and the nature of foreign direct investment, transport infrastructure and the efficiency of public administration.

To sum up, the uncertainty surrounding the nature of the underlying driving factors only allows for a rejection of the basic neoclassical growth model. Further research would have to be done, however, to test the empirical validity of the endogenous growth model, as the fact that technological spillovers do indeed drive our result cannot be extracted directly from our study.

One interesting question would be whether our results allow implications about the EU enlargement process. In terms of pure GDP per capita levels, some countries (Slovenia, the Czech Republic, Hungary and Slovakia) have already reached a GDP per capita level (in percent of the EU-15) which is similar to or even above the one Greece showed at its EU entry in 1981. But as our study is based on historical data for the current EU Member States, we cannot directly apply the findings to the potential accession countries. The structural and institutional differences in these economies, as compared to the current Member States, are sometimes huge, and even the fact that the income levels of all candidate countries currently lie below our estimated threshold does not allow for the conclusion that these countries will indeed profit more than average from EU membership. Additionally, one should take into consideration that these economies not only undergo an accession, but also a transformation process. This also limits the applicability of our results.

Finally, let us draw some policy conclusions. There seems to be a growth bonus associated with the formal EU membership. Our model indicates the presence of knowledge spillovers, so it is not only trade that matters. This growth bonus gains importance over time, underpinning the fact that European integration is a long-term concept and, even more importantly, that the growth bonus in the EU is still working. Additionally, we have found an asymmetric effect on long-term growth, so obviously European integration drives convergence. The results fit into the picture that nominal and real convergence stand next to each other as equal goals of the EU and are being successfully pursued.

References

Andrews, D. K. and Ploberger, W. (1994) Optimal tests when a nuisance parameter is present only under the alternative, *Econometrica*, 62: 1383–1414.

Badinger, H. (2001) *Growth Effects of Economic Integration – The Case of the EU Member States (1950-2000)*, Research Institute for European Affairs (Vienna: Working Paper 40, University of Economics and Business Administration).

Baltagi, B.H. (1995) *Econometric Analysis of Panel Data* (Chichester: Wiley).

Barro, R.J. (1991) Economic growth in a cross section of countries, *Quarterly Journal of Economics*, 106(2): 407–43.

Barro, R.J. (1995) *Inflation and Economic Growth*, NBER Working Paper Series, 5326.

Barro, R.J. (1997) *Determinants of Economic Growth: A Cross-country Empirical Study*, Harvard Institute for International Development (Discussion Papers, 579).

Barro, R.J. and Lee, J.-W. (2001) International data on educational attainment: updates and implications, *Economic Papers*, 53: 541–63.

Barro, R. J. and Sala-i-Martin, X. (1992) Convergence, *Journal of Political Economy*, 100(2): 223–51.

Bernard, A.B. and Durlauf, S.N. (1996) Interpreting tests of the convergence hypothesis, *Journal of Econometrics*, 71(1-2): 161–74.

Carree, M. and Klomp, L. (1997) Testing the convergence hypothesis: A comment, *The Review of Economics and Statistics*, 79(4): 683–86.

De Melo, J., Montenegro, C. and Panagariya, A. (1992) L'integration regionale hier et aujourd'hui, *Revue d'Economie du Developpement*, 0-2: 7–49.

Durlauf, S.N. and Quah, D.T. (1998) *The New Empirics of Economic Growth*, NBER Working Paper, No. 6422.

European Commission (1999) *The European Regions: Sixth Periodic Report on the Socio-Economic Situation in the Regions of the European Union* (Luxembourg: Official Publication Office).

European Commission (2001) *Allocation of 2000 EU Operating Expenditure by Member States* (European Commission, Budget, Own Resources, evaluation and financial programming).

Fölster, S. and Henrekson, M. (2001) Growth effects of government expenditure and taxation in rich countries, *European Economic Review*, 45: 1501–20.

Hansen, B.E. (1996) Inference when a nuisance parameter is not identified under the null hypothesis, *Econometrica*, 64: 413–30.

Hansen, B.E. (1999) Threshold effects in non-dynamic panels: Estimation, testing, and inference, *Journal of Econometrics*, 93: 345–68.

Harrison, A. (1995) *Openness and Growth: A Time Series, Cross-country Analysis for Developing Countries*, NBER Working Paper Series, 5221.

Henrekson, M., Torstensson, J. and Torstensson, R. (1997) Growth effects of European integration, *European Economic Review*, 41: 1537–57.

Landau, D. (1995) The contribution of the European common market to the growth of its member countries: an empirical test, *Review of World Economics*, 131(4): 774–82.

Levine, R. and Renelt, D. (1992) A sensitivity analysis of cross-country growth regressions, *American Economic Review*, 82(4): 942–63.

Moucque, D. (2000) A survey of socio-economic disparities between the regions of the EU, in: *Regional Convergence in Europe: Theory and Empirical Evidence* (EIB Papers, 5-2, 13-24).

Romer, P.M. (1990) Endogenous technological change, *Journal of Political Economy*, 98: S71–S102.

Sachs, J.D. and Warner, A. (1995) Economic reform and the process of global integration, *Brookings Papers on Economic Activity*, 1: 1–118.

Sala-i-Martin, X. (1996) Regional cohesion: Evidence and theories of regional growth and convergence, *European Economic Review*, 40: 1325–52.

Solow, R.M. (1956) A contribution to the theory of economic growth, *Quarterly Journal of Economics*, 70: 65–94.

Vanhoudt, P. (1999) Did the European unification induce economic growth? In Search of scale effects and persistent changes, *Review of World Economics*, 135(2): 193–220.

Chapter 6

Towards a European Economic Constitution

Renato Brunetta

The possible roles of a constitution: procedures, aspirations, credibility and values

The constitution of a State or community of States can be defined as a collection of fundamental rules of law that lay down the values and basic organisation of that State or community of States.

Early modern constitutions, such as the United States' Constitution, were primarily concerned with defining a model of government. They set out the general principles of government, leaving the exact content to be determined by ordinary law. The US Constitution, signed in Philadelphia on 17 September 1787 and which became law the following year, was amended by the Bill of Rights, in the form of 10 amendments ratified in 1791, to which a further 17 were later added, aimed at safeguarding the freedoms of its citizens. According to the Founding Fathers, particularly Madison, the effectiveness of the procedures and not the statement of principles was the key to safeguarding the freedoms of citizens. In France, the constitutional model is in many respects similar to that of the US, at least from a formal point of view. The Gaullist Constitution of 1958 is content neutral. For a declaration of fundamental values, reference is made to the Declaration of the Rights of Man and of the Citizen of 1789 and the preamble to the 1946 Constitution (cit).

Over time, and in developing countries in particular, constitutions have become increasingly lengthy and 'ambitious'. One of the contributing factors has been 'second-generation' social and economic rights, which emerged at the beginning of the last century, some time after 'first-generation' civil and political rights. The implementation of these social and economic rights requires action by the State in the form of benefits and thus increased government expenditure. Intervention by the legislator is thus necessary for these rights to be enforced.

The aim is to add substantial equality in terms of living and working conditions to the formal equality granted by civil and political rights. Certain Constitutional Courts, including the Italian Constitutional Court, have been forced to admit that the nature of some of these constitutional requirements – including the right to work – is rather like a policy statement; in other words, indicating the objectives for the State and public administration as a whole, without being directly applicable.

Usually, content biased constitutional models lead to an institutional impasse and the creation of expectations, which are inevitably ignored. Examples of such degeneration can be found in the post-colonial Indian Constitution, with its 395 articles, and in the Brazilian Constitution, which has 245 articles plus a further 200 provisional regulations.

Some countries, such as the UK, do not have written constitutions. Despite the claims of certain scholars that a constitution could practically be reconstructed merely by cutting and pasting from the Statute Book (Mitchell, 1968), the fundamental principles at the very heart of UK institutions rely on tacit constitutional conventions. These are the fruit of a long and gradual evolutionary process, the architects of which are not easily identifiable (unlike the authors of written constitutions).

Apart from its form (written or unwritten, rigid or flexible, long or short), two principal objectives can be identified with the drafting and subsequent promulgation of a constitution.

First, there is the objective of providing citizens and institutions with the assurances of an instrument that is less flexible than normal legislation. It is harder for a constitution to be manipulated by the political majority and thus it is more able to protect the rights of the minority. This is the fundamental premise of liberal constitutions, such as the substantial British Constitution, which has evolved over the centuries, and the US Constitution of 1787, which claim to limit sovereign power credibly. In the language of economic essays on credibility, constitutions (at least in their liberal form) bind the hands of a State or supranational authority, protecting the rights of citizens from potential abuse or interference. In modern democracies, liberal constitutions protect the minority from the tyranny of the majority, rather than from the free will of absolute power (Tocqueville, 1848), a hazard descried by Madison, who in Issue 10 of the *Federalist* writes that 'Either the existence of the same passion or interest in a majority at the same time must be prevented, or the majority, having such coexistent passion or interest, must be rendered, by their number and local situation, unable to concert and carry into effect schemes of oppression'. Hence the checks and balances of the US Constitution.

Thus, in a liberal constitution, the essence is not so much in the list of fundamental rights of the individual, but above all in the statement of institutional rules protecting the individual's freedom.

This is the case with the English tax reforms introduced following the Glorious Revolution of 1688. These changes reflected the need to make more credible the government's promise to honour its debts.

The English government increased its credibility by expressly limiting the powers of the Crown to alter unilaterally the financial conditions of loans awarded by private companies. This required the introduction of a special procedure, whereby in order to renegotiate the debt, the Crown needed permission from Parliament (which primarily represented the interests of the holders of wealth, to coin a socio-economic phrase).

Therefore, in order for government to be credible, a set of constitutional rules must be introduced to modify the structure of incentives at the very heart of the institutions. Citizens should be persuaded that the constitution is robust enough to withstand changes from one day to the next, except under exceptional circumstances and subject to near-unanimous approval.

As well as providing assurances, constitutions may need to create or formalise an identity based around a common citizenship or ideology.

Instead of a bottom-up liberal model, which allows citizens to limit the discretionary powers of governments, we now have a top-down constitution (fostered by governments to direct their citizens). In this case, the constitution is not concerned with defining synthetically the principles of government, but is the vehicle by which values are instilled to inspire social and individual relationships. This is the case with socialist constitutions or constitutions of former colonies, which fulfil almost exclusively the functions of propaganda or decisiveness, deliberately kindled by the dominant political or economic elite.

Having briefly examined the history of this debate, the question we now need to ask ourselves is whether a constitution has a place in Europe today.

In a European Constitution, set out in a clear, concise document, some discern the opportunity to promote European citizenship via the declaration of a common identity. However, this vision does not appear to be fully endorsable, if construed as the top-down promotion of something that does not currently exist or which exists only in the minds of an elite minority, because, according to a code that has evolved to differing degrees in the various Member States, only if the rules and institutions provided by a single constitutional document allow the European machinery to operate freely and unerringly could this have a positive impact on the future of European unification.

For this reason perhaps, it might be preferable to follow the US and French examples, separating the concept of values from the European Constitution per se, construed as an institutional structure. Similarly, still following the example set by France and the US, the Charter of Fundamental Rights of the European Union, ratified on 7 December 2000 at the European summit in Nizza, could serve as a preamble for the future European Constitution.

The Fundamental Rights Charter actually has the advantage of rendering visible and explicit in the construction of Europe the fundamental rights already enjoyed by European citizens: human dignity, liberty, equality and solidarity.

At the same time, the Charter unites under a single law, rights that are currently dispersed across a heterogeneous group of sources. As stated in the preamble,

> This Charter reaffirms, with due regard to the powers and tasks of the Community and the Union and the principle of subsidiarity, the rights as they result, in particular, from constitutional traditions and international obligations common to the Member States, the Treaty on European Union, the Community Treaties, the European Convention for the Protection of Human Rights and Fundamental Freedoms, the Social Charters adopted by the Community and by the Council of Europe and the case-law of the Court of Justice of the European Communities and of the European Court of Human Rights.

To strengthen the role of fundamental rights in the European constitutional system it would be right to draft a simplified and shorter text of the Charter, along with a more hierarchical structure of the rights in order to highlight the role of the fundamental rights with respect to the rights having a secondary status. In this way it could be possible to create a stronger legal certainty and to reduce the risk of proliferation of constitutional contentiousness.

The Role of an Economic Constitution: the Individual or State First?

An economic constitution is responsible, within a broader constitutional framework, for regulating economic relationships.

It is possible to identify schematically two fundamental ideological reference matrices. The liberal model is aimed at limiting the public role in the economy. It adheres to the principle that everything not expressly prohibited is allowed.

The socialist model limits the role of intermediate individuals and organisations, placing the authority of the State before the free will of the citizens and thus negating the principle of horizontal subsidiarity.

Both models fulfil the same requirement of producing a more stable legal framework, even if this is for distinctly opposing reasons.

According to Petroni, in the liberal (or ius naturalist) version, a constitution is a set of laws and procedures aimed at protecting citizens' rights. These rights are not generated by the constitution itself but precede it. Both the constitution of powers and the organisation and exercise of such powers are justified insofar as they are demonstrated to be suitable instruments for protecting the rights of the individual in various historical circumstances (Petroni, 2001). This is generally referred to as a *bottom-up* model, since it originates from a bottom-up requirement that is common and pre-existent.

At the furthest extent of the powers of central government vis-à-vis the individual, according to the principle of horizontal subsidiarity that we have been describing, a second constraint emerges, this time concerning the powers of central government compared with those of local government. This is a vertical interpretation of the principle of subsidiarity, which nonetheless has the same objectives as the principle of horizontal subsidiarity: increased protection of the individual from the will of governments. Reducing the size of the constituency actually gives citizens greater control over governments. In the words of Albert Hirschman, this can be expressed either in terms of *voice* (by voting and by the citizen's participation in public life) or in terms of *exit* (moving from one jurisdiction to the next according to convenience, a kind of 'voting with one's feet' approach, as defined figuratively by Tiebout, 1956).

This is a concept with which the US constituents who met in Philadelphia were closely acquainted, and which has only recently taken root in European soil (Bognetti, 2001).

In a socialist (or ius positivist) model therefore, the rights of the individual appear to be a creation of the State. The principal vehicle for this creation is the law, as a declaration of the will of the State to protect the individual's rights. Above the law, constitutions copy this model and found their own validity on it. Beneath the law, regulations follow the same legislative approach (Monateri, 2001).

Here, the constitution does not claim to limit the public leviathan, and thus it assumes a special importance, even though it represents the ne plus ultra of systems of law. The socialist (or ius positivist) model is therefore a top-down model, where governments determine the rights of citizens and the organisation of society, based on a common goal. This is the same paternalistic vision that, taken to its furthest extreme, produced the totalitarian monsters of the twentieth century.

In practice, a mix of ius naturalism and ius positivism is the most common approach, at least among European constituents.

The German Basic Law affirms in fact in Article 20 that 'Germany is a democratic and social federal state'.

Some scholars believe that from this principle derives the imposition of all three powers of the State upon social justice (Haberle, 2001), and that other European constitutions thus present similar compromises between opposing ideologies.

Article 1 of the post-Franco Constitution declares that 'Spain constitutes itself into a social and democratic state of law which advocates liberty, justice, equality, and political pluralism as the superior values of its legal order'.

This ambiguity is particularly evident where relations between the public and private sectors are described.

Article 41 of the Italian Constitution is an obvious example of this, where it declares that 'The private economic initiative is free. It cannot operate in conflict with social utility or undermine safety, freedom or human dignity. The law determines the appropriate programmes and controls for public and private economic activity to be targeted and coordinated for social purposes'. Similarly worded provisions can be found in other European constitutions, such as those of Spain and Germany.

Nevertheless, articles with such ambiguous meanings ultimately have little impact on the characteristics of the economic system, and may even qualify the exercise of rights. In fact, the rights of ownership and economic initiative are in this way subordinate to an entire series of ex-ante conditions, which render the actual exercise of such rights difficult.

The procedural elements, however, are likely to have greater impact on the characteristics of the economic system.

More specifically, these elements include procedures governing public finances and the budgetary process and, as we will see later, procedures affecting market operation. This assessment is based on a correct interpretation of horizontal and vertical subsidiarity, two disparate yet complementary versions of the same principle. Without a clear indication of constraints and procedures, the principle of subsidiarity risks remaining an empty vessel, lending itself to a wide range of interpretations and leaving an enormous margin for discretionary power in terms of defining the exact limits of functional powers (Petroni and Caporale, 2000).

The principal role of a European Constitution should be to fill this empty vessel with precise, unambiguous content (restricting only the scope for manipulating the constitution), a necessary condition that must be met before the people of the European Union can become citizens in every respect, rather than mere subjects.

The European Constitution Debate: Form and Substance

In the Laeken Declaration of 15 December 2001, the European Council summoned the Convention, an assembly with powers of democratic representation of national governments and parliaments, the European Parliament, the Commission and the Council (as well as observers representing countries wishing to take part in the enlargement process). The Convention will have the task of examining the fundamental questions raised by any future development of the EU and identifying their respective solutions.

The essential objective of the entire process is to devise a true European Constitution. The Laeken Declaration also indicates the general issues with which the European Convention must concern itself for the purpose of identifying solutions that will, in turn, serve as a foundation for the Intergovernmental Conference to be held at the end of 2003 or beginning of 2004.

The instrument of the Convention, which follows the model used to draw up the Fundamental Rights Charter, therefore satisfies the need to strengthen the role of the people in the construction of a Union that is both a Union of States and a Union of peoples.

The Convention is actually a more transparent and participative instrument, bringing Europe closer to the people and capable of overcoming the constraints to be highlighted in Nizza by the Intergovernmental Conference.

With the Convention, Europe's enlightened or perhaps bureaucratic elite will make way for a Europe of the people. The bottom-up constitutional model accordingly represents the only feasible option.

Having said that, the institution of a Convention, which many believe prefigures the drafting of a European constitutional charter, suggests that there is neither a de facto nor a legitimate European Constitution in place today. This theory is backed by those who, like the German constitutionalists Paul Kirchhof (1992) and Dieter Grimm (1996), point out that the Treaties on which the legal system of the European Union is based do not possess the characteristics of a true constitution from either a legal or political point of view, because fundamentally there is no true European people.

In this interpretation, the term 'constitution' belongs only to the fundamental law of the State and expresses the political choice of the only legitimate constituent according to democratic principles: the sovereign people.

On the other hand, the same Charter of Fundamental Rights of the European Union refers in its opening lines to 'European peoples' in the plural.

Therefore, as long as no European citizenship prevails over national citizenship, there is no point in creating a European constitutional charter in the immediate future. Champions of this view, including, notably, Lord Dahrendorf, are vocal in their denouncements of a European Constitution, present or future.

Others state that in the absence of a focal point represented by a single law and a set of legal rules able to determine a pre-established order, the constitution is the result of contingencies and mutual compromises, a flexible interface between law and politics. Hence, it is rather a case of a constitutional arrangement than a constitution (Scoditti, 2001).

Theoretical issues aside, the prevalent doctrine holds that, in Europe, a substantial constitution has already existed for some time, and more specifically since the Treaty establishing the European Economic Community was first introduced in 1957. The reasons for this are twofold. First, contrary to the fundamental principles of international law, the Treaty of Rome provides the Community with powers that are applied directly by citizens of the States concerned. The Court of Justice has furthermore adopted this doctrinal approach, affirming that the EC Treaty represents the true fundamental constitutional charter for the Community and that, in addition, the Treaties have introduced a new legal system in favour of which the States are limiting their sovereign rights in an increasing number of sectors, and that therefore the subjects of this new legal system are not only the Member States, but also the citizens themselves. Secondly, in interpreting the Treaties, Court of Justice jurisprudence has constantly expressed itself in favour of the supremacy of the Treaties themselves over national law (Petroni and Caporale, 2000).

Given the almost unique nature of these considerations, it could be said that the concept of a constitution may be applied with due care outside its original jurisdiction – the State – and be extended to other legal systems and to Community systems in particular.

Yet legal concepts cannot remain clear-cut. Although historically laws have been enacted within a state, national or international framework, we are now faced with a new, solitary subject, the European Community, which differs from both the State and classic international organisations (Weiler, 1995).

Conversely, the State does not represent the only legal system (Kelsen 1962). If the legal system comprises a set of rules and institutions that govern internal rules within a human society, then *ubi societas ibi jus*. Since every society spontaneously generates its own set of rules, then it stands to reason that every society also has its own legal system, provided that this is autonomous; that is, that it derives exclusively from this society. For a legal system to be autonomous, it must lay down its own rules and be the sole judge of their validity. In addition, there must be a system that generates these rules; in other words, there must be sources of law. The primary source of any legal system is its constitution. The Community legal system, as recognised by the Court of Justice, consists of an autonomous legal system integrated with national legal systems, as is the case in existing federal models (Kovar, 1993).

Apart from the Treaties, a European Constitution would essentially consist of the Fundamental Rights Charter ratified at the end of 2000 at the European summit in Nizza.

In this respect, three fundamental principles have been identified (Parisi, 2001) as being at the root of existing European constitutional architecture.

These consist of the principle of subsidiarity (in its vertical form only), the principle of fair collaboration (both between States and between States and supranational institutions) and the principle of mutual recognition.

The construction of a single European constitutional pillar is anything but unnecessary. As affirmed by Quadrio Curzio (2001) it is necessary for the existing Constitution 'to be simplified, clarified and integrated in a single document able to give certainty to all the actors'.

As soon as the functionalist choice on which thus far the process of European unification has been based prioritises the establishment of common economic institutions, any future European Economic Constitution must not only have qualitative importance, as in the case of the economic constitutions of the Member States of the European Union, but also a quantitative procedural dimension without comparison in individual Member States, due to the fact, totally *sui generis* compared with traditional State constitutional processes, that the European Union already has a single currency, without (yet) having a common economic policy.

This does not mean that other competencies, like foreign, defence and security policy should be ignored in the European constitutional framework.

What to Include in any Future European Economic Constitution: From Intergovernmental to Community Decision-making in the Interests of Dual Devolution, Bottom-up versus State Opportunism, Top-down for Increased Flexibility

As we saw earlier, the principles of subsidiarity and mutual recognition require a series of decisions to be taken at a potentially constitutional level in economic terms by EU Member States. This is the case for example with decisions concerning welfare and labour. In these and in other areas, long-term and universally applicable objectives have been identified, requiring procedures to be introduced at a national level, as explicitly stated in the Luxembourg process on labour. The key is to avoid wherever possible renouncing the model of competitive federalism, which relies on competition at a systemic and institutional level (a salient characteristic of the liberal project for Europe in the definition given by Petroni and Caporale, 2000). The European model should therefore remain beyond dirigist temptation, such as the harmonisation of tax rates, confined in any case to harmonisation of an administrative nature. It is another matter entirely to agree on procedures and principles allowing fair competition between fiscal systems and labour markets for example, without duplication (in the case of taxes, for example) or hazardous social dumping.

In this context, common standards in social policy are acceptable as far as they can encourage a major labour mobility within Europe and they can offer an easy-reading benchmark to European citizens who wish to judge the quality of different national systems (Tabellini, 2002). As for the rest, welfare policies must be submitted to national or sub-national level.

Using similar arguments, some propose a further extension of the principle of mutual recognition to other markets, such as the labour market, in the interests of diversity (see ISAE, 2001, report on the state of the European Union). This proposal would prove difficult to implement, at least for the time being, but has the advantage of focusing the attention on the need for the European system to remain a flexible institutional work in progress, not only for reasons of efficiency, but also to minimise possible cultural attrition.

Neo-institutionalism reminds us that cultural constraints are a real impediment to the success of large-scale top-down social reforms (North, 1994). To ignore the specific needs of each country would in fact have serious adverse effects and risk frustrating any attempt at reform, insofar as it would clash with the inevitable phenomenon of *path dependence*, which demonstrates that the workings of the institutions can be altered only in the long term and often only by accident. This type of social analysis is light-years away from the Cartesian rationalism professed by a significant majority of the European political and bureaucratic elite.

These economic and cultural reasons serve as an excellent pretext for omitting from the supranational constitution numerous issues that will be discussed and resolved lower down, according to the principle of vertical subsidiarity.

However, anything that, if left in the hands of national governments, could give rise to opportunistic or free-riding behaviour, must be constitutionalised. This kind of behaviour tends to occur in situations where there are intrinsic limits to the ability for voluntary collaboration to produce efficient results (information asymmetry and public assets), situations moreover that are incompatible with the credibility of the single currency and the building of the single market.

Credibility of the single currency and the guaranteed basic conditions for growth are thus two positive results of meeting the basic conditions for creating a European Constitution.

It should also be pointed out that opportunistic behaviour and free-riding are in themselves factors that undermine social cooperation. They end up becoming a barrier to market efficiency, which should be characterised by voluntary cooperation.

This resembles the argument put forward by Alesina *et al.* (2002), who suggest a criterion that, in their opinion, would enable European construction to be reconciled with the effective application of the principle of vertical subsidiarity. The assumption is that the European institutions should concern themselves exclusively with those activities that have clear economies of scale or external effects (that is, interdependent effects) and with respect to which there are only slight differences of opinion between Member States.

For this reason the European constitution should be rigorous enough to reduce to silence the opportunistic voices that play at national level, but at the same time flexible enough to adapt to new middle- and long-term needs. As long as 'growths and decreases of the powers of EU are equally probable' (Micossi, 2002).

All this by avoiding the creeping centralisation that took place in many states with a federal structure (such as the USA) and by allowing the reversibility of some centralist choices (as, for example, in agricultural matters, where the common policy has today less meaning than it had at the time of the creation of the EEC). Therefore, the task of a European constitution should also be to force the future top-rulers of our continent to use formal procedures that are subjected to democratic control in case they intend to give to Brussels further executive duties. This should be done by enhancing a clear constitutional process that increases in the long-term the credibility of macroeconomics policies and the efficiency of pan-European markets – all elements that, as we will see, represent the basic conditions of the growth and, as a consequence, of the competitiveness of the new Europe.

The opportunism of national governments, even in the (rare) event of this benefiting the population or part of the population in that state, ultimately and inevitably harms other citizens in the European Union and future generations, slowing growth and thus hampering cohesion. To correct these policy loopholes is therefore an essential task, if not *the* essential task, of a liberal constitution, responsible for reaffirming the principle of fair collaboration between Member States and between Member States and Community institutions.

There is currently an increasing awareness in literature and among economic policymakers that a strong political bias either underpinning the tendency for governments to accumulate excessive deficits and debts… or limiting government expenditure and deficits has led governments in the majority of industrialised countries to consider adopting (if they have not already done so) fiscal discipline measures in a bid to minimise the negative fiscal behaviour that ties their hands (Buti and Sapir, 1999).

At the root of fiscal indiscipline by governments in an economic community are three types of free-riding behaviour, two of which are internal (national) and one of which is external (international). First, since public spending benefits tend to be concentrated, while the costs are diffuse (Olson, 1965), private interests form coalitions to exploit fully government subsidies to their advantage. This clearly has repercussions on the government budget (at least up until the point where the marginal benefit of the lobbyist effort exceeds the marginal cost). Secondly, in the absence of altruism between the generations, current generations tend to dump accumulated debts on future ones (Buchanan and Wagner, 1997). Since the latter have no vote, in a democracy (and in other nation states, if we accept that even dictatorships need popular consensus), the will of current generations prevails. Finally, in the case of monetary union, a third threat is added to the risks of free-riding. A country in debt may be able to use its influence within the central bank or may benefit from other governments seeking to prevent a default situation, thus obtaining lower interest rates on the debt than those it would otherwise have paid. This gives rise to the need for an independent central bank and exemplary government budgets. For a start, the risk of free-riding increases with the number of players (in this case, Member States participating in the single currency). Therefore, the imminent enlargement of the EU (and the prospect of European Monetary Union) strengthens considerably the need for stringent fiscal policy.

Furthermore, in a reality such as Europe where the political cycle lacks continuity and the weighting of the votes of individual countries in Community decisions is non-proportional, the self-imposition of rules should take place at the least amendable level possible, so as not to be affected by the frequency of electoral appointments, which ultimately present similar opportunities for spending. If governments introduce generous fiscal policies to stimulate the economy and win elections, the solution is not to look the other way or surrender to Messianic moralism. On the contrary, armed with a healthy dose of realism, the rules need to be rewritten in order to render policy incentives compatible with exemplary finances and individual welfare, along the lines of the kind of liberal constitutionalism that limits the discretionary powers of the State over currency and budgets.

Maastricht and the Stability and Growth Pact

So far in Europe, constitutionalisation from the point of view of demand has been asymmetrical, dealing only with currency. The next step is to downsize and repackage this in the form of a future European Constitution, confirming the autonomy of the European Central Bank from undue political pressure.

In order to do this, and in view of the enlargement, it would be necessary to re-design the institutional structure of the European Central Bank. The spectre of decisional paralysis, as a consequence of the entry of candidates countries into the euro area, could materialise in case this would lead to a proportional numerical increase in the board of the European Central Bank, without any changes in the rules. From now on, we should consider – as suggested by Baldwin *et al.* (2000) – the introduction of some correctives, such as, for instance, the strengthening of decisional powers of the executive board (more protected from national opportunistic short-term interests than the board of directors) or the introduction of some kind of weighted vote that takes into account the dimensions of single countries' GDP (single countries have today the same weight in voting).

The Maastricht Treaty, which handed exclusive monetary power over to an independent European Central Bank, makes explicit reference to the stability of public finances only in Article 104c. Based on this, the Stability and Growth Pact (SGP) was drawn up, instituted by Council Regulation (EC) No 1466/97, Council Regulation (EC) No 1467/97 and the Resolution of the Council of Europe of 17 June 1997.

As we already know, Council Regulation (EC) No 1466/97 provides that Member States in the euro area must submit stability programmes, while those not participating in the single currency must implement policies aimed at attaining a high level of convergence with participating Member States, submitting the appropriate convergence programmes. Among other things, the stability programme must indicate the medium-term objective of budgetary positions of close to balance or in surplus and the targeted adjustment path of the government concerned, as well as satisfying the debt-to-GDP criterion. Budgetary estimates and other economic policy measures adopted or proposed in order to attain the programme objectives, must be described in detail and, in the most critical cases, their quantitative effects on public finances explained.

The Council will alert a Member State at an early stage to the need to take the necessary corrective budgetary action in order to prevent a government deficit from becoming excessive; if this deviation persists, the Council may enforce and publish its recommendation.

The assessment should clarify whether the medium-term budgetary objective of each stability programme makes provision for a safety margin to prevent excessive deficit, whether the economic assumptions on which the programme is founded are realistic and whether the measures adopted and/or proposed are suitable for following the targeted adjustment path for the medium-term budgetary objective.

Council Regulation (EC) No 1467/97 also sets out the provisions for speeding up and clarifying the implementation of the excessive deficit procedure to deter excessive government deficit and to further their prompt correction.

The 3 percent deficit-to-GDP reference value may be exceeded only if the annual fall in GDP exceeds 2 percent or if the fall is less than 2 percent (but at least equivalent to 0.75 percent) but is exceptional and temporary.

Sanctions may involve payment of a mandatory non-interest-bearing deposit of 0.2 percent plus one tenth of the difference between the deficit as a percentage of GDP up to a ceiling of 0.5 percent.

However, and this is the Achilles heel of the entire construction of the SGP, not only are none of these measures automatic, but they require qualified majority voting by EU Member States. Some authors (Von Hagen and Strauch, 2001) fear the possibility of undesirable cooperation (or at best collusion) between the various Member States, with a tendency to reciprocate favours. This self-indulgence ultimately undermines the credibility of the institutional structure of the SGP (which partly occurred recently with ECOFIN in February 2002, regarding the Commission's decision to reprimand Germany and Portugal, recommended to the Council).

The objective laid down by the SGP for budgetary positions of close to balance or in surplus is an important objective that many Member States have not only not yet attained, but appear to be having trouble in attaining before the deadline. The attainment of this objective is critical for the success of EMU, since it guarantees observance of the 3 percent of GDP deficit criterion and allows the automatic stabilisers to operate freely in the case of an economic downturn..

It is important therefore that the SGP objective is met in accordance with the commitments undertaken within the framework of broad economic policy guidelines and that its realisation is not constantly deferred, at the risk of undermining the credibility of the euro. For this reason, a SGP untainted by collusion and thus free from ongoing tactical manipulation by Member States seems the only real guarantee able to safeguard financial stability in the euro area. Otherwise, we run the serious risk of government budgets slowly but inexorably going into the red, with grave repercussions for inflation and growth. As underlined by the joint statement given by Tony Blair and Silvio Berlusconi at the recent Anglo-Italian summit on 15 February 2002, 'maintaining macroeconomic stability is crucial in helping to deliver lower interest rates and higher investment leading to more jobs, sustained growth, and the right framework for innovation and entrepreneurship'.

That is not to say that budgetary policy has not played an increasingly important role in attenuating the effects of country-specific shock on real production, particularly following the failure of national monetary policy within EMU. A means of safeguarding the automatic stabilisers in the spirit of the SGP is represented by the attainment of a medium-term objective allowing a safety margin that gives sufficient room for manoeuvre for the automatic stabilisers so that these can act freely without infringing the 3 percent limit. For most EU countries, this would result in the attenuation of cyclical fluctuations to between 20 percent and 30 percent. The importance of automatic stabilisers could also increase: the SGP, while credible in its constitutionalisation, would be internalised by economic agents with a positive impact on private consumption and on the efficiency of the stabilisers themselves.

A budget that is, on the whole, structurally balanced would also allow most countries to meet the SGP objective, in that it would allow them to address both the budgetary risks linked with an economic downturn and unforeseen budgetary events. The attainment of this objective is particularly important so that countries with the highest debt levels (Belgium, Greece and Italy) can reduce their levels of debt to below 60 percent of GDP within a reasonable space of time. Conversely, in countries with no shortage of automatic stabilisers (the Netherlands, Finland and, outside the euro area, Denmark and Sweden), a slight structural surplus is appropriate (approximately 1 percent of GDP). In fact, as studies have shown (Van den Noord, 2000), the cyclical safety margin is in the region of 1.5–2 percent of GDP for the large majority of EU countries and in the region of 2.5–3.5 percent for Scandinavian countries and the Netherlands. Using a similar method, the International Monetary Fund and OECD both reach the conclusion that a structural deficit of between 0.5–1.5 percent of GDP (IMF) and below 1.5 percent of GDP (OECD) would be enough to allow the automatic stabilisers to operate without infringing the 3 percent of GDP deficit criterion, even during a severe economic downturn. Therefore, all of the conditions necessary to render the constitutionalisation of the SGP as the founding, credible and inviolable principle underpinning the single currency are already in place today.

However, to achieve sound budgetary results requires efficient institutions; in other words, efficient decision-making procedures, objectives and rules of conduct. In a recent communication on the strengthening of the coordination of economic policy in the euro area, the Commission advanced concrete proposals to improve budgetary surveillance in the EU within the existing legislative framework. Four of these proposals merit closer examination: (a) to establish the principle whereby Member States inform the Commission and Council before definitively adopting key budgetary decisions; (b) to ensure that stability and convergence programmes are submitted every autumn; (c) to improve the information content of these programmes; (d) to cover the issue of the long-term sustainability of public finances in these programmes.

Most of these proposals were assimilated by the new code of conduct on the content and format of stability and convergence programmes adopted by the ECOFIN Council on 9 July 2001. The most noteworthy relate to the submission of (updated) programmes between 15 October and 1 December each year, the adoption of a model to be followed when preparing these programmes and the use of tables to present the data in a complete and comparable form. However, observance of a code of conduct is dependent upon the goodwill of the parties. Even a non-sceptic can see that a more robust means of enforcement is required for the code to be able to withstand the electoral winds of change that continue to buffet Europe.

The budgetary rules and procedures of individual nation states help budgetary objectives to be attained at an EU level. Evidently the budgetary authorities in the various Member States are influenced in different ways by the need to remain aligned with EU surveillance mechanisms. Using the SGP, several Member States have adopted a pluri-annual budgetary planning framework or other mechanisms or approaches that help define and control public spending priorities in the medium term.

Commitments undertaken at EU level also determine relationships between the various national institutions responsible for budgets, or central government, parliament and the State/local government. In this respect, many Member States have adopted measures to strengthen the responsibility of each level of government in accordance with the budgetary objectives assigned to public administrations by the stability or convergence programmes. The conclusion of internal stability pacts in many Member States has been a welcome development. In Germany, the absence of explicit agreements between the federal government and the Länder was the determining factor in the exceeding of the 2001 budgetary objectives.

The credibility of the SGP in its current form is therefore seriously undermined by its unconstitutional elements and not by its rigidity. Its structure is in fact changeable from one day to the next, depending upon majority and national interests, despite being bound to the political and electoral cycles of individual Member States. Therefore, since the content of the Stability and Growth Pact may be fully credible, it seems appropriate to transcribe the salient characteristics of the Pact into the Constitutional

Charter, so that the expectations of economic agents can be stabilised around certain values and objectives and the effectiveness of fiscal policy increased.

In short, as far as any European Constitution is concerned, it is a question of emphasising the third and fourth paragraphs of Article 81 of the Italian Constitution, as advocated by Luigi Einaudi and Ezio Vanoni ('No new taxes or new expenditures may be established by the law approving the budget. All other laws implying new or additional expenditures must set forth the means for covering them').

Due to Einaudi's vigilance during his seven-year term of office, supported at a policy-making level by Vanoni and at a doctrinaire level by Constantino Mortati, the interpretation of Article 81 was initially rather intransigent (on the intractable interpretation of Article 81 by Italian President Einaudi, see *Lo scrittoio del Presidente*, 1956). The deficit-to-GDP ratio was maintained until the end of the 1960s at around 2.5 percent (in line therefore with the deficit criterion fixed at Maastricht, which only decades later would prove so difficult to meet). Thereafter, the constitutional mechanism proved much less robust than expected. A change in economico-cultural paradigm, corresponding to the consolidation of a Keynesian-statist ideology, did not find much resistance in a vague constitutional principle such as Article 81.

In actual fact, the wording of this Article, interpreted to the letter, provides for the coverage of expenditure forecast during the prevailing financial year, and not for subsequent financial years. It has been easy therefore to fudge the issue, forecasting minimum expenditure for the prevailing financial year and increased expenditure for subsequent financial years, particularly after the Constitutional Court endorsed such practices.

Moreover, Article 81 fails to take proper account of the financial profile of entitlements (e.g. pensions, subsidies, etc), which have led to a rise in expenditure equivalent to that provided by law. In other words, the expansion of the welfare state was the Trojan horse used to expunge Article 81 and to render it inoffensive (Longobardi and Pedone, 1994). The principle of balancing budgets having been thus undermined, by the latter half of the 1970s it was being ignored completely (Zaccaria, 1999).

Europe would do well to heed this lesson. It is far better to have modest yet clear and transparent objectives than rules that are easily overturned. For this reason, the introduction of variants such as the 'golden rule', which makes a distinction between ordinary expenditure and capital expenditure, should be treated with caution. For capital expenditure, the fiscal criteria would become more flexible, making an allowance for deficits; the risk, however, is of encouraging governments to engage in creative accounting that ultimately distorts the spirit, if not the letter, of budgetary rules.

It is a misconception that in other Member States, such as France and Germany, balancing budgets has been achieved by clear rules of procedure. If there is no exact equivalent to Article 81 in other European constitutions, then the alternatives have proven more than adequate.

We only need to look at Article 113 of the German Basic Law, where it states that 'statutes increasing the budget expenditures proposed by the Federal Government or involving or likely in future to cause new expenditures shall require the consent of the Federal Government', or Article 40 of the French Constitution, which prescribes that 'Private members' bills and amendments shall be inadmissible if their adoption would have the effect of reducing public revenue or of creating or increasing an item of public expenditure'. In France, this law has since been strengthened by the fact that 'Parliament shall pass finance bills under the conditions stipulated by an organic act' (Article 47 of the French Constitution), which means among other things that 'in the absence of agreement between the two Assemblies, a bill may be adopted by the National Assembly on final reading only by an absolute majority of its members' (Article 46 of the French Constitution).

In the case of Germany and France, the constitutional requirements have also been bolstered by the unequivocal accountability of executive power in the event that budgets are exceeded. A government may continue to spend, tax and run into debt, but under this provision, it may no longer pass the buck, accusing parliament of financial demagogy. There is no longer any doubt that the government, and the government, alone is responsible for public debt. In this case, there are essentially two conditions for compliance with the constitutional rules: clear rules of procedure and government incentives compatible with financial stability. The Italian fragmentation of responsibility and therefore of blame, together with the opaqueness of the Constitution, has hindered rather than helped the implementation of Article 81.

The constitutionalisation of the SGP at a European level, according to the various procedures laid down by Article 81 of the Italian Constitution, which takes to heart Italy's mistakes, therefore represents a return to the strict financial principles that inspired our constituents. As was said earlier, this is to be applied taking account of the trade-off between credibility and flexibility, with the ultimate goal of promoting growth, cohesion and competitiveness.

From the SGP to Medium to Long-term Financial Sustainability

However, the Stability and Growth Pact on its own is not sufficient to guarantee financial sustainability in the long term. Budgets that are close to balance or in surplus in the short to medium term do not necessarily mean sound public finances in the long term. External factors such as population ageing and advances in medical technology (with the increased costs that these entail) can undermine long-term financial stability.

Alongside the constitutionalisation of laws derived from the Stability and Growth Pact, it is necessary therefore to introduce a series of measures aimed at safeguarding the sustainability of public finances in the medium to long term also. Only a credible fiscal policy in the long term could have a positive influence on the behaviour of citizens and industry.

With this in mind, four criteria have already been drawn up in Europe to guide Member States in their financial policy-making (ECOFIN decision of 22 February 2000): (1) if a budgetary balance has not yet been reached in structural terms (a situation that is common to nearly all euro area countries), tax cuts should be reflected in corresponding spending cuts, which cannot only balance the fall in revenues (caused by the tax cuts), but also safeguard the medium-term objectives set out in the stability pact; (2) the tax cuts should not be pro-cyclical. In fact, during the positive cycle, an equivalent reduction in the tax burden to spending tends to increase demand, which may trigger runaway inflation. In other words, if we allow a growth deficit during an economic downturn, then controls must continue to be tight during periods of economic recovery; (3) countries with high levels of public debt should fix and maintain ambitious budgetary objectives. Simply put, before introducing tax cuts, these countries should give clear indications of debt convergence in the medium term; (4) tax cuts should form part of a wider packet of reforms. Since interaction between fiscal and welfare systems actually has a dominant influence over the success of the labour market, tax cuts should be introduced in close association and synchronous with other key structural reforms (such as education, schools, welfare and social buffers).

Laws that prescribe the transparency of government budgets in countries signed up to the euro, based on common standards, may prove a better solution for integrating these four criteria, thus realising (and constitutionalising) a true fiscal decalogue.

European constituents should devise a system of rules and principles that can act in place of the state without however immobilising it entirely, placing European fiscal policy at the forefront of the trade-off between credibility and flexibility within a context of sustained growth.

The Building of Pan-European Markets

Monetary and fiscal legislation must also correspond with laws aimed at strengthening market integration by means of a European policy aimed at promoting and safeguarding competition. The theory of optimal currency areas (Mundell, 1961) dictates that in the presence of a common monetary policy and a decentralised fiscal policy (two characteristics of the current European architecture), an asymmetric shock in terms of demand may be mitigated only by the increased mobility of production factors (particularly labour) and price and wage flexibility, not to mention the key role played by budgetary policy (at a federal level) in terms of redistribution, three conditions that fall short of being met in the euro area.

Market integration could either align EMU with the first two conditions or (and perhaps more probably) prevent asymmetric shock. The rebalancing role of the exchange rate may be replaced by flexibility of supply, either in terms of price and wage fixing mechanisms, or by market integration (Secchi and Altomonte, 2002).

Furthermore, in a truly integrated area, trade between Member States is likely to be intra-sectorial (De Grauwe, 1997). This means that the likelihood of economic shock affecting more than one country at a time is increased, rendering futile any recourse to exchange rate adjustment. This is even more meaningless since an increase in competitiveness (particularly in the public utilities sector) should reduce inflation differentials between exemplary and less exemplary European countries.

As Secchi and Altomonte point out, the European Council (Lisbon, March 2000) called upon the Commission, Council and Member States 'to speed up liberalisation in areas such as gas, electricity, postal services and transport'. This was echoed the following year by a virtually identical exhortation at the Stockholm European Council, which urged that, in the absence of specific commitments and binding enforcement mechanisms, good intentions were dissolving, and that resolving this deadlock would not prove easy due to skewed economic and political cycles.

Here too, the short-term requirements of *politique politicienne* fail to take account of the longer-term view. As a result, constitutional reforms extending the life of the policy would appear necessary, even from the point of view of supply, so much so that while, in terms of demand, the Maastricht Treaty and EU regulations provide a solid enough foundation (even if somewhat ill-equipped for economic recession) for the implementation of monetary and fiscal policy, in terms of supply, we must trust for now to the good intentions of Member States and to the promptings of the Commission, rather than to any enforcement by a third authority.

The fundamental principle whereby businesses in Europe should be able to compete in any country on an equal footing therefore remains a dead letter in many sectors; sectors moreover where, nearly 10 years on from the inception of the single market, the free movement of people and capital continues to be a chimera.

The Commission also talks of a delivery gap between intentions and achievements in areas such as European patents, financial services and energy. Some Member States are bound by the commitment undertaken in Stockholm to assimilate at a national level 98.5 percent of European legislation by March 2002. Most of the 1500 cases of infringement of Community legislation brought against Member States relate to barriers to the free provision of cross-border services (Commission of the European Communities, 2002).

Short-lived national egoism therefore risks damaging the credibility of European governance in key areas of our economy.

If long-term choices must remain the exclusive competence of the political sphere, then observance of regulations must reflect the SGP and remain untainted by opportunism.

This is echoed by the Lamfalussy Report (Commissione Lamfalussy, 2001), which recommends the adoption of a series of measures and institutions in order to complete the harmonisation of the financial services sector by 2005.

The solution prescribed by the Committee of Wise Men chaired by Baron Lamfalussy (increased transparency, common standards and improved dialogue between national authorities) could prove a sound model worthy of adoption in other sectors, such as the crucial energy sector, where 'an integrated EU energy market is essential to ensure the future supply of energy at reasonable prices to Europe's citizens and businesses. In order to avoid unfair competition, the liberalisation process must be fair and balanced across all member states'. The same principle applies to rules governing mergers, whereby, according to the paper prepared jointly by the UK and Italian governments, clarity and coherence are required 'in order to facilitate the creation of an integrated capital market in the EU, to enhance wealth creation and exploit synergies'.

At stake is the reconciliation of the independence of European governance institutions with the accountability of these institutions, and common standards with the principle of subsidiarity. Only in a situation of dual equilibrium between these principles will we achieve effective market integration in Europe, where fair competition between country systems (in the form of competitive federalism) will be able to cohabit with effective competition between businesses. This means for example that the protection of monopolistic revenues cannot be justified by any common principle of subsidiarity.

To What Extent should the EU be Open to Migratory Flows?

The free movement of people and the removal of frontiers within the EU call for the reconsideration of immigration policy in Europe.

Top on the agenda is the need to reach an agreement on a core of essential and common principles inspired by national and/or regional policy in this area. The Commission recently tabled a proposal for a directive on the conditions of entry and residence of citizens in third countries intending to find paid employment or to be self-employed. One of the principal objectives laid down by the directive is the definition of common criteria and procedures on the conditions of entry and residence of non-EU citizens based on the national legislation in force.

This effort is noble yet inadequate, unless it is protected by constitutional laws. The number of immigration applications varies according to the point in the economic cycle. In times of plenty, demand is above average, and vice versa when times are hard, with serious repercussions on the propensity to invest.

In the absence of common rules of entry, based on constitutionally ratified principles, the opportunism of nation states is likely to prevail, leading to an incessant manipulation and interpretation of Community legislation, which would not only result in widespread spillover (with immigrants that, deported from one country, would simply be transferred to another), but in a situation of uncertainty that would penalise both EU production and the immigrants themselves.

What Action should be Taken?

As we have already seen, the institutional design of the EU thus far in terms of regulatory requirements induced by the single currency in a non-optimal currency area (Mundell, 1961) seems to take account of the issues raised but is wanting as regards the robustness of its procedures.

In terms of demand, fiscal policy is not sufficiently coordinated to have an impact on the economic cycle, nor does the Stability and Growth Pact seem credible enough to be able to govern deviant behaviour in fundamental areas such as budgetary deficit in individual Member States. The outlook is even more gloomy for supply, since the EU suffers from endemic and widespread rigidity, lack of modernisation and growth gaps, in spite of the numerous declarations made from time to time by the various European Councils (at Lisbon in March 2000, Nizza in December 2000 and Stockholm in March 2001).

In short, while there are sufficient legal bases for effective governance both in terms of supply (competition and the single market) and demand (the SGP), the instruments to hand have been proven utterly incapable of withstanding the oft-reciprocated opportunism and national egoism associated with the diverse conditions of sectorial competitiveness in Member States (e.g. energy, telecommunications, etc) and individual electoral and political cycles.

To free the process of European construction from the egoistic short-sightedness of the Member States has thus supplanted the abstract affirmation of shared values to become the primary and perhaps the only goal of a future European Constitution.

Towards the Creation of a New Hierarchy of Sources of Law: More Constitutional Procedures, Laws and Regulations, and Fewer Treaties

The European Constitution (if and when this comes to fruition) will inevitably lead to a definition of the hierarchy of sources of law.

The hierarchy of sources of law is vital for understanding who does what both at a Union level and in relationships between the EU and other levels of government.

Since the Spinelli Treaty of 1984, the European Parliament has been highlighting the need to embark upon a restructuring process of sources of law. This need was echoed in Declaration 16 attached to the Maastricht Treaty, to a certain extent following on from a paper presented by Italy to the ICG. The 1992 declaration assigned the task of assessing the feasibility of introducing a hierarchy of sources of law to the ICG of 1996. Since then, little or nothing has been done, save a few attempts at restructuring by the European Parliament, attempts that have amounted to nothing.

The Community legal system does not lay down, particularly with respect to secondary legislation, a system of formal priorities by virtue of which one law prevails over another, such that conformity with the former is a prerequisite for the legality of the latter, and such that the latter may not depart from the former unless within the bounds permitted by the same. In reality, the absence of a hierarchy of sources of law is a direct consequence of the choices of procedures and instruments made by the Treaties in relation to the exercise of powers.

In actual fact, the Treaties do not allow the EU to operate through legislative instruments that can be tailored and moulded to the nature and level of action chosen (legislative, statutory or executive act). Conversely, laws should be transposed by specific and typical instruments defined analytically by the Treaties themselves. These include regulations, directives, decisions and recommendations within the framework of the EC treaty (Article 249), common positions, framework decisions, decisions and conventions within the framework of judicial and police cooperation in criminal matters (Article 39 of the Treaty on European Union), and lastly guidelines, common strategies, joint actions and common positions in terms of Community foreign and defence policy (Article 12 of the Treaty on European Union).

These instruments are defined in terms of their nature and effects, but not in terms of their rank or reciprocal relationships in terms of legislative force, therefore it is not possible to organise them into any kind of hierarchy.

The choice of the type of instrument is not linked with the force that this should have so much as with the objectives to be attained. Often the type of instrument is not stipulated, leaving the choice to the discretion of the institutions. Accordingly, the procedure for adopting the instrument does not derive from its nature so much as the legal basis chosen.

This has led to some confusion, since institutional acts often do not correspond to the type defined by the Treaty (e.g. detailed directives that resemble regulations, regulations that, instead of being directly binding, make provision for national implementing provisions, etc).

Furthermore, the various flexibility requirements have generated a series of atypical instruments, such as resolutions, declarations, inter-institutional agreements and communications, the nature and effects of which are unclear, to the point that even the Court of Justice does not view them as legally binding.

The decision not to structure the system of sources of law also derives from a desire not to clarify the limits and roles of the institutions and levels of government in relation to their legislative and executive functions. This in turn is due to the fact that the Community legal system has a federal role, even though it does not possess all of the characteristics that this might imply.

In truth, the intergovernmental method by which the majority of functions are in practice discharged by the Council of Ministers and by Member States is becoming increasingly commonplace.

The confusion has been to the detriment of the Commission, which holds and delegates the executive function, and the European Parliament, which sees its role as primarily concentrating on the legislative and control functions.

A hierarchy of sources of law would instead have the effect of ending the confusion and thus limiting the powers of the Council, which, as the dominant institution, holding both legislative and executive functions, has largely profited from the current ambiguity.

Moreover, the voting mechanisms within the Council should be revised, by reaching a solution more effective than the one arisen from the summit of Nice, a solution that takes into account in a realistic way the danger, in terms of institutional paralysis, of the enlargement of the European Union (Baldwin *et al.*, 2000).

However, as soon as the co-decision making procedure has become the ordinary legislative procedure and a constitution is drawn up, organising the system of sources of law will become unavoidable.

The restructuring process should take place at a constitutional, legislative and executive level.

In fact, a future European Constitution would have neither the form nor the scope or level of detail or language of the Treaties, which by their very nature still formally come under the heading of international law.

The constitution must define the fundamental principles and legal reserves, while it is left to ordinary legislation to define the general regime applicable to sectors and areas, and in some cases the procedures of application. Ordinary laws should assign responsibility for application both at a Community level and at a national level, in accordance with the principle of subsidiarity.

At a Community level therefore, legislation would be implemented by the Commission, fully responsible for executing the instruments and defining issues of an exclusively regulatory nature, without prejudice to the powers of other levels of government.

For each instrument, there should be a specific decision-making process that is fundamentally unique to each level.

From a constitutional point of view, this entails a repositioning in the hierarchy of sources of law matters that come within the remit of the EU, without in any sense prejudicing the current distribution between levels of government provided by the Treaty.

The hierarchy should have no effect on the vertical distribution of powers between levels of government. It should be confined to rationalising the exercise of powers to be assigned to the EU.

Conversely, the impact on horizontal distribution is certain. Repositioning within the hierarchy of sources of law will primarily affect measures relating to Community policy and the single market, which are currently over-elaborated in the Treaties and have no place in the Constitution.

However, the impact is also closely linked with new inter-institutional balances that see the European Parliament becoming a proper legislator, essentially on an equal footing with the Council of Ministers. Current provisions laid down by the Treaty governing the assignment of implementing powers (Article 202) have in fact become obsolete since the acquisition of new legislative powers by the European Parliament.

Furthermore, the need for restructuring has emerged clearly in recent months in terms of regulating the European financial services market.

While not wishing to stand in the way of responsive regulation, which is often 'technicistic' in nature, involving Member States directly, the European Parliament has confirmed its role in the legislative procedure and in the definition of implementing powers. As for the implementing powers of the Commission, these are governed in such a way as to limit them specifically in terms of scope and duration. The Commission has undertaken to respect the powers of the European Parliament, keeping it regularly informed and giving it sufficient time to analyse the implementing measures.

Within the hierarchy of sources of law, co-regulation as well as self-regulation should find an adequate role. These are in fact fundamental instruments to give effective and flexible rules to markets that otherwise could appear blocked within the hierarchy of the sources.

Co-regulation and self-regulation, by involving directly the interested parts in the process of creating the rules of a market, especially where cutting-edge technologies play a fundamental role, introduce the necessary amount of dynamism, adjusting the rules themselves to the changes of facts.

It is clear that co-regulation as well as self-regulation must be included into a public framework of legislative nature that defines general and binding principles and consents to the intervention of the public authority as last resort in the case where co-regulation and self-regulation are unable to give the necessary juridical certainty.

Conclusions

Based on this analysis, how is a European Economic Constitution to be structured? The answer is simple. First, a clear distinction needs to be made between 'values' and 'procedures'. Only by siphoning off the set of founding, common values into a preamble, following the lead of the Fundamental Rights Charter, can the series of constitutional principles and procedures relative to both economic and foreign and defence policy be free from useless, indeed dangerous, divisions.

Having made this distinction, we will need to address the issue of formalisation of general principles, the constitutional procedures at the root of the construction and cohesion of the EU and its international position.

The aforementioned principle of *subsidiarity*, both in its vertical form, among the various possible levels of government, and in its horizontal form, among the public and private sectors, the principle of *fair collaboration* between Member States and between Member States and supranational and infranational institutions, and the principle of *mutual recognition*, insofar as these have a founding nature, no longer seem sufficient, indeed necessary.

In order to achieve complete, enduring economic governance accompanied by a single currency in a non-optimal currency area, it will be necessary to resort to the constitutionalisation of all those procedures already present chaotically to varying degrees in the regulatory system of the EU; procedures, moreover, that are capable of freeing the architecture of the EU from the inevitable short-sightedness of the political electoral cycle.

In short, it is simply a matter of constitutionalising well-defined areas and subjects and releasing the Community decision-making process from the stranglehold of individual governments.

In terms therefore of the role and functions of the European Central Bank and the Stability and Growth Pact, in terms of the building of pan-European markets and in terms of the internal revenue, stock markets and financial markets, the principles and procedures that are and will increasingly be at the root of the new Europe will be identified and explained more clearly in order to be exploited at a constitutional level, not only in the current phase of consolidation and development of the EU, according to agreements reached during the Lisbon Summit in 2000, but also and above all in relation to the long and complex transition represented by the enlargement of the EU and its international status. With respect to this latter point, particular attention should be paid in constitutional terms to the procedures of governance opening the EU up to migratory flows. Although the four fundamental freedoms of the Treaty of Rome – the movement of goods, services, capital and people – as well as the values expressed in the Fundamental Rights Charter are enough to characterise the internal position of the EU in terms of mobility of human capital, there is however an absence in this respect of a relationship between the EU and the rest of the world, a clear regulatory framework, free from the egoism and/or short-sightedness of the nation states from the point of view of the qualification and quantification of immigration policy. In other words, how can we establish the principles, rules and procedures that will stop individual countries or manufacturing sectors from using immigration as a competitive advantage in the short term during times of plenty and then dumping it on other partners as a social cost during periods of economic decline?

These values, principles and procedures thus represent the essential components of the new European constitutional charter, taking account however of the need, on the one hand, not to confuse plans and, on the other, the need to treat with the proper impartiality the set of principles and procedures capable of rescuing the European building process from the threat of opportunism, which has been the greatest barrier to its complete and linear realisation so far.

Acknowledgements

Angelo Maria Petroni, GianPaolo Galli, Carlo Altomonte and Antonio Preto provided valuable comments. In addition, Stefano da Empoli contributed significantly to this paper.

Appendix: Suggested Constitutional Definitions from an Economic Perspective

Economic Policy

The economic policy of the EU and Member States satisfies the principles of an open market economy with free competition, in which economic and social progress, competition, a high level of employment and balanced, sustainable development are all encouraged.

European Central Bank

The European Central Bank is independent from any other power. It defines and implements EU monetary policy with a view to safeguarding price stability. In achieving this objective, it supports the overall economic policy of the EU.

Budgetary Balance

The EU and Member States seek to limit government deficit in accordance with regulations ratified by ordinary law.

Any instrument establishing new expenditures or reducing projected revenues must indicate the means of maintaining the overall budgetary balance. Any instrument providing for expenditures across more than one financial year must comply fully with the pluriannual economico-financial plan laid down by common agreement of the EU and Member States.

The European Commission and the European Central Bank are responsible for surveillance of budgetary positions and for implementing the measures necessary to prevent infringements of economico-financial planning tools.

Market

The single market posits the free movement of goods, services, capital and people. The EU pursues a policy of total market liberalisation.

Any barrier to trade is prohibited. Member States may introduce restrictions only when these are in the public interest. Any restriction must first be ratified by the European Commission after consulting the Council of Ministers.

The single market operates according to the principle of mutual recognition between national legal systems. Harmonisation of legal systems will be confined to that strictly necessary for the purpose of rendering effective mutual recognition and preventing the distortion of competition in accordance with the principles of proportionality and subsidiarity.

Within principles established by legal measures, the use of co-regulation and self-regulation will be provided.

Market Surveillance

The EU and Member States may establish central and national authorities responsible for market surveillance and regulation in areas within their respective remit. The central authority has the task of coordinating national authorities for the purpose of ensuring the overall satisfactory operation of the market.

Internal Revenue

EU and Member State fiscal policy is governed by progression criteria. It is implemented in accordance with the principle of budgetary balances and the objectives of European economic policy.

Stock Markets, Finance and Regulation of Companies

The regulation of financial markets is governed by the criteria of transparency, responsibility and consumer protection. Decisions relating to implementing measures may be delegated to the European Commission, the central authority and national supervisory authorities to ensure complete respect of the powers assigned to the legislative authorities.

The regulation of listed companies is based on the principle of proportionality between the risk capital held by investors and the locus of decision-making powers. Equality of treatment of minority shareholders is guaranteed in the event of transfer of control.

Mobility of Human Capital

The EU encourages worker mobility and labour market flexibility. It lays down common standards for access, establishment and movement within the EU of workers from third countries.

References

Alesina, A., Angeloni, I. and Schuknecht, L. (2002) What does the European Union do? CEPR Working Paper No. 3115, European University Institute Working Paper No. 2002/61.

Baldwin, R., Berglof, E., Giavazzi, F. and Widgren, M. (2000) *EU Reforms for Tomorrow's Europe*, working paper n.2623 (London: CEPR).

Bognetti, G. (2001) L'evoluzione del federalismo moderno e i diversi modelli dello Stato federale, in A.M. Petroni (ed) *Modelli giuridici ed economici per la Costituzione europea* (Bologna: il Mulino).

Buchanan, J.M. and Wagner, R.E. (1997) *La Democrazia in Deficit* (Roma: Armando Armando).

Buti, M. and Sapir, A. (1999) *La politica economica nell'Unione economica e monetaria europea* (Bologna: il Mulino).

Commission of the European Communities (2002) *The Lisbon Strategy – Making Change Happen* (Bruxelles: Commission of the European Communities).

Commissione Lamfalussy (2001) *Final Report of the Committee of Wise Men on the Regulation of European Securities Markets* (Bruxelles: Commission of the European Communities).

De Grauwe, P. (1997) *The Economics of Monetary Integration* (Oxford: Oxford University Press).

Einaudi, L. (1956) *Lo scrittoio del Presidente* (Torino: Einaudi).

Growe C. and Fabri Ruiz H. (1995) *Droits constitutionnels européens* (Parigi: PUF).

Gerkrath, J. (1997) *L'emergence d'un droit Constitutionnel pour l'Europe,* (Bruxelles: Universitè de Bruxelles).

Grimm, D. (1996) Una Costituzione per l'Europa? In: G. Zagrebelsky, P.P. Portinaro and J. Luther (Ed.) *Il futuro della Costituzione* (Torino: Einaudi).

Haberle, P. (2001) Saggio introduttivo sulla costituzione tedesca, in *Le Costituzioni dei paesi dell'Unione Europea* (Padova: Cedam).

Hagen, J. von and Strauch, R. (2001) Budgetary consolidation in EMU, in *European Commission Economic Papers*, No 148.

Kelsen, H. (1962) *La dottrina pura del diritto* (Utet:, Torino).

Kirchhof, P. (1992) Der deutsche Staat im Prozeß der europäischen Integration, in: J. Isensee and P. Kirchhof (Hrsg.) *Handbuch des Staatsrechts der Bundesrepublik Deutschland. Band VII: Normativität und Schutz der Verfassung – Internationale Beziehungen* (Müller).

Kovar, R. (1993) *La contribution de la Cour de justice à l'édification de l'ordre juridique communautaire* (RAE).

ISAE (F. Padoa Schioppa Kostoris, Ed.) (2001) *Rapporto sullo stato dell'Unione Europea* (Bologna: il Mulino).

Longobardi, E. and Pedone, A. (1994) La politica tributaria, in: F.R. Pizzuti (Ed.) *L'economia italiana dagli anni Settanta agli anni Novanta* (Milano: McGraw-Hill).

Micossi, S. (2002) *The Mandate of the Convention*, in *Institutional Reforms in the European Union* (Roma: Europeos).

Mitchell, J.D.B. (1968) *Constitutional Law* (Londra: Green&Son).

Monateri, P.G. (2001) La circolazione dei modelli giuridici e le sue conseguenze per l'Unione europea, in: A.M Petroni (ed.) *Modelli giuridici ed economici per la Costituzione europea* (Bologna: il Mulino).

Mundell, R. (1961) A theory of optimal currency areas, *American Economic Review*, 51.

Noord, van den (2000) The size and role of automatic fiscal stabilizers in the 1990s and beyond. OECD Economic Department Working Paper, No. 230.

North, D.C. (1994) *Istituzioni, cambiamento istituzionale, evoluzione dell'economia* (trad. it.) (Bologna: il Mulino).

Olson, M. (1965) *The Logic of Collective Action* (Cambridge: Harvard University Press).

Parisi, N. (2001) L'attuale organizzazione dei pubblici poteri nell'Unione europea, in: A. Quadrio Curzio (Ed.) *Profili della Costituzione economica europea* (Bologna: il Mulino).

Petroni, A.M. (2001) L'analisi economica del federalismo e la sua applicazione alla struttura costituzionale dell'Unione europea, in: A.M. Petroni (Ed.) *Modelli giuridici ed economici per la Costituzione europea* (Bologna: il Mulino).

Petroni, A.M. and Caporale, R. (2000) *Il federalismo possibile* (Soveria Mannelli: Rubbettino).

Quadro Curzio, A. (2001) Introduzione: Riflessioni per una Costituzione economica europea, in: Alberto Quadro Curzio (Ed.) *Profili della Costituzione economica europea* (Bologna: il Mulino).

Scoditti, E. (2001) *La Costituzione senza popolo* (Bari: edizioni Dedalo).

Secchi, C. and Altomonte, C. (2002) *L'euro: una moneta, una Europa* (Venezia:, Marsilio).

Simon, D. (2001) *Le système juridique communautaire* (Parigi: PUF).

Tabellini, G. (2002) The allocation of tasks, in: *Institutional Reforms in the European Union* (Roma: Europeos).

Tiebout, C.M. (1956) A pure theory of local expenditures, *Journal of Political Economy*, October.

Tocqueville, A. de (1948) *De la Démocratie en Amérique* (Parigi).

Vertice Regno Unito-Italia (2002a) *Dichiarazione congiunta*, (Roma, 15 Febbraio).

Vertice Regno Unito-Italia (2002b) *Temi chiave per Barcellona* (Roma, 15 Febbraio).

Weiler, H.H. (1995) *The State 'über alles'. Demos, Telos and the German Maastricht Decision* (Cambridge MA: Harvard Jean Monnet Working Paper).

Zaccaria, F. (1999) La copertura delle nuove o maggiori spese: un approccio di economia pubblica in termini di evoluzione delle istituzioni politiche, *Atti XI Conferenza Società italiana di economia pubblica* (Pavia).

Part 2

Chapter 7

Fiscal Discipline and Policy Coordination in the Eurozone: Assessment and Proposals

Jean Pisani-Ferry

Introduction

This chapter is about what can be improved in the policy system of the Eurozone. It focuses on current challenges and makes proposals for change. It is therefore by nature critical of current arrangements.

It could be objected that there is no reason to look for changes, because there is much to praise in what has been achieved in the first years of EMU: the transition to the new currency and the new policy regime has been a major success for the EU; macroeconomic management in Europe has improved significantly; and further microeconomic gains can be expected from this new step in integration.

Whereas this is obviously true, complacency would be a misguided attitude. Just because the EMU system is still in its infancy, economists and policymakers have to learn from the early experience, to assess what the next problems could be and to discuss how they could be addressed. With only a few years of experience behind us, there is certainly no point in considering wide-ranging reforms, but there is room for serious discussions on what we have learned. We should aim at developing a vision of the direction for change that would help clarifying issues in current policy discussions and making proposals for step-by-step changes. The pace of change will depend on political and economic conditions. But to be able to respond to unexpected events and opportunities, policymakers need a roadmap.

The paper, which partially draws on my previous research on the same issues (Jacquet and Pisani-Ferry, 2001; Pisani-Ferry, 2002), focuses on two main topics, fiscal discipline and policy coordination. In a way, these are two aspects of the same broader question: what are the channels of policy interdependence in a monetary union and how should the policy system be designed to deal with externalities arising from this interdependence? But the distinction is nevertheless useful:

(a) the notion of fiscal discipline deals with the specific externalities associated to the adverse spillover effects of excessive deficits leading to potentially unsustainable debt accumulation in member countries. Among economists and policymakers, there is not much disagreement, either on the risk an irresponsible fiscal behaviour would create for monetary union, or on the need for common rules or mechanisms that ensure fiscal discipline. However, there are controversies on the proper design of those rules and mechanisms. Hence, the discussion focuses on issues of design rather than of principle;

(b)   the notion of policy coordination refers to other externalities that are not dealt with through mechanisms devoted to ensuring fiscal discipline. The key question here is whether national fiscal policies should be granted full autonomy, provided they abide by fiscal discipline, or whether there is a need for further coordination over and above what is required to avoid irresponsible fiscal behaviour. This has been a matter for discussion within the EU since the Delors report of 1989. The topic remains controversial, as some economists argue that coordination is simply not necessary (if not counterproductive) while others claim that it is required. The issue here is thus of principle as well as of design.

The chapter is organised as follows: the main conclusions are first summarised in the next section. The section after then focuses on discipline and the fourth section on coordination.

Main Conclusions

Problems

A good starting point is to draw up a list of the problems we are facing. My own selective list is as follows.

(1)   *There is wide agreement on the need for fiscal discipline in a monetary union, but there are several problems with our current definition of it.* The three main difficulties are (i) a focus on actual rather than cyclically adjusted deficits, which results in insufficient constraints on lax fiscal policies in good times and excessively tight constraints on responsible fiscal policies in bad times (this shortcoming is however being addressed, as the assessment of the budgetary situation is increasingly based on cyclically-adjusted data); (ii) a focus on the deficit rather than on the debt situation, i.e. on short term constraints rather than on long term sustainability. This strong emphasis on the deficit is not based on the provisions of the treaty, but on the interpretation they were given in the specific context of the mid-1990s, when a decision on EMU membership had to be taken; and (iii) as regards the debt ratio, a narrow approach to the long term sustainability of public finance, which leaves aside off-balance sheet liabilities. Furthermore, doubts about the credibility of the Stability Pact, which had been around since the beginning, have increased as a consequence of the Spring 2002 decision on Germany.

(2)   *We still lack a generally accepted doctrine on the role of macroeconomic policy instruments in the Eurozone.* Asymmetric developments are clearly not of the responsibility of the central bank, however there is not much agreement on what fiscal policy should do to counter shocks hitting individual member

states. The lack of a common doctrine on the role of discretionary fiscal policy was highlighted on the occasion of the Council recommendation to Ireland of 2001. As regards symmetric shocks, uncertainty about the strategy of the ECB leaves room for questions about the mix of monetary and fiscal reactions that is deemed appropriate in response to adverse shocks affecting the Eurozone as a whole. The slowdown of 2001–2002 was the occasion of reaching a common understanding on the role of automatic stabilisers in response to a slowdown in world demand; however, this falls short of providing a complete response to uncertainties.

(3) *The EU does not yet have a clear doctrine on why and when coordination is necessary.* Policy coordination remains a disputed issue, intellectually and institutionally. Some scholars claim that it is unnecessary, while others call for it. The aggregate fiscal stance and the aggregate fiscal position of the Eurozone were only recently recognised as relevant policy variables and the ECB is unwilling to take part in any exercise that could require that it commits on its future policy actions. Furthermore, member states, while paying lip service to coordination, are reluctant to relinquish their freedom to make discretionary choices. Finally, procedures for coordination are excessively complex and tangled, which weakens their impact on actual policy decisions.

(4) *As the interaction between EU procedures and national decisions remains generally weak, implementation is not satisfactory.* The Broad Economic Policy Guidelines (BEPGs) are discussed in detail by government representatives, but their impact on national policy discussions is frequently negligible. The Eurogroup itself still lacks visibility (seen from, say, Singapore, it is not clear what it is supposed to do). It is difficult to escape the impression that a large part of the energy that is devoted to EU procedures is simply wasted.

(5) *Structural reform ranks high on the agenda of the EU, but interaction between structural reform and macroeconomic policy remains weak.*

Proposals

(1) Structural deficits and output gaps measured according to a common methodology should be published by the Commission and serve as a basis for the evaluation of the budgetary situation in the member states. The methodology, its implementation and proposals for improvements should be regularly audited by an independent panel.

(2) When possible, the emphasis of fiscal discipline should be shifted away from the year-by-year monitoring of the deficit to a more medium-term oriented approach that focuses on the long run sustainability of public finance. This could be done through offering member states the option to subscribe to a 'Debt Sustainability Pact'. Countries participating in this new pact would have (i) to publish comprehensive public finance accounts according to improved EU accounting standards that allow us to assess the potential future impact of off-balance sheet liabilities; (ii) to keep their public debt ratio (Maastricht definition) below, say, 50 percent of GDP; and (iii) to set a

five-year target for this ratio, that would serve as a benchmark for assessing their budgetary policy. Countries satisfying these three conditions would automatically qualify in the no-excessive deficit procedure and be exempt from the fines envisaged in the Stability Pact. Failure to comply with any of the above three conditions would automatically activate the standard excessive deficit procedure and, if relevant, trigger sanctions.

(3) An economic policy charter for the Eurozone (a code of conduct) should be prepared for adoption by the Eurogroup. This code of conduct would not have a binding character, but would represent a common understanding on economic policy principles.

(4) The Stability programmes should be developed into fully-fledged instruments of surveillance and coordination. They should spell out how it is intended to alter budgetary policy in response to output and price surprises, as well as in case of revenue shortfall or surpluses. Those presumptive responses would not need to be identical across countries; however, they would have to be consistent with common principles as spelled out in the code of conduct. They would serve as a benchmark against which policy decisions would be assessed by EMU partners and market participants. The interaction between European procedures and national budgetary procedures should be both streamlined and reinforced in order to make sure that domestic policy decisions are consistent with commitments made in Brussels. In particular, decision on the Stability programmes should be made part of the national budget preparation procedures, including as regards the role of national parliaments.

(5) Coordination among the members of the Eurozone should be strengthened. It has been agreed that the budgetary position of the Eurozone as a whole should be regarded as a relevant variable. The Eurogroup should begin its surveillance exercise with an assessment of it. Further steps could be:

(i) a reciprocal binding agreement by the member of the Eurozone to consult their partners and the Commission before significant economic policy decisions are taken, as proposed by the Commission;

(ii) the replacement of the rotating presidency system by the designation of a Eurogroup president for a fixed period; and, which is more controversial,

(iii) the transformation of the Eurogroup into a collective executive body with the ability to make decisions by qualified majority voting.

(6) A constructive dialogue should be developed between the ECB and the Eurogroup on the interaction between structural reform and macroeconomic policy.

Fiscal Discipline

As already mentioned, there is not much disagreement on the need for fiscal discipline in a monetary union. Controversies about the Stability Pact nevertheless began as soon as it was agreed upon (Eichengreen and Wyplosz, 1998) and they have not ended. It is generally recognised that the Pact has triggered reductions in the deficits within the Eurozone, but it is frequently claimed that it is too rigid and prevents fiscal policies from fully playing their stabilisation role. It is also claimed that it does not bind fiscal policy choices enough when tax receipts abound. Furthermore, the Spring 2002 Council decision not to issue a formal early warning as the projected German fiscal deficit was getting close to the 3 percent limit has revived old doubts about the credibility of sanctions.

The question is thus not whether we need a Stability Pact, but whether the design of the current one provides the appropriate incentives to national governments while achieving the right mix between short-term flexibility and long-term constraint. A discussion on these issues requires clarity about the rationale for and the aim of fiscal discipline. In what follows, I thus start by summarising the main arguments for fiscal discipline. Next, I turn to the design of rules and to proposals for improvement.

Rationale

The main arguments for fiscal discipline rules are:[1]

(a) *moral hazard.* Although the provisions of the Maastricht treaty explicitly spell out that EMU members should not expect any form of bail-out, the potential costs of a default on public debt by a member state (especially a large one) could constrain the ECB in its policy choices. For example, the central bank could be forced to refrain from raising interest rates if it anticipates that this would aggravate the risk of a financial crisis.[2] Hence, high, potentially unsustainable debt ratios are to be avoided;

(b) *macroeconomic spillovers.* In an integrated capital market, public debt accumulation may exert an upward effect on the long term interest rate. It also impacts short term interest rates if monetary policy targets inflation and fiscal policy affects prices. Hence, there is an externality that national fiscal policy may fail to take into account. As a result, debt ratios and the long term interest rate both tend to be too high. Fiscal rules are needed to correct this;

(c) *political failures.* Democratic governments are short-sighted and tend to run excessive deficits. With separate currencies, this political failure is (at least partially) taken care of by the threat of exchange crises (in a fixed-but-adjustable exchange rate regime) or the inefficiency of fiscal reflation (in a floating exchange rate regime). In a monetary union, there is no automatic

---

1 Beetsma (2001) provides a summary of the arguments.

2 The consequences of a default on the public debt would obviously depend on the country's size. Arguably, a default on German or Italian public debt would have a systemic character while a default on the Irish debt would not. However, the ECB could hesitate to precipitate the default of a small member state because it could have both serious political consequences and a strong signalling effect. This is a justification for requiring that all member states abide by the same fiscal discipline rules.

check on the risk of fiscal profligacy.

I regard argument (a) as the most convincing of the three because it puts an emphasis on a potential threat to monetary and financial stability, i.e. on what EMU was made to achieve. It is important to stress that the type of externalities it puts an emphasis on are of a long run nature. The corresponding analytical setting is the standard long run one in which prices are flexible and have their level determined by monetary policy alone, while output is supply-determined. In such a framework, monetary and fiscal policies can be used independently provided the public debt remains sustainable. Thus, there is no case for coordination to go beyond avoiding the build up of unsustainable fiscal positions.[3]

In view of the distinction between discipline and coordination, argument (b) has more to do with the latter than with the former, because while it is true that spillover effects exist, there is no reason to focus exclusively on the excessive deficit–interest rate channel. Other channels of interdependence – e.g. through goods market linkages, the common exchange rate and the common balance of payment, or the average inflation rate of the Eurozone – can also be significant. Taking all these channels into account, it is disputable that what is needed is a rule that exclusively aims at preventing excessive deficits.

Argument (c) builds on evidence accumulated by the political economy approach to fiscal policy. However, it is not clear to what extent a possible political failure that results in excessive government borrowing, but does not have adverse effects on partner countries, should be addressed through common rules rather than reforming national institutions and procedures. It may be true that governments behave in a less responsible manner when the threat of a crisis is absent, but from that observation does not follow that this failure should be corrected through European disciplines.

The main rationale for fiscal discipline rules is thus that excessive debt accumulation with possible consequences on other member states should be avoided. This admittedly rather narrow definition of the goal has the advantage of providing guidance to address the issues of design.

Design

The significance of argument (a) was recognised in the preparation to the Maastricht negotiations, with the result that emphasis was put on debt sustainability issues[4]. But as the debt ratio of several member states exceeded 100 percent of GDP in the mid-1990s, debt had to be put aside as a practical criterion to assess the ability of member states to participate in EMU. It was still true when the Stability Pact was negotiated in 1997 and, as a consequence, the pact simply overlooks the debt criterion. As a result, fiscal discipline has so far been essentially assessed and enforced on the basis of the deficit rather than on the debt situation. This raises several difficulties.

---

3   von Hagen and Mundschenk (2001) develop the argument.
4   This is apparent in Emerson et al. (1990). See also Italianer (1993) and Bini-Smaghi et al. (1994).

What Deficit?

The most obvious problem arises from the monitoring of the deficit on the basis of headline rather than cyclically adjusted figures (in part because of disagreements on how to take cyclical factors into account). This approach results in insufficient constraints on lax fiscal policies in good times and excessively tight constraints on responsible fiscal policies in bad times, which is unfortunate, since it has been observed (Buti and Sapir, 1998) that fiscal policy precisely tends to behave pro-cyclically in periods of above-trend growth.

The latest cycle has confirmed this tendency: major mistakes tend to be made in 'good times' rather than in 'bad times'.

A reason for the initial focus on headline figure is that there was no agreement on how to take cyclical factors into account. In recent years, the EU has made progress towards a refined approach to budgetary surveillance. The Ecofin (2001) now explicitly states that:

> "the assessment of the appropriateness of the member states' medium term objectives and the examination of their fulfilment have to take explicit account of the cyclical position and its effect on the budget". At the initiative of the Economic Policy Committee, it was recently agreed to change the measure of the output gap from a purely statistical methodology to a more economically-based one. Member states have also agreed that automatic stabilisers should be allowed to play their role in both directions, provided the deficit remains below the 3% threshold. Several of them have adopted expenditure targets that have the advantage of insulating public spending from the effects of cyclical economic fluctuations and of letting fluctuations in receipts play their stabilisation role. The resulting system can thus be described as "cyclically-adjusted approach when possible, and nominal when necessary".

What Role for the 'Benchmark'?

A refined approach to budgetary surveillance is certainly a positive development, however there are some remaining difficulties. A budgetary policy that is geared to avoiding breaching the 3 percent limit during a slowdown may lead the debt ratio to converge on significantly different debt levels, depending on the short run elasticity of tax receipts and the sensitivity of the country to macroeconomic shocks. For example, according to the Commission, the so-called 'cyclical safety margin' varies from 1.5 percent of GDP in France to 4.3 percent of GDP in Finland (Artis and Buti, 2001). Assuming a 0.5 percentage point additional margin, this translates to 'benchmark' budgetary balances of, respectively, -1 percent and +1.8 percent of GDP. With, say, 2.5 percent growth and 1.5 percent inflation, this implies steady state values of -26 percent and +47 percent for the net wealth of the public sector.

The 'benchmark' interpretation of the SGP thus had the uncomfortable effect of implying significantly different steady state values for the public debt ratio. To instruct, implicitly at least, member countries to converge on such different levels of public debt and therefore to confront the associated consequences for intergenerational redistribution, can hardly be justified on the basis of a parameter as inconsequential as the short term elasticity of tax receipts.

Why Zero Debt?

Partly as a consequence, the EU has moved away from relying on the 'benchmark' that was used in the late 1990s to assess the budgetary situation in the member states. In its July 2001 Opinion on the content and format of the stability and convergence programmes, the Ecofin stated that the minimal benchmarks are 'an additional working instrument, but not a target per se'.[5] The emphasis is now put on the achievement of (structural) budgetary balance by 2004, an objective that was endorsed by the European Council in Barcelona. This means that the net wealth of the public sector should converge on a positive or zero value in all member states.

The paradox is however that as member states get closer to this objective, it becomes less and less justifiable to impose strict limits on their short term borrowing. Assuming that a country whose government is, say, 20 percent of GDP would run for a short period of time a budget deficit of 3 or even 4 percent of GDP, it is hard to imagine how the Council could claim that its policy threatens monetary and financial stability and thus how it could justify fining that country.

This would especially apply to a government that borrows to finance public investment. For example, could the EU claim that there are overriding reasons why an accession country with a low public debt ratio should not finance investment in infrastructures, education or the cleaning up of the environment through public borrowing? On both efficiency and intergenerational equity grounds, it may be a perfectly sensible policy to front-load such expenditures and to make future generations pay for the investments they will benefit from. This argument is especially relevant for catching-up member states and the accession countries.

The Risks of the Status Quo

It is a fact of life that a law that has lost justification is not considered legitimate anymore and cannot be credibly enforced for long. The same could happen to the Stability Pact in a not-too-distant future. Actually, this was already implicitly recognised in the Council decision of February 2002 on the convergence programme of the UK: although the British government envisaged a deficit of 1 percent of GDP in 2005/2006, the Council approved the programme. This is a recognition that the same rules may be applied differently when the debt ratio is 100 percent of GDP and when it is below 40 percent.

To focus on the short-term limits rather than on long-term intertemporal constraints was certainly justified in the context of the run-up to and the first years of EMU. However, it is less and less the case. At end-2001, already 8 of the 12 countries participating in the euro and 11 of the 15 current EU member states were below the 60 percent debt threshold. The proportion is roughly the same for accession countries (at end-2000, the debt ratio remained below 60 percent in 9 of the 12 candidates), and some of them such as Estonia, Latvia and the Czech Republic are hardly indebted at all. This suggests that time has come to consider a more balanced approach to fiscal discipline.

---

5   Ecofin Press release of 10 July 2001.

Proposals

Whatever its shortcomings, the Stability Pact is an asset because it embodies the commitment of the EU to fiscal discipline. Reforms should build on what has been achieved, and be phased in a way that preserves the credibility of the system. Thus, options for change should address both long term perspectives and issues of transition.

Cyclical Adjustment

A straightforward avenue for improvements is to rely on a common methodology for measuring the output gap and the budgetary impact of cyclical factors. As progress has been achieved recently in this direction and the EU now agrees on a methodology, structural deficits measured according to it should now be published by the Commission and serve as a basis for the evaluation of the budgetary situation in the member states. The methodology should also be communicated to the markets and the public. Finally, in order to make these figures as indisputable as possible and in order to preserve the comparability of structural deficits across countries, the methodology, its implementation on a country-by-country basis, and proposals for improvements, should be regularly audited by an independent panel.

A Debt-based Approach

The main direction for change should however be to focus more on debt sustainability and to reward countries whose public finance situation is fundamentally sound with a relaxation of short term constraints. This would be in accordance with the essential rationale for fiscal discipline that has been outlined.

For this approach to be operational, however, two difficulties must be addressed. First, the Maastricht debt criterion as it is measured is much too crude to be relied upon to assess the soundness of public finance in the member states. This was already pointed out in Commission studies and the need for a more developed approach was endorsed by the European Council in Barcelona. Off-balance sheet liabilities must be taken into account, especially implicit liabilities resulting from the prospective imbalance in the financing of pay-as-you-go pension systems. According to European Commission (2001) calculations, over the next 50 years the burden of old-age pensions should increase by more than 3 percentage points of GDP in the EU as a whole, but by several times more in some member states. Depending on discount rate assumptions, this implicit liability may represent as much or more than the market debt. It would thus make little sense to shift the emphasis on debt sustainability without improving the public accounting framework.

Reforming the public accounting framework in order to represent better the existing and potential future claims on public resources is obviously fraught with difficulties. But this could not be a reason not to act. To focus exclusively on the deficit as it is measured in the national accounts could only lead member states to develop innovative financial techniques to circumvent common constraints.

Whatever the definition of discipline that is adopted, progress is needed on the public accounting front.

The second difficulty is that even when the debt ratio is made the target variable, the deficit remains the control variable. In practical terms, focusing on debt limit alone could result in significant slippage as member states could not adjust their deficit fast enough to meet their commitments. This implies, first, that any reformed arrangement should include safety margins and, second, that the consistency between the current and projected deficits and the debt target should be monitored closely.

A Debt Sustainability Pact

Taking these elements into account, a practical proposal would be to offer to member states the option to subscribe to a 'Debt Sustainability Pact'. Participation in this new pact would be voluntary. Those countries who would choose to take part in it would have:

(i)   to publish comprehensive public finance accounts according to improved EU accounting standards that allow assessment of the potential future impact of off-balance sheet liabilities;

(ii) to keep their public debt ratio (Maastricht definition) below a certain threshold, say 50 percent of GDP (the safety margin should be large enough to ensure that the debt ratio remains below 60 percent even in the case of a significant slippage);

(iii to set a five year target for this ratio, which would serve as a benchmark for assessing their budgetary policy. The target level should take into account the existence of implicit liabilities and be subject to multilateral surveillance, as for the Stability programmes. It would then become part of the medium term commitments of the member state's Stability programme. The consistency between current fiscal policy and this medium term commitment would be assessed annually in the framework of budgetary surveillance.

Countries that choose to opt for this pact and satisfy the three conditions would automatically qualify in the no-excessive deficit procedure of Art. 104 (ex 104c) and would thus be exempt from the fines envisaged in the Stability Pact (but they would still have to prepare Stability programmes). However, failure to comply with any of the above three conditions would automatically activate the standard excessive deficit procedure and, if relevant, trigger sanctions as envisaged in the Stability Pact.

Why offer an option rather than reform the Stability Pact? First, because there is still wide dispersion in the public finance situation of the member states; for the countries whose debt ratio remains above 60 percent of GDP or close to that threshold, it would be hardly appropriate to move from a deficit-based approach to a debt-based approach. Second, because an attempt to reform the pact would immediately be regarded as an attempt at softening discipline. Third, offering an option could serve as an incentive for member states to improve their budgetary situation and reform their accounting procedures in order to qualify as 'tier 1' countries.[6]

Adopting this approach would have the advantage of restoring a degree of subsidiarity in public finance decisions, while addressing the externality the Stability Pact was created to deal with.

Coordination

Rationale

The issue of policy coordination in EMU has been a matter for discussion since the Delors report of 1989, which stated that national fiscal policies would have to abide by 'binding rules' that 'would permit the determination of an overall policy stance'. It has become a topic for analytical research, but remains a disputed one. Numerous authors (of which Gros and Hobza, 2001; De Grauwe and Polan, 2001; Alesina *et al.*, 2001; Beetsma *et al.*, 2001) argue that it is not necessary, and can even be counterproductive. Others (such as Artus, 1999; Jacquet and Pisani-Ferry, 2001; von Hagen and Mundschenk, 2001, 2002) maintain that it would significantly improve the policy outcome. *The Political Case*

Before summing up the main economic arguments put forward in the controversy, it may be useful briefly to discuss the political case for coordination. As Paul De Grauwe (1998) once eloquently argued, the legitimacy of the ECB does not rest on its isolation. On the contrary, it comes from its shareholders and gains strength from the fact that ministers are able to talk to each other and to take collective responsibility for what belongs to governments (and not to the central bank): fiscal policies, tax policies and structural policies, to mention only three major aspects. An ECB that would be perceived as acting in isolation, without the backing of its shareholders, would lack legitimacy. An ECB that would be perceived as the only policy player of the EMU system would risk being held responsible for whatever does not work in the Eurozone[7] – which could only result in a clash with public opinion.

---

6   It must be said, however, that an approach could be devised that would address the same concerns while leaving the Stability Pact nominally unchanged. A possibility would, for example, be to make the 'close to balance or in surplus' target dependent on a country's debt level and on its off-balance sheet liabilities. Member states whose debt and implicit liabilities are low would be able to run higher deficits than those who do not meet that condition

7   The argument was also used by Strauss-Kahn (1998) as a reason for the creation of the Eurogroup.

More generally, a policy system in which no one could be held responsible for the overall policy outcome would be vulnerable to attacks on the ground that such a functioning is not compatible with the responsiveness citizens are entitled to expect from democratic governments. To use a provocative analogy: a French convict recently committed suicide in police offices after he had killed eight members of a municipality. An official report concluded that all rules and procedures had been respected and that no specific responsibility could be invoked. Citizens were understandably unconvinced, to say the least: having respected rules and procedures cannot exempt those who are in charge from their responsibility when something goes badly wrong. This also applies to the proper functioning of the policy system of the Eurozone.[8]

The Economic Case

Turning to the economic side of the discussion, a first line of argument (Gros and Hobza, 2001; De Grauwe and Polan, 2001) stresses that as monetary union increases both the positive spillover effects of fiscal policy (through goods markets integration) and the negative ones (through capital markets integration), the resulting net effect is indeterminate. Thus, it is argued that monetary union does not increase the need for fiscal coordination in comparison to a floating exchange rate regime.

It is obviously correct that in a Mundell-Fleming setting, the sign of the spillover effects of fiscal policy is a purely empirical issue. But the argument is not really convincing:

(a) to claim that an issue can only be settled at the empirical level (as opposed to the theoretical one) does not prove that it is irrelevant;

(b) the argument does not show that the policy outcome could not be improved through better coordination, it only says that the case for coordination may not be higher after EMU than before;

(c) by focusing on horizontal spillover effects, the argument misses that the common inflation rate, the common exchange rate and the common current account balance are 'club goods' that are specific to a monetary union. This does not come from any increase in horizontal spillover effects but simply from the fact that those variables are or may be regarded as common policy objectives. Examples include the common inflation rate, which is treated as a policy objective by the central bank and can, at the same time, be affected by fiscal policies. Other relevant variables are the exchange rate and the current account (or the overall saving rate) if they become regarded as policy objectives. The existence of such club goods creates a channel of interdependence that is both specific to EMU and unambiguous in sign.[9]

This, however, does not end the discussion. The recent literature on EMU policy coordination (for example Beetsma *et al.*, 2001, Dixit and Lambertini, 2002, Uhlig,

---

8   Similar points are made by British officials in their description of the UK policy system. See for example O'Donnel (2001).

9   Jacquet and Pisani-Ferry (2001) and von Hagen and Mundschenk (2001) develop the argument.

2002) on which Alesina *et al.* (2001) draw recognises the existence of interactions through common objectives, or 'club goods'. However, several authors rely on a well-known result from game theory to emphasise that a coordination that is limited to a subset of players (the governments) and does not involve a major one (the central bank) could be counterproductive. While it is in effect possible that coordination among a subset of players reduces global welfare, it is important to stress that this is not a general result.[10] Depending on the assumptions on the structure of the economy as well as on the governments' and the central bank's objective, coordination can have positive, negative or neutral effects on welfare.

From a practical standpoint, Alesina *et al.* (2001) claim that coordination among fiscal authorities or between them and the central bank is 'not necessary if the monetary and fiscal authorities (independently) follow appropriate and prudent policies', by which they mean that the central bank follows an inflation targeting strategy and the fiscal authorities maintain a cyclically-adjusted balanced budget.

Alesina and his co-authors provide a clearly articulated view of how EMU should work, but one that is valid only if a number of implicit assumptions are satisfied. The most significant are the following:

(a) monetary policy is entrusted with the task of managing aggregate demand in the Eurozone according to its inflation target. This implies that monetary and fiscal authorities do not have conflicting policy objectives and that governments trust the ECB enough to refrain from actively managing the aggregate demand of the Eurozone. These would certainly be positive developments. The ECB, however, has been reluctant to explicitly recognise that it has a responsibility in managing aggregate demand beyond its mandate to ensure price stability, because it perceives that this kind of commitment would risk jeopardising its independence. It has not acknowledged that it follows an inflation targeting strategy and that it is willing to counter potentially deflationary shocks with the same energy as inflationary ones. And it stresses that potential output growth in the Eurozone is between 2 and 2.5 percent while the European council has set a 3 percent target;

(b) the policy-mix is irrelevant. In Alesina *et al.*'s view, monetary policy and fiscal policy are perfect substitutes, so there is no point in trying to change the balance between the fiscal and the monetary stance. In other words, the aggregate public saving ratio of the Eurozone is an irrelevant variable (or at least there is no reason why it should deviate from zero). As a first approximation, it is certainly correct to focus on the level of aggregate demand. However, the policy mix may matter, at least in an open economy setting, first because it has an impact on the interest rate and the exchange rate, thereby on the

---

10 Artus (2002) provides a nice overview of the results that can be expected from coordination among budgetary players when the central bank's objective differs from the social objective. He shows that when the central bank is more conservative (i.e. inflation-adverse) than society, while the governments' objective function corresponds to the social objective, then whether budgetary coordination improves or deteriorates social welfare depends on the sign of the fiscal policy externality.

inflation/output balance, and second, because the policymakers' objectives may include other variables than inflation and output, for example the current account or the real exchange rate.

Coordination sceptics often claim that while the policy mix may be relevant in theory, it is irrelevant in practice because of our inability to determine how exchange rates would respond to changes in the fiscal/monetary mix. While it would certainly be hazardous to attempt to fine-tune the exchange rate in this way, there are circumstances in which it is reasonable for policy makers to decide on the policy mix. Recent examples include the Japanese case, where interest rate policy has become ineffective due to liquidity trap effects, the celebrated 'Clinton–Greenspan' policy mix, or German unification. Looking ahead, the large and persistent current account imbalances within the G7 may lead to situations where controlling aggregate public saving would become a policy objective.

The view against coordination thus rests on significant assumptions that may not be satisfied in practice. An important element in the argument of Alesina *et al*. is, however, to recall that well-designed rules of behaviour reduce the need for discretionary coordination. This has relevance because the respective merits of the rules-based approach and a discretionary approach to coordination depend on the institutional environment. Between the US Treasury Secretary and the Federal Reserve Chairman, periodic, discrete meetings may be enough to organise co-ordination. But in Europe, where decision makers are numerous and diverse – Finance ministers, for example, do not all have the same responsibilities – discretionary co-ordination inevitably implies high transaction costs. It is thus advisable for the EU to try to reap the maximum benefit from ex-ante (i.e. rules-based) coordination, while keeping in mind that there are limits to what a rules-based approach can achieve and that procedures for effective discretionary action are needed.

Design

There is a considerable degree of confusion in Europe as regards the objectives, the scope and the procedures of coordination. Official documents pay lip service to it but fall short from defining why it is required, when it should be activated and how it should be implemented. For example, the end-1999 report by the Ecofin to the European Council in Helsinki, which was an early attempt at taking stock and defining avenues for progress, is full of vague statements and short on specifics. It mentions the principle of 'close co-ordination' among the 'fundamental principles' [of economic policy in EMU]. The motive for it originates in the fact that 'the completion of the Single Market and the single currency accelerate economic integration in the Community and give rise to more and more spill-over effects' (without further precision), which means that 'the relevance of policy co-ordination is particularly cogent within the euro area, especially, but not only, as regards macro-economic policies'. Such general statements do not provide a roadmap for making decisions.

Objectives

The official literature examined in Pisani-Ferry (2002) does not convey the impression that EMU has converged on a stable set of policy principles and on a broadly accepted doctrine on the role of macroeconomic policy instruments. While the core rules of monetary union such as price stability or the need for fiscal discipline are firmly established, there remain a number of open issues as regards the role of fiscal policies, the assignment of instruments to objectives, the extent of spillover effects or the response to shocks of various types that should be expected from the policy system. Successive versions of the Broad Economic Policy Guidelines (BEPGs) have, for example, outlined different sets of principles for assigning instruments to objectives.

Progress has certainly been achieved in recent years. Eurozone policy makers have embarked on a 'learning by doing' exercise and have made efforts to clarify their understanding on policy principles. Welcomed clarifications have occurred on the occasion of common macroeconomic shocks. This first occurred in 1998 in the aftermath of the Asian crisis, when the Eurogroup endorsed the view that the appropriate response to the expected slowdown in world demand would be to keep on reducing the deficits while relying on monetary policy to counter the effects of the slowdown; another important clarification occurred in Autumn 2001, also in response to a (more severe) slowdown, when the European Council decided that automatic stabilisers had to be allowed to play their role in full, unless there was a threat to exceed the 3 percent deficit threshold. The recent decision by the European council to regard the aggregate fiscal position of the Eurozone as a relevant policy variable (a notion that not long ago was anathema to some member countries) is also notable.

However, there was much less coordination in responding to favourable shocks such as the unexpected rise in fiscal revenues in 1999–2000 and the windfall gain from the sale of UMTS licences. The Council was also rather unsuccessful when dealing with asymmetric shocks, as illustrated by the 2001 controversy on Ireland.

A reason for this state of affairs is that the treaty and accompanying legislation does not (and could not: international treaties are obviously not economic textbooks) spell out how the policy system of the Eurozone is expected to work. While the objectives and the broad definition of responsibility are clearly defined, important policy principles are missing. For example, it is not clear from the provisions of the treaty how fiscal and monetary policies should respond to a symmetric drop in aggregate demand, nor is it clear how fiscal policy should respond to an asymmetric price shock. The resulting uncertainty is compounded by the absence of a policy authority who is clearly entrusted with the role of a 'decision-maker of last resort' that is able to respond in a discretionary fashion to unexpected developments. This strongly contrasts with, for example, the UK setting, where the Treasury explicitly sees its role as that of a Stackelberg leader (Allsop, 2002; O'Donnel, 2001).

The paradox of the EMU policy system is thus that it is long on rules and short on principles.

Procedures

The EMU system relies heavily on ex ante rules but it also includes procedures for defining a common approach to economic policy choices (the BEPGs) and a body, the Eurogroup, which was explicitly conceived as a forum for elaborating a joint economic assessment and consulting on discretionary policy choices.

Experience with the rules-based approach suggests that in addition to the rigidity it implies, implementation is more complicated than anticipated. A key issue here is the degree of 'ownership' by the various member states of the commonly agreed rules and the Stability programmes. The budgetary procedures of the member states have not yet fully adjusted to the new EMU environment and national policymakers still ignore, at least in part, what their country may be committed to vis-à-vis its partners. While the Pact and the programmes have in general had a significant influence on domestic budgetary policy choices, implementation has been more effective when they have explicitly been made part of the national framework for budgetary decisions.

The experience with the BEPGs can hardly be considered positive. The guidelines are discussed in detail by the representatives of the member states but they are frequently ignored by national policy makers. They are more the result of a line-by-line negotiation than the expression of a common strategy. They are furthermore difficult to enforce since Art. 103 does not have 'teeth' and this was exemplified by the 2001 Council recommendation on Ireland, which was ignored by the Irish authorities.

As regards the Eurogroup, it is generally considered by participants to be a useful forum for policy discussions. A small number of participants, confidentiality of discussions and an informal atmosphere make it a body very different from the Ecofin. However, its external visibility is very limited and it has not yet produced noticeable results. Part of the difficulty lies in the rotating presidency, which prevents leadership and continuity in external representation. Part also lies in the inability of the Eurogroup to make decisions.

Proposals

'Coordination' involves both uncontroversial and controversial proposals. Among the relatively uncontroversial suggestions that could be implemented are those that could contribute to clarifying the common doctrine, to achieving a better information of the different players, and to making sure that commitments made in Brussels are put into practice at home. More controversial are the reinforcement of the Eurogroup and its transformation into a collective executive body.

A Code of Conduct for Economic Policy

To clarify the common doctrine, Jacquet and Pisani-Ferry (2001) have proposed drawing up an 'economic policy charter' for the Eurozone that would develop principles to guide economic policy decisions as well as market expectations.

A similar idea has been put forward by the Commission in its communication of February 2001 under the name of a 'code of conduct'. This code of conduct would not have a binding character, but would represent a common understanding on economic policy principles. It should especially include:

(i) assignment principles for responding to (favourable or adverse) shocks of a symmetric or asymmetric nature. In the European Commission's (2001) words, the code would 'lay down the principles on the basis of which the different policy instruments could be activated to increase the area's economic growth potential and to cope with shocks affecting the area or some of its member states';

(ii) rules of conduct for the management of public finance over the cycle and on how national budgetary policies are expected to respond to favourable or unfavourable shocks to the tax receipts (contingent rules);

(iii) the common understanding on the rationale of and the scope for coordination.

From a policy standpoint, an approach based on state-contingent rules of conduct would represent a third way between a coordination model based on rigid rules and numerical thresholds (as in the Stability Pact) and a discretionary approach to coordination. The adoption of such rules would help market participants and, more generally, economic agents to form expectations on the likely policy reactions to shocks. It would thus improve the predictability of macro-economic policy.

An important issue is whether this code of conduct would include elements on the ECB strategy. As the above discussion has made clear, the definition of fiscal policy principles could hardly made much progress in the absence of predictability of the monetary policy behaviour. However, the ECB would certainly be reluctant to participate in an exercise that might jeopardise its independence. A practical way out would be for the central bank to clarify its own strategy simultaneously. As already advocated by many economists, this clarification should include the abandonment of the 'first pillar' and the adoption of a symmetrical inflation target.

As regards the method, the preparation of this code could draw on the recent experience of EMU and the progress made in the formulation of policy responses to events. But its elaboration should not be left to the negotiation. In order to preserve analytical clarity, it would be preferable that the Commission requests a panel of outside experts to draw up a proposal.

The Stability Programmes as Instruments of Coordination

A second step would be to develop the Stability programmes into fully-fledged instruments of surveillance and coordination. This could be especially useful if short term constraints on deficits are relaxed as suggested in the third section. Apart from enhancing their role in national budgetary decision making, this approach implies that the Stability programmes should spell out how it is intended to alter budgetary policy in response to output and price surprises, as well as in the case of revenue shortfall or surpluses. A simple example of such presumptive responses is the adoption by several member states of public spending targets that are not revised in reaction to revenue shortfalls or surpluses.

Those presumptive responses would not need to be exactly identical across countries; however, they would have to be consistent with common principles as spelled out in the code of conduct. There would still be room for discretionary choices by the national authorities, but the presumptive responses would serve as a benchmark against which policy decisions would be assessed by EMU partners and market participants.

For the Stability programmes to play their role, the interaction between European procedures and national budgetary procedures should be both streamlined and reinforced. Simple reforms could include:

(i)   grouping the EU annual coordination and surveillance processes around two main procedures, a 'structural' one and a 'budgetary and macroeconomic' one, each of which would be the main focus of a Semester and result in a synthetic report to be submitted to the European parliament. The Ecofin (2001) decision to shorten the period for submission of the Stability programmes and to cluster their examination is a step in this direction;

(ii)   including in national budgetary bills a 'first chapter' on the zone's perspectives and policy choices that would be debated by parliament ;

(iii)   making the decision on the Stability programmes part of the national budget preparation procedures, which means that the programmes would have to be adopted by parliament.

A More Effective Eurogroup

These proposals would help in clarifying the EMU rules of the game. However, they would not eliminate the need for concerted discretionary action in certain circumstances.

Since it has been agreed that the budgetary position of the Eurozone as a whole should be regarded as relevant variables, the Eurogroup should begin its surveillance exercise with an assessment of it (for this to take place, national public finance programmes had to be submitted to the Commission in time for their impact on the fiscal prospects and policy stance of the Eurozone as a whole to be discussed before individual country programmes are assessed. This is now the case). Further steps could be:

(i)   a reciprocal binding agreement by the member of the Eurozone to consult their partners and the Commission before significant economic policy decisions are taken, as proposed by the Commission;

(ii)   an institutional reinforcement of the Eurogroup through the replacement of the rotating presidency system by the designation of a president for a fixed period.[11] Such a change would open the way for a more effective leadership

---

11 Whether this president would be one of the ministers belonging to the Eurogroup or a commissioner depends on the directions for reforming the EU institutions and goes beyond the scope of this paper.

and for a greater external visibility of the Eurogroup.

A certainly controversial change would be to transform the Eurogroup into a collective executive body by giving it the ability to take decisions by qualified majority voting (Jacquet and Pisani-Ferry, 2000). The idea behind the proposal is not that the Eurogroup should each year decide on the budgetary policies of the member states, but that it should have the capacity to set guidelines when it agrees that a change in the overall fiscal stance is needed. The corresponding procedure should be designed order to ensure that such guidelines are only issued when there is a clear case for joint action. It should also preserve the exclusive role of the Ecofin as a co-legislator, which implies that the Eurogroup should only be given the capacity to adopt policy guidelines.

A practical possibility would be to give to the Eurogroup the ability to adopt policy guidelines by qualified majority upon Commission proposal, after it has determined that the situation requires a common policy response. To remain credible, such guidelines should not be used too frequently, rather they should only be adopted when there is a clear case for joint action. The Council should refrain from instructing member states to modify their policy choices in the absence of explicitly defined externalities.

Interactions between Macroeconomic Policy and Structural Reform

This paper has focused on macro-economic policies. However, the interaction between macroeconomic and structural issues is just as important. A good illustration of this state of affairs is the already mentioned gap between the Council's growth target and the ECB's evaluation of the growth potential of the Eurozone l. How this gap is supposed to be filled has not been spelled out – or, in other words, it is neither clear whether the structural reforms that are currently contemplated are expected to raise the growth potential by 0.75 percentage points in the coming years, nor whether implementing those reforms would lead the ECB to revise its own estimates of potential output. The risk is that uncertainty about the strength of the governments' commitment to reform leads the ECB to adopt an excessively cautious attitude and that uncertainty about the monetary policy reactions to bold structural policy actions weakens the governments' incentive to reform.

A constructive dialogue should be developed between the ECB and the Eurogroup on the interaction between structural reform and macroeconomic policy. The key policy variables around which this dialogue could take place are, on the one hand, the NAIRU (or more refined concepts of the equilibrium unemployment rate) and the output gap of the Euro zone, and on the other hand the growth rate of potential output. The Commission could provide a significant input to this dialogue in the form of evaluations of the non-inflationary growth potential and of the impact of structural reforms implemented in the member states or at the Union level.

References

Alesina, A., Galí, J., Giavazzi, F., Uhlig, H. and Blanchard, O. (2001) Defining a macroeconomic framework for the Euro Area, in *Monitoring the European Central Bank*, (n.3, CEPR).

Allsopp, C. (2002) The *Future of Macroeconomic Policy in the European Union*, External MPC Unit Discussion Paper n. 7, (Bank of England, February).

Artis, M. and Buti, M. (2001) *Setting Medium-Term Fiscal Targets in EMU*, in: A. Brunila, M. Buti and D. Franco, *The Stability and Growth Pact: The Architecture of Fiscal Policy in EMU* (Hampshire, UK: Palgrave).

Artus, P. (1999) *Indépendance de la banque centrale et conflits portants sur les politiques monétaires et budgétaires* (Caisse des dépôts: n. 39/MA, juillet).

Artus, P. (2002) *Une présentation générale de quelques résultats concernant la coordination des politiques budgétaires et monétaires* (Caisse des dépôts: n. 96/MA, April).

Beetsma, R. (2001) *Does EMU need a Stability Pact?*, in A. Brunila, M. Buti and D. Franco, *The Stability and Growth Pact: The Architecture of Fiscal Policy in EMU* (Hampshire, UK: Palgrave).

Beetsma, R., Debrun, X. and Klaassen, F. (2001) *Is Fiscal Policy Coordination in EMU Desirable?* (IMF: Working Paper n. 01/178).

Bini-Smaghi, L., Padoa-Schioppa, T. and Papadia, F. (1994) The transition to EMU in the Maastricht Treaty, *Essays in International Finance* (Princeton, November).

Brunila, A., Buti, M. and Franco, D. (2001) *The Stability and Growth Pact: The Architecture of Fiscal Policy in EMU* (Hampshire UK: Palgrave).

Buti, M. and Sapir, A. (1998) *Economic Policy in EMU* (Oxford: Oxford University Press).

Buti, M. and Sapir, A. (Eds) (2002) *The Functioning of EMU: Challenges for the Early Years* (London: Edward Elgar).

De Grauwe, P. (1998) Law unto itself, *Financial Times*, 12 November.

De Grauwe, P. and Polan, M. (2001) Increased capital mobility: a challenge for national economic policies, in: H. Siebert (Ed), *The World's New Financial Landscape: Challenges for Economic Policy* (Springer).

Dixit, A. and Lambertini, L. (2002) *Symbiosis of Fiscal and Monetary Policy in a Monetary Union*, mimeo.

Ecofin (2001) *Opinion on the Content and Format of Stability and Convergence Programmes* (2001 Code of Conduct), July, reprinted in *Public Finance in EMU 2002* (European Economy n.3/2002).

Eichengreen, B. and Wyplosz, C. (1998) The stability pact: more than a minor nuisance? *Economic Policy*, 26.

Emerson, M. *et al.* (1990) One market, one money, *European Economy*, 44.

European Commission (2001) *Commission Communication on Strengthening Economic Policy Co-ordination within the Euro Area* (COM 82: 7 February).

Gros, D. and Hobza, A. (2001) *Fiscal Policy Spillovers in the Euro Area: Where are they?*, mimeo.

Italianer, A. (1993) Maastering Maastricht: EMU issues and how they were settled, in: K. Gretschmann (Ed.), *Economic and Monetary Union: Implication for National Policy Makers* (Maastricht: European Institute of Public Administration).

Jacquet, P. and Pisani-Ferry, J. (2001) *Economic Policy Co-ordination in the Eurozone: What Has Been Achieved? What Should Be Done?* (London: Centre for European Reform, January).

O'Donnel, G. (2001) *UK Policy Coordination: The Importance of Institutional Design*, mimeo.

Pisani-Ferry, J. (2002) The EMU's economic policy principles: words and facts. Paper prepared for the European Commission (Directorate-General ECFIN), in: M. Buti and A. Sapir (Eds) *The Functioning of EMU: Challenges for the Early Years*.

Strauss-Kahn, D. (1998) Le Conseil de l'euro: un forum pour la coordination des politiques économiques, *Revue d'économie financière*, 45.

Uhlig, H. (2002) One money, but many fiscal policies in Europe: what are the consequences? Paper presented to the DG ECFIN workshop on *The Interactions between Fiscal and Monetary Policies in EMU*.

von Hagen, J. and Mundschenk, S. (2001) *The Political Economy of Policy Coordination in EMU*, mimeo.

von Hagen, J. and Mundschenk, S. (2002) *The Functioning of Economic Policy Coordination*, in: M. Buti and A. Sapir (Eds) *The Functioning of EMU: Challenges for the Early Years*.

Chapter 8

EU Institutions: The Challenges of the Enlargement Process

Vieri Ceriani

The enlargement process induces strong pressures for reforming EU institutions. As an example, the effects of the unanimity rule in decision-making will be very different under a membership of 25 (or 30) with respect to the actual membership of 15, not to mention the original one of six. The enlargement process underlines and aggravates some of the problems that exist under the present arrangements. The setting up of the Convention on the future of Europe is the clearest evidence of the importance of institutional reforms. The ongoing discussion involves practically all aspects of the EU decision-making procedures; the very roles of the Commission, the Council and the Parliament are under scrutiny. The goal is to overcome the so-called *democracy deficit*, the imbalances, sluggishness and slowness of the decision making process (partly but not solely due to the heavy reliance on unanimity voting).

This chapter will concentrate on a few aspects of the institutional reform: far from completeness, it will simply review some of the issues that appear more closely related to the conduct of economic policy, without drawing conclusions.

The Current Status: A Pre-federal Arrangement ?

It is well known that the institutional nature of the EU is peculiar and difficult to compare both with existing federal states and with other international entities. Member States retain full sovereignty on almost all their prerogatives. However, no international union has ever had an autonomous legislative process; never has union law had prevalence on national law or been directly applicable; and never have the sentences of an international court been directly mandatory. A purely intergovernmental decision process, stemming from an international treaty, does not need a system of co-decision with a Parliament, which is elected by all the peoples of the Member States. Recently, Member States have decided to renounce their prerogatives on monetary policy and decided to adopt a single currency. They have also decided on the creation of an internal market (with four basic freedoms) and to have a common foreign and security policy.

A discussion of the exact nature of the European institutions is out of the scope of this Chapter. The soundest conclusion is that these institutions have evolved over time, continue to evolve, and from the outset had a built-in dynamism that was intended to move towards stronger and tighter supra-national relations among Member States.

Other historical examples show a pattern of gradual build-up, from national states to super-national entities of the federal type. Nevertheless, it is not a necessity that the EU follows the same evolutionary process, or that it ends up with the features of a federal state of the kind we are today familiar with. So far, the build-up of the EU has followed very original paths; it is likely (and even desirable) that it will continue to do so.

New Federal Tasks and Institutional Changes

From the economic point of view, the fundamental issues addressed by the literature on fiscal federalism are the assignment of the tasks to the different levels of government, and the decision making process in the fulfilment of those tasks and their financing.

The current debate considers defence and foreign policy as natural candidates to for the competence of the Union. Internal security and immigration are part of the same broad task. This change in the allocation of responsibilities is generally viewed as consistent with the principles of subsidiarity: the tasks under consideration can be more efficiently carried out in a centralised way. It seems obvious that, speaking with one voice, the bargaining power at international level should be augmented. Other considerations in favour are the need to combat more efficiently terrorism, smuggling, and organised crime, and to protect more effectively the external borders while guaranteeing the fundamental freedoms of movement in the internal market. In these areas, the presence of spillover effects assigns the competence to the upper level of government.

The point of debate is whether an enhanced intergovernmental coordination would suffice, or a formal assignment of these tasks to the Union is necessary. After years of fatiguing efforts at coordination, it seems that the second solution is gaining ground. 'In this sphere, power-sharing amounts to relying on the goodwill of national leaders [...] Recent events have confirmed only too clearly that in today's Europe the media coverage afforded to a national leader who appears individually on the international stage is irresistible compared with a team approach' (European Parliament, 2002). The difficulties of intergovernmental coordination clearly will not diminish – quite the opposite – with an increased number of actors.

In the case of a formal assignment of tasks to the Union, the institutional setting is open to discussion. Who will be responsible for foreign policy and defence and which procedures will be followed? The debate is open between two opposite views: the so-called *community* method and the *inter-governmental* method.

The key features of the community method are:

- the European Commission has the monopoly to introduce legislative initiatives, in the general European interest;
- the Council of Ministers, representing Member States (national governments) is the legislative power; it decides by qualified majority in most cases (except

those where unanimity is required); it can amend Commission proposals by unanimity;
- the European Parliament, directly elected by European citizens, co-legislates or at least is consulted;
- Member States implement EU policy;
- the EU institutions, Member States and interested parties can take a case to the European Court of Justice; the Commission may take Member States to the Court for implementation failures.

The community method currently applies to issues related to the 'first pillar' (largely economic, social and environmental matters, including international trade). It does not apply to the Common Foreign and Security Policy and to Justice and Home affairs, which were introduced as second and third 'pillars' in the Maastricht Treaty of 1992. On these matters, the right of initiative is mostly shared by all Member States and the European Commission, and unanimity mostly applies as a decision rule.

The community method is supported by the Commission and favoured by smaller Member States. The main consideration is that the decision-making process is transparent, based on legal procedures, open to public debate, and guarantees accountability. The Commission plays an important role in balancing different policy issues in the general European interest and acts as 'guardian of the Treaty'.

The Commission has advanced proposals to apply the community method to the second and third pillars. The functions of High Representative for CSFP should be brought into the Commission and merged with those of the Commissioner for External Relations. This position should be charged with representing Europe internationally and should set the agenda on international affairs. The decisions should be taken by the Council at majority, except for security and defence, where unanimity should apply. Foreign policy should be given the necessary resources: budget, new procedures, and a network of external delegations.

The intergovernmental method (supported by some European governments) focuses on an enhanced role of the Council and of its Presidency, which should no more be rotating on a six-months basis, but should be stable for several years, and elected by the members of the Council. The President of the Council would officially represent the Union in its international relationships and assume the functions of the High Representative for CSFP.

No new resources would be given to the Union, because the responsibility of carrying out policies would be on the Member States.

Under the intergovernmental method, the driving force of European policy would be national governments, and the role of the Commission would be seriously reduced. As regards the coordination of policies, this solution might be less effective than the other. In terms of democratic accountability, this solution presents some weaknesses. The appointment of the President by the Council itself (heads of government) is the critical aspect. In addition, the Commission is appointed by the Council, but the Parliament confirms this appointment. Proposals have been put forward to have the Commission appointed by Parliament, and confirmed by the Council, or even to have direct elections by European citizens. The Conference will propose ways forward on these issues. It is worth nothing that new tasks might be given to the Union and, under some solutions, new resources might be needed.

A New Financing of the 'Federal' Budget?

Currently, the budget of the Union relies heavily on transfers by Member States. In origin, custom duties, agriculture contributions and a percentage of the harmonised VAT base formed the 'own resources'. Custom duties have decreased over time, and continue to do so, because of the successive enlargements of the Community and of the conclusion of several free trade agreements. The VAT receipts are also decreasing, due to the reduction of the rate. In 1988, new receipts were needed to face the increase in the expenses for the common agricultural policy, for the social fund and for regional development, linked to the accession of new Member States (Greece, Spain, Portugal). It was decided to phase-out VAT gradually and to introduce a new source of financing, based on GNP. The gap between total expenditures and the existing 'own resources' was to be filled through transfers by Member States, in proportion to their share of the Community GNP (with the exception of the special UK arrangement). By 2006, the GNP resource will come close to financing 75 percent of the budget of the EU.

The current method of financing lacks transparency and accountability. EU citizens do not perceive how and how much they are contributing to the EU budget. Custom duties are collected by national customs and transferred to Brussels. The VAT and the GNP resources are both calculated through statistical methods, assessed through an administrative procedure between officials of the Member States and the Union, and take the form of transfers to the Union.

The decision process is typically intergovernmental: Ecofin adopts a decision at unanimity, which is then ratified by the European Parliament and by national Parliaments. These ratification have a formal content. The decision is taken after rather fatiguing negotiations among Member States. The discussion is focused entirely on which Member States gain or lose, which are the net beneficiaries and the net contributors, and by how much.

It has been pointed out that the European Parliament has prerogatives over expenditures, but not over receipts. From this point of view, it is unique with respect to all other Parliaments in the world. And this state of affairs is at odds with the basic principles of democracy ('no taxation without representation').

In addition, subsidiarity may work effectively only if every level of government has effective financial autonomy.

Today, the size of the EU budget is very limited: roughly 1 percent of EU GNP. It is mainly devoted to the Common Agricultural Policy and other forms of regional redistribution: cohesion funds and structural funds. The forthcoming accession of 10–15 states will require some increase of the budget, as happened with previous enlargements. Also, new expenditures might arise if the institutional reforms assign new and enlarged responsibilities to the Union, in the fields of foreign policy and security. A decision on expenditures cannot go without a decision on financing.

The EU Commission and the EU Parliament have put forward the proposal to move away from the current method of financing the Union and replace it with own taxes, voted for by the EU Parliament. The transparency, the accountability and the legitimacy of the budgetary process would increase. The discussion in Parliament and among EU citizens would be more responsible, would focus on the priorities of EU action and on the best means to finance them. The redistribution across countries will then not be the almost-exclusive issue of discussion.

As regards the type of revenues to be levied, proposals have been put forward to reserve a share of the VAT base or of the income taxes base for a specific EU tax. Probably income taxes would be preferable on the grounds of accountability. Recent proposals (Commission, 2001) move from the consideration that, for ameliorating the functioning of the internal market, some convergence of the corporation tax is needed: the corporation tax base might be harmonised (at least, as an optional regime for business), leaving Member States free to fix the rates. In this context, it might be considered to levy a European tax on the same tax base as the national tax. Environmental taxes might also be candidates: the protection of the environment is the typical task which, due to the presence of spillover effects, is more efficiently assigned to the upper level of government.

The Budget and Stabilisation Policy

It has been advocated that a common monetary policy needs to be complemented by a common fiscal policy. The Union has a common monetary policy; fiscal policy remains a prerogative of Member States, but is subject to the rules of the stability and growth pact. A coordination on major economic policy guidelines is achieved through screening and monitoring of national policies. These arrangements ensure fiscal discipline on Member States and some coordination on major economic policy themes. They tend to rule out discretionary fiscal policies, both at national and Union level.

In this framework, it is out of question that an enlarged Union budget may become an instrument of stabilisation policy. In the first place, the size of the European budget will remain very small with respect to the EU economy. Even if new expenditures and revenues were added, they will be of a minor scale. Furthermore, the Union cannot raise debt and is forced to manage a balanced budget. There will be no room for discretionary fiscal policy, which in any case would be quite ineffective.

The functioning of the stability and growth pact and of the major economic policy guidelines may be streamlined. The Commission has proposed to the Convention a strengthening of its role in the enforcement of the pact and in proposing macroeconomic policy cooperation. The major economic policy guidelines and the opinions on the stability and convergence programmes should be drafted on the basis of proposals by the Commission (from which the Council could depart only by unanimity), rather than mere recommendations from which the Council may depart by qualified majority. When the economic policies pursued by a Member State deviate from the major guidelines approved, or jeopardise the smooth running of the economic and monetary Union, the Commission wants to be in a position to address directly the Member States concerned, through warnings, rather than submit recommendations to the Council. It is likely that Member States will strongly oppose these proposals.

On the whole, it seems that the institutional reforms currently under discussion will not bring significant changes in the area of stabilisation policies. National and EU policies will remain anchored to fiscal discipline and very little room will be allowed for discretionary policies. The EU budget, although it might be enlarged if some proposals are approved, will be balanced.

Redistribution Policies: Cohesion and Structural Funds

The redistribution policy of the EU is aimed at enhancing the economic convergence of poor regions. It is based on cohesion funds and structural funds: the formers are directed to States, the others to individual regions, which present lower levels of per-capita GDP.

These funds, although limited in their global amount, constitute roughly a third of the EU budget and are quite important for the receiving regions. Together with common agricultural policy, they have played a role in the decision to apply for EU membership. Typically, accession countries expect to be (and will be, to an extent that is to be decided) net gainers from joining the Union.

With the accession, the centre of gravity of these policies will shift significantly towards the East. Many regions, which today are recipients, will no longer benefit from these funds, funds that will be destined to the new entrants. This will put strains on the regions and the states interested. The redistribution policies will have to be redesigned: a tough bargaining process between Member States will take place, based on the usual issue of who are the net losers and by how much.

Leaving aside this aspect, the discussion has focused on two other issues related to enlargement. Although no clear evidence is available, the effectiveness of the distribution policies in fostering convergence has been questioned, especially in comparison with national regional policies. The correspondence to the subsidiarity principle has also been questioned, claiming an excessive interference of the Commission in the implementation of these policies.

At one extreme, it has been proposed to reduce drastically these funds, keeping them only for accession countries: they would be abolished for existing Member States, which, according to subsidiarity, might develop their own regional policies. This proposal seems very radical, and not perfectly in tune with the institutional setting. If fostering convergence is a task of the Union, these policies should, in principle, be independent of the date of accession to the Union. Such an interpretation of subsidiarity will bring more reliance on Member States regional policies, with the risk of a less coordinated action. In addition, regional policies have much to do with competition and State aid. If the motivation is to diminish the 'interference' of the Commission in the implementation of EU redistribution policy, this solution may well prove ineffective, because of the strong powers of the Commission in the area of competition. Instead of a 'cooperative' policy between Member States and the Commission, we might end up with a less friendly scrutiny by the Commission under the State Aid rules. Although it must not be overemphasised, there is a risk of increased litigation between the Commission and the Member States, which might induce some uncertainty for investment decisions.

There exists a widespread feeling that current procedures may and should be streamlined, leading to more effective implementation of redistribution policies, which could be focused on few major priorities and implemented with a more precise and effective division of competence between the Commission and the Member States. The Commission should concentrate on policy design and on monitoring the implementation, while Member States should take care of the actual implementation.

Regulation: Between Legislative and Administrative Solutions

In the last few decades governments have devoted greater attention to the tasks of regulation and have significantly reduced their direct involvement in the management of the economy. In Europe, the creation of the internal market has enhanced the attention to regulation and has created specific problems, related to the institutional setting of the EU.

The EU has considerably increased its prerogatives with respect to national governments, and is now charged with very important tasks in the enforcement of the internal market, in the common trade policy, in the enhancement of competition, and in contrasting state aid.

Nevertheless, a fundamental problem exists. In many areas the regulatory policies of the Member States lead to solutions that differ from each other and create obstacles to the functioning of the internal market. In some cases, regulations are intentionally aimed at creating barriers and discriminations to protect national interests. But in many other instances the fragmentation of the internal market is simply the result of different national regulations.

The enlargement process, due to the large number of new entrants, will aggravate the problem of an uneven regulation in the internal market. In addition, the accession countries by definition have no experience in implementing Community law. Many of them are economies in transition and lack a consolidated tradition in regulation.

It is a common belief that in fields such as public utilities, financial services, environment and consumer protection, health security, trademarks and the like, a better coordination of regulatory policies is needed.

At the root of the problem lies the fact that, in accordance with the principle of subsidiarity, the implementation and the application of the EU legislation is left to Member States, which transfer the content of EU directives into national legislation, and apply national regulations; the national regulations are mutually recognised. The very application of the subsidiarity method is the cause of discrepancies in the application of EU policies, and these discrepancies create obstacles to the functioning of the internal market.

Improving the coordination of the regulatory policies may be pursued in different ways. One is the legislative way: more EU legislation would produce more coordination. By reducing the area of discretion for Member States, the amplitude of the discrepancies is obviously reduced. Undoubtedly some legislation on the principles and guidelines of regulatory policies would be helpful. But it is questionable that increased legislation would be the most effective solution in general. By its nature, legislation may not define every aspect. Pervasive legislation introduces excessive rigidities and it is difficult to amend. Beyond certain limits, administrative measures are necessary and constitute the appropriate solution.

One way forward could be the strengthening of the administrative power and action of the Commission. A unified administrative power would certainly prove effective in providing uniform regulatory policies. This has been the case for competition policy, a field in which the Commission holds substantive powers of control and implementation. The application of this solution to other areas has been resisted, mainly because it entails a significant shift of power from the Member States to the Commission. But also because of the difficulties and costs of acquiring adequate professional and technical expertise.

One alternative administrative solution is the use of independent EU agencies and the creation of a network of national agencies.

In the last decade, a number of EU agencies have been created, basically in response to the increased need for information and coordination, and to lighten the Commission's workload in various policy areas. They operate in a broad range of fields: training, environment, drugs and drug addiction, pharmaceutical, trade marks, design and model, safety and health at work, food safety, aviation safety, and so on. These agencies are not super-national entities that take over the responsibilities of national agencies. They act as a net of the national agencies responsible domestically for the specific policy that they are in charge of. Often they have taken over the responsibilities of existing committees within the Council. Their task is to support EU and national authorities to identifying, preparing and evaluating specific areas and policy measures. The EU agency is a sort of permanent secretariat of national agencies, which gives continuity and support to a constant exchange of data, information, experiences, opinions, discussions. These EU agencies have, in only a few cases, decisional powers (e.g. the authorisation of pharmaceuticals or the registration of trademarks). They rather create a background of common information, orientation and mutual thrust, which is essential for policy decisions at EU level and for coordinated regulatory decisions at national level. They encourage uniform interpretation and implementation of Community law. In terms of transparency and accountability, they seem better than a Committee or a Commission division.

Nevertheless, an expanded role of the agencies has limits on grounds of legitimacy and democratic accountability, and has to be viewed in the overall framework of checks and balances.

In conclusion, no single solution seems adequate to address satisfactorily the issue of a consistent and uniform regulation of the internal market. Not by chance, perhaps, the Committee of Wise Men (chaired by A. Lamfalussy), charged with investigating the functioning of the European securities market and of advancing proposals for its improvement, has come to the conclusion that the best way forward is a four-level approach to regulation policy. This approach, that was endorsed by the European Council in 2001 and (February 2002) by the European Parliament, is to work as follows.

Level 1 will consist of legislative acts, namely directives or regulations, proposed by the Commission following consultation with all interested parties and adopted under the co-decision procedure by the Council and the European Parliament. In adopting each directive or regulation the Council and the Parliament will agree, on the basis of a Commission proposal, on the key principles, nature and extent of detailed technical implementing measures to be decided in Level 2.

In Level 2, the Commission and the European Securities Committee, the future regulatory committee, will decide the relevant implementing measures, and will update them when necessary. These measures will form part of Community Law and be binding for all Member States. The Committee will be chaired by the Commission and formed by representatives of all Member States. The European Parliament may object (adopting a resolution) if it considers that the measures taken at this level exceed the implementing powers provided for in Level 1.

In Level 3, the European Securities Regulators Committee will act as a fully independent committee of national regulators to ensure a common and uniform interpretation of Level 1 and 2 acts in the Member States. The Committee will produce consistent guidelines for administrative regulations to be adopted at the national level; issue joint recommendations and set common standards on matters not covered by EU legislation; compare and review regulatory practices to ensure effective enforcement throughout the Union, and define best practice; and conduct peer review. The ESRC will also act as an advisory committee to the Commission in Level 2.

In Level 4, the Commission will strengthen the enforcement of EU legislation, by checking Member States' compliance and taking legal action if required.

This four-level approach is a very thorough attempt to address the problem of inconsistent and disharmonious regulation in the internal market. It melds different solutions and tries to achieve the goal in ways that take into consideration the institutional roles of the various actors (Parliament, Commission, Member States, national regulators) and the principles of legitimacy, transparency and accountability.

A similar approach is under way in the field of competition policy. The Commission has prepared proposals to enforce EU legislation through a net of national competition authorities, headed by the Commission.

Reference

Commission (2001) *Towards an Internal Market Without Tax Obstacles* (Brussels: COM, 582).

Commission (2002) *A Project for the European Union* (Brussels: COM, 247).

European Parliament (2002) *Draft Report on the Division of Powers between the EU and the Member States*, rapporteur: Alain Lamassoure.

Europeos (2002) *Institutional Reforms in the European Union – Memorandum for the Convention* (Rome).

Goulard, S. and Nava, M. (2002) *Un financement plus démocratique du budget européen: un défi pour la Convention européenne*, mimeo.

ISAE (2002) *Rapporto annuale sullo stato dell'Unione Europea* (Giugno).

Lamfalussy Committee (2002) *Final report of the Committee of Wise Men on the Regulation of European Securities Markets* (Brussels).

Oates, W. (1999) An essay in fiscal federalism, *Journal of Economic Literature*, September.

Schaub, A. (2002) *The Commission's Position within the Network* (Florence: April).

Vos, E. (2000) Reforming the European Commission: what role to play for EU agencies? *Common Market Law Review*, 37: 1113–34.

Chapter 9

Let Social Europe(s) Compete!

Tito Boeri

Introduction

The EU Convention is experiencing a slow start. It is quite unlikely that the Convention will actually take-off before the German elections. So far, the reference document is the 'Project for the European Union' issued in 2002 by the Commission, which argues in favour of a coordination of social policies. Coordination is a rather loose concept, which can be located along a wide spectrum, ranging from the 'open coordination' method of the Luxembourg process to something in a close neighbourhood of a harmonisation of social policies. In this chapter we propose to reduce this indeterminacy. In particular, we take a clear stance in favour of coordination as a way to promote a more effective competition across systems. While it may sound as a contradiction in terms, it is not. Insofar as our notion of coordination allows for more mobility of the European workforce, it implies that EU citizens can 'vote with their feet' enhancing competition among systems.

These issues are typically dealt with by economists as a problem of allocation of tasks among different levels of Government. Fiscal federalism theory, in particular, offers a powerful framework to assess what should be assigned to central, supra-national, bodies and what should instead be left as a prerogative of de-centralised policy-making, such as national governments.

When dealing with social policies, however, this framework may appear too narrow. The relevant issues in this domain concern more the governance structure, the rules of coordination, than the degree of centralisation or de-centralisation by themselves. Due to the absence of significant spillovers and economies of scale in social security provision, the case for reallocating tasks to EU supra-national authorities is weak. The most relevant issues concern, instead, the scope of competition that should be promoted and allowed across the various 'Social Europe(s)' nowadays characterising the institutional landscape of the Old Continent.

The plan of the paper is as follows. The next section characterises the different Social Europe(s) and discusses whether or not they are converging to a unique model. Once established that this is not the case, the subsequent section discusses whether or not EU-level decision-making should pursue a harmonisation of these different Social Europe(s). Since the answer is no, the fourth section concludes by arguing about the scope of competition among the different restrictions that should be imposed on competition among the different social security systems and the role that EU supra-national authorities may play in this context.

Are Social Europe(s) Converging in any Event?

In order to assess better the implications of a coordination of social policies in the EU area it is important to evaluate the scope of the adjustment that would be required to level out differences in the size and composition of social spending in Europe. Equally important is to assess whether or not a convergence is occurring across the various systems that can nowadays be identified in Europe.

Four Social Europe(s)

It is customary (for example see Ferrera, 1998, and Bertola *et al.*, 2001) to divide Europe into four social policy models. The first group is represented by the *Nordics* (Denmark, Finland and Sweden, plus the Netherlands – a hybrid between the Scandinavian and the Continental models and has recently moved Northwards[1]), which features the highest levels of social protection expenditures, and universal welfare provision based on the citizenship principle. Extensive fiscal intervention in labour markets, based on a variety of 'active' policy instruments, substantial tax wedges, and relatively extensive employment in the public sector also belong to this model while unions' presence in the workplace and involvement in the setting and administration of unemployment benefits generates compressed wage structures.

The second cluster includes the *Anglo-Saxon* countries (Ireland and the UK), which are closer to the Beveridgian tradition and feature relatively large social assistance of the last resort schemes. Cash transfers here are primarily oriented to people of working-age. Activation measures are important as well as schemes conditioning access to benefits of regular employment. On the labour market side, this model is characterised by a mixture of weak unions, comparatively wide and increasing wage dispersion and relatively high incidence of low-pay employment, half-way between Europe and the US.

Continental European countries (Austria, Belgium, France, Germany, and Luxembourg) are the third group, relying extensively on insurance-based, non-employment benefits and old-age pensions. Large invalidity benefit schemes are also present, which draw on contributions on employment income, along the Bismarckian tradition. While unions' membership rates have been falling quite dramatically in the last 20–25 years (Boeri *et al.*, 2001b), a strong union influence has been, to a large extent, preserved in these countries by regulations artificially extending the coverage of collective bargaining much beyond unions' presence.

Finally, we have the Mediterranean countries (Greece, Italy, Spain and Portugal), concentrating their spending on old-age pensions and allowing for a high

---

[1]   We refer, in particular, to the decision, made in the year 2000 in the Netherlands, to adopt a universal pension scheme and extend the sickness insurance scheme to the self-employed.

segmentation of entitlements and status.[2] Their social welfare systems typically draw on employment protection and early retirement provisions to exempt segments of the working age population from participation in the labour market. Also in this case, a strong union influence has been preserved by practices (e.g. jurisprudence) artificially extending the coverage of collective bargaining. As a result, wage structures are, at least in the formal sector, covered by collective bargaining and strongly compressed in these countries.

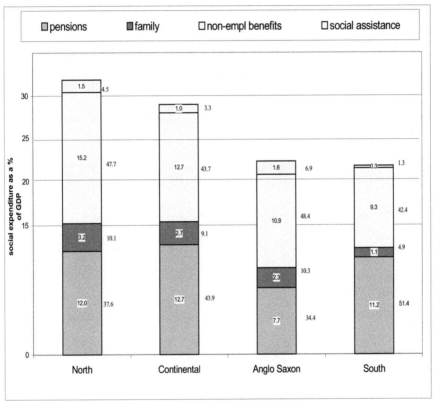

Figure 9.1   Social policy items divided into four main policy domains

Figure 9.1 provides a simple characterisation of the four models, grouping the various social policy items into four main policy domains: pensions (encompassing old-age and survivors' provisions), non-employment benefits (unemployment benefits, sickness benefits, invalidity pensions and early retirement, whenever listed separately from old-age pensions), family allowances (child-care benefits and family benefits) and social assistance (including means-tested housing benefits). Social expenditure is normalised by GDP, while information on the percentage distribution

---

2   Note that these countries implemented universal national health care systems between the 1970s and the 1980s. However, we do not deal with health spending in this paper.

of social spending is provided next to each histogram. Data are drawn from the EC ESSPROS database which offers, to date, the best framework to assess the size and composition of social spending in the EU area.

As is apparent from Figure 9.1, differences in levels and composition are not of a second order of magnitude and are broadly in line with the taxonomy offered above (although not all institutional features can be measured). In particular, universal non-employment benefits are what distinguishes the Nordic model (and makes it larger in scope than the others) from the Continental model, which is slightly less large in scope and focused more on pensions than on transfers to individuals in working age. The Anglo-Saxon world (mostly the UK as we are dealing with a GDP-weighted average) displays a smaller welfare state and one that devotes comparatively more resources to social assistance of the last resort. Finally Southern Europe displays the smallest welfare state, more than half of which goes to public pensions, whilst social assistance is negligible.

Table 9.1   Average yearly growth rate in socal spending over GDP

unconditional beta convergence	Average growth rate of social spending over GDP 1980–1990		Average growth rate of social spending over GDP 1990–1999	
constant	0.0438	***	0.0463	**
social policy exp over GDP 1980	-0.0015	*	–	
social policy exp over GDP 1990	–		-0.0014	*
EU15* base year soc.exp/GDP	0.0001			
euro11*base year soc.exp/GDP			-0.0003	
R2	0.45		0.26	
number of observations	22		18	

These country groupings should not conceal important differences in the policy mix which are present within each model. Yet, in three policy areas out of four, differences across models capture from 45 to 60 percent of the total variation in the composition of social spending. This can be gauged by decomposing the total weighted (by GDP) sum of squared deviations of social expenditure shares (to social expenditure, rather than GDP in order to eliminate variation due to income levels) into a within-models and a cross-models mean variation (Figure 9.2). The only area where the within models variation dominates is non-employment benefits, which is the most heterogeneous set of measures of the four and the one most affected by the underlying labour market conditions (e.g. differences in the incidence of unemployment).

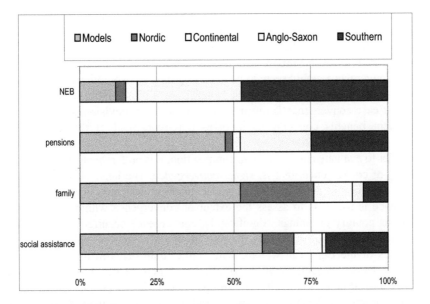

Figure 9.2   Decomposition of the differences in the social policy mix

Converging?

Are these four Social Europe(s) converging in terms of size and composition of social spending?

To shed some light on convergence in social spending, we regressed the growth in social expenditure as a percentage of GDP over two sub-periods: the period 1980–90 (where we can draw on the OECD Social Expenditure database) and the period 1990–99 (where ESSPROS data are available). In particular, we regressed the average yearly growth rate in social spending over GDP against its initial level for the cross-section of countries provided by the two datasets. Convergence in the unconditional sense is implied, according to this methodology, if the coefficient for spending in the base year is negative and statistically significant.

The results of this exercise are displayed in Table 9.1. We cannot reject this *beta* unconditional convergence for the OECD countries as a whole. However, the beta coefficient implies a very low convergence rate (-0.0015) and is barely statistically significant. The same type of conclusions can be obtained with reference to the second sub-period and for the ESSPROS country panel (which includes the EU-15, plus Iceland, Norway and Switzerland). Furthermore, in both cases the interaction variables for the EU area (or the EMU group) and the initial level of social spending are not significant, which suggests that there has not been an additional effect of European integration or the Monetary Union on the convergence in the size of the welfare state.

We also analysed convergence in terms of specific programmes and we tested another type of convergence, that is, *sigma-convergence*, i.e. whether the standard deviation in the logarithm of social spending had decreased or increased over time. These results are available, upon request from the author. Finally we looked at qualitative information on the nature of reforms, by drawing on a recent inventory of social welfare reforms in Europe.

Beta convergence would seem to be occurring only in two policy areas, namely social assistance and non-employment benefits. At a closer look, it appears that in the first case convergence is towards the top levels of provision while for non-employment benefits convergence involves a retrenchment of this programme category (Bertola *et al.*, 2001).

In order to evaluate convergence in composition, it is preferable to adopt another definition of convergence, that is, *sigma-convergence*. The latter occurs when the standard deviation in the logarithm of social spending decreases over time. Sigma convergence is useful is to assess the extent of convergence within and between the various country groupings. Significantly, convergence occurred mainly *within* the various social Europes, namely the four groups of countries typically used by taxonomies of the European welfare states rather than between them: the cross-country variation between social expenditure as a percentage of GDP decreased over the 1996–1980 period in all these groups of countries. In conclusion, there are some indications that the cross-country variability in the size of the welfare states is decreasing. However, this is occurring mainly within the various 'Social Europes' rather than across them.

Finally, we looked at an inventory of reforms assembled at Fondazione Rodolfo Debenedetti. The latter is based on a variety of sources (including country economic reviews carried out by OECD, Income Data Source studies, EC-MISSOC reports, etc), and takes stock of reforms carried out in Europe over the period 1987–1999 in three domains: non-employment benefits, employment protection and pensions. Reforms are classified on the basis of their broad orientation, that is, whether they tend to reduce or increase the generosity of non-employment benefits and make employment protection more or less stringent, and their radical or marginal nature.[3]

Contrary to popular wisdom and to the belief that labour market and social welfare institutions cannot be modified, many institutional changes have occurred over the observation period. I counted almost 200 reforms, that is, more than one per year and country. However the changes have often been marginal (172 out 198 reforms, that is roughly 85 percent of the regulatory changes did not pass our two-stage procedure identifying radical reforms). Moreover the reforms are almost evenly split between those reducing generosity and protection (107 out of 198, that is, about 55 percent) and those increasing generosity and employment protection. It is also not infrequent to find reforms going one against the other just a few years apart. These inconsistencies and the marginal nature of most reforms have significantly increased the institutional complexity of the European landscape.

To summarise the results in this section, there are at least four different Social Europe(s) and a very mild convergence in the size of social programmes is occurring among them. To the extent that the cross-country variability in the composition of

---

3   Details on the inventory of social policy reforms produced at the Fondazione Rodolfo Debenedetti are available at www.frdb.org.

the welfare states is decreasing, this is occurring mainly within the various 'Social Europes' rather than across them. Institutional changes are occurring at (unexpectedly) high frequencies, but reforms are rarely comprehensive. Overall, there are no indications that differences in the size and composition of social spending across EU member states are being levelled-out automatically.

Should we Artificially Impose Convergence?

Given that convergence is not occurring automatically, the frequently asked question as to whether the various Social Europe(s) should be harmonised or not is a relevant one. There are no a priori arguments for having EU supra-national authorities levelling out differences in the size and composition of social spending across EU member states. The two standard arguments for centralised provision of public goods (Oates, 1999) – the presence of economies of scale and spillovers across jurisdictions – would seem to have limited application to the case of social policies,[4] as discussed below.

Economies of Scale in Social Policy: Lessons from the Small EU Countries

The relevance of the economies of scale argument can be assessed by comparing the performance of social welfare systems of small and large EU countries. Performance can be assessed by making references to the three main functions typically assigned to social policies, namely:

(i) reduce poverty and, more broadly, income inequalities,
(ii) protect against labour-market-related uninsurable risk (including the interactions between unemployment and longevity risk)
(iii) increase the rewards from labour market participation.

The first is perhaps the most important function attributed to social welfare cum tax systems. The effectiveness of the redistribution operated in the different EU countries is visually assessed in Figure 9.3. The latter plots differences between pre and post tax/transfers Gini coefficients (vertical axis) against the social policy expenditure to GDP ratio.[5] As one would expect, redistribution is larger in the countries devoting more resources to redistributive policies. More importantly, the most effective redistribution (the larger difference between pre and post tax/transfer inequality per any given level of social spending) is observed in the relatively small European countries, while the largest nations – with the exception of the UK – perform rather

---

4   See Fatàs (1998) for an assessment of the economies of scale attainable by adopting a common European social security model.

5   Pre-tax and transfer incomes are constructed making use of the European Community Household Panel, a longitudinal dataset providing income and labour market information on about 60,000 individuals across the entire EU. Pre-tax and transfer income is calculated as total disposable income minus social transfers divided by a 'net/gross ratio' factor provided by EUROSTAT in the ECHP.

poorly in this respect, as they all lie below the regression line. This conclusion is supported also by analyses with micro data, notably (probit) regressions of the probability of receiving different types of cash transfers against family characteristics and income. Targeting on the basis of income and house ownership typically works better in the Nordics, Ireland and the UK.

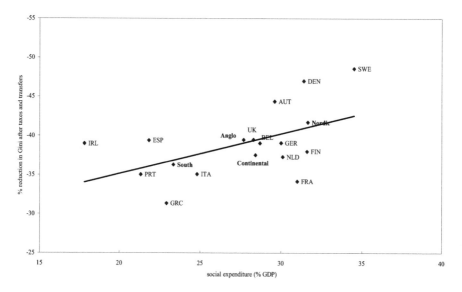

Figure 9.3   Redistributive efficiency of social expenditure. Entire population

Moving to the second criterion, *protection against uninsurable labour market risk* is typically provided in two ways: (i) by imposing legal restrictions against firing – the so-called employment protection legislation (EPL); (ii) by providing unemployment benefits in addition to those established by collective bargaining (UB). The differences between these two systems are clear: EPL protects those who already have a job, and does not impose any tax burden; UB can also be targeted to specific groups, but generally provide insurance to the population at large and are typically financed by a tax on those who work. Thus insiders, those with a stable and regular job, typically prefer EPL to UB. EU countries employ both tools, although to varying degrees. As discussed in Bertola and Boeri (2002), EU member states have chosen very different points in the trade-off between the two main instruments to protect individuals against unemployment risk.

How efficient are these combinations of EPL and UB in protecting workers against labour market risk? One way to assess this is just to let workers decide. A section of the ECHP questionnaire is particularly useful in this respect insofar as it asks employees with a permanent contract whether and to what extent they are satisfied with their present level of job security (rather than simply asking as other questionnaires about the perceived stability of their current post).

The histograms in Figure 9.4 measure the fraction of working individuals in the survey stating that they are dissatisfied with their present level of job security in the various countries. Small EU countries, such as Austria, Denmark, the Netherlands, Portugal, Ireland, Belgium and Finland, come out once more as those providing stronger protection against labour market risk.

Finally, incentives to work, the third social policy objective listed at the outset, vary

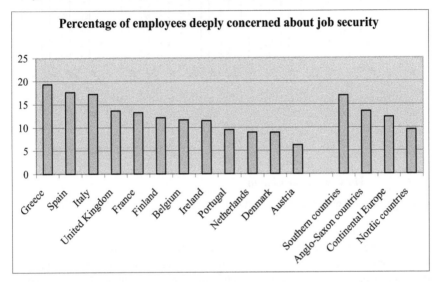

Figure 9.4   Efficiency in providing protection against labour market risk

significantly from country to country as hinted at by the large dispersion within the EU of employment-to-population ratios and unemployment rates. As shown by Figure 9.5, to attain the target set at the Lisbon Summit of at least a 70 percent employment rate by the year 2010 (65 percent by 2005), some countries would have to increase their employment to population ratios by about 2 percentage points per year. More importantly, in many countries this will require increasing labour force participation rather than simply absorbing unemployment. Once more, with the notable exception of the UK, we find small EU countries displaying the best performance.

An explanation for this better performance in redistribution of the smallest EU countries is that local provision of social security can better exploit local information and deal with the large informational asymmetries jeopardising the effectiveness of redistributive policies. Needless to say, all this work is in favour of a de-centralisation of social policy, rather than the other way round.

Do Different Social Europe(s) correspond to Different Preferences?

There are also important political and political-economic counter-indications to imposing convergence 'from the top'. First, there is evidence of path dependency and status quo bias in social welfare reforms. They also work better when they are

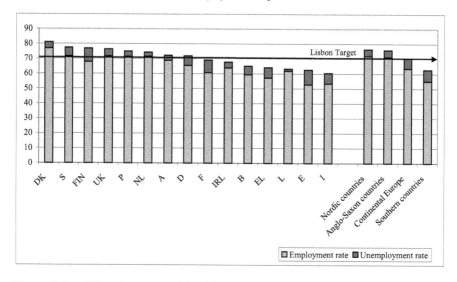

Figure 9.5   'How far from Lisbon?'

Source: Eurostat, Labour Force Survey (2001)

comprehensive (Coe and Snower, 1997), which means that they need to operate on country-specific institutional clusters.[6] As Social Europes are so different (and still so) from each other, reforms ought to be respectful of the initial conditions, and by imposing the same pattern of adjustment to the different European social policy models there is a high risk of jeopardising reform efforts altogether. Secondly, interactions among different tiers of Government may drive decisions and the actual implementation of policies far away from the theoretical fiction of a benevolent planner.

Thirdly, insofar as differences in Social Europe(s) reflect differences in preferences of EU citizens, such a harmonisation would run against democratic rules on highly sensitive issues, given that most EU supranational authorities lack, as yet, political accountability. This may result in stronger pressures for the break-up of the Union.

Ongoing work assessing attitudes of European citizens towards the size and composition of welfare state (Boeri *et al.*, 2001a and 2002), however, does not support the view that EU citizens have heterogeneous preferences as to the size and composition of social spending.

In general, citizens of countries with the smallest welfare states (e.g. Spain) are more prone than others to support an increase in social security contributions and taxes than French and German citizens who already have a generous welfare system. Preferences over reform options in specific areas are also in line with similarity in preferences. To give an example, an increase in retirement age finds a majority in Italy, where the effective retirement age is lower, whilst it sounds as a rather unattractive option to German workers. Similarly, a reduction in the replacement rate

---

6   See Bertola and Boeri (2002) for a discussion of institutional interactions within the various Social Europe(s).

offered by public pensions finds a slim majority in Germany, where pension benefits are higher, but it is the most disliked option among Italian workers. However, these differences are not as marked as to create a majority in favour of reforms and there is evidence of a form of status quo bias.

Other indications on attitudes of EU citizens come from a special wave of the Eurobarometer survey entirely devoted to elicit preferences over social welfare reforms. Unfortunately, many questions/answers are not very informative insofar as they do not put the interviewees in front of the relevant trade-offs. Those that do so, confirm that preferences are not inconsistent with convergence. Figure 9.6, for instance, displays answers to a question embodying the budget constraint ('Current pension levels should be maintained even if this means raising taxes or contributions'). Interestingly enough, the countries where there is a stronger support for a retrenchment in pension expenditure are just those (we know from earlier that it is Continental and Southern Europe) where pension spending over GDP is larger. The above example is relevant because pension expenditure is what is ultimately preventing the weaker institutional clusters in Europe – the Southern and the Continental models – to get closer to the Nordic and/or the Anglo-Saxon welfare systems, offering a better performance on many grounds, as discussed earlier.
Finally, the case for a harmonisation of social policies on pure equity grounds is rather weak. In the presence of large differences in productivity levels, harmonisation of policies does not imply harmonisation of outcomes. The experience of the Italian Mezzogiorno and the German unification episodes testify to this.

Overall, there is a strong case for maintaining prerogatives over social policies

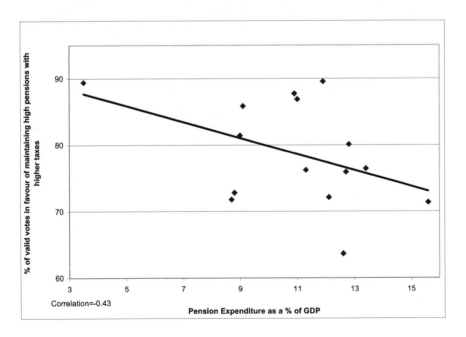

Figure 9.6   Answers to a question embodying the budget constraint

to national Governments, and preserving the unanimity rule in EU-level decision-making in this area. Small EU countries typically obtain the best performance in terms of effectiveness in redistribution, protection against uninsurable labour market risk and employment rates, which may point to diseconomies of scale in social welfare provision. Majority voting on these issues may just end-up providing the worse of each welfare system with the countries with the best social policies in place being always in the minority. Yet, there is no evidence that heterogeneity of preferences is what drives the different Social Europe(s). The various countries may just be caught in different politico-economic equilibria, which do not necessarily correspond to the best ones from the standpoint of their citizens.

Rules for Competition

Does the above mean that there should be only 'negative integration' or veto-bargaining (Cameron, 1999) in the field of social policy? A number of arguments can actually be made to reduce the scope of competition across European welfare systems, which are very much in the spirit of 'positive integration'.

Spillovers, Race to the Bottom and Migration

A quite popular argument in favour of policy coordination at the EU-level in this field is that closer integration and more intense competition may induce 'social dumping' and set in motion a 'race to the bottom' in social welfare provision (Sinn, 2002). Evidence in support of the view that the European welfare state is threatened by such type of pressures is weak to say the least (Boeri, 2001) and the discussion in the second section suggests that cross-country differences in social welfare systems are far from being 'arbitraged' away by competitive pressures. Europe is a Continent whose citizens are much less keen to change residence than in the US: less than half-a-percentage point of the European labour force changes region of residence within a year (compared with 2.5 percent moving across states in the US).

The problem of European labour markets is, after all, one of low mobility rather than the other way round. More mobility of the European workforce would be required to deal with the huge and persistent regional labour market asymmetries. Acute skill shortages and high labour slack tend to become chronic conditions of specific regions, they coexist within the same country even a few kilometres apart. Migrants tend to play this spatial arbitrage function (Borjas, 2002). Those from Eastern European countries to Germany jumped over the eastern Länders to find a residence in the western part of the country, which offers better chances of finding a job and higher wages. Similarly, migrants from North Africa moved far to the North-East regions of Italy, where there is virtually full employment, 'jumping over' the depressed labour markets of the Mezzogiorno. It is just because of this spatial arbitrage that migration prevents overheating in local labour markets, contributing to containing inflationary pressures.

Migrants play an even more important role in allowing for non-inflationary and productivity-enhancing employment growth in the presence of wage compressing institutions such as those characterising the European landscape. This additional role of migration is visually characterised in Figure 9.7. The left-hand side diagram shows the market-clearing wage prevailing in the dynamic regions (the North) which is also used – due to the imposition of the same contractual minima throughout the country – also in the South. At the initial equilibrium, the South experiences unemployment as the Northern wage acts as a binding minimum wage. Migration flows, in this context, play two useful functions. On the one hand, they increase employment and reduce wages in the North by shifting to the right labour supply (as shown by the bold line, S^1). On the other hand, migration, by acting on Northern wages, reduces labour costs also in the South (from W^* to W^1) allowing it to partially absorb its unemployment pool (which shrinks from u to u^1).

This provides a more subtle reason for coordination of social spending than the so-called 'race-to-the-bottom'. To the extent that differences in the generosity of

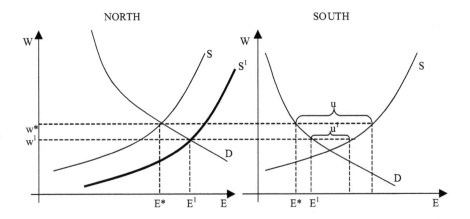

Figure 9.7   Effects of migration in countries with centralised bargaining structure and no mobility

welfare states do not replicate the differences in the strength of local labour markets, this important function of migration in promoting non-inflationary growth in Europe may be jeopardised. There is some evidence that 'welfare shopping' may be occurring within the migrant population, if not among the European population at large. Immigrants to the EU from non-EU countries tend to receive proportionally more social transfers than the native population (Sapir, 2000). Moreover not all the differences in access to welfare can be explained by observable characteristics of migrants (i.e. the number of dependent children, their marital status and skill level). In some of the European countries with the most generous welfare states (Denmark, Belgium, the Netherlands, Austria and France) there are indeed indications that a rather mild form of 'residual dependency' is present, thereby non-EU citizens receive social transfers more than can be predicted on the basis of their characteristics (McCormick *et al.*, 2002).

Against this background, the adoption of a common EU-wide safety net, adjusted to reflect cross-country and cross-regional differences in the cost-of-living, can be envisaged as a way to avoid distorting the distribution of Enlargement-related migration over Europe.[7] It is a one-time opportunity to receive migrants who, because of cultural and historical ties, can be assimilated relatively easy within Europe. This opportunity should not be lost by inducing migrants to choose the country or region of destination based on criteria – such as access to relatively generous safety nets – which are unrelated to labour market fundamentals.

Coordinating the Experiments and dealing with Politico-economic Constraints

An additional reason for having a mild form of positive integration is related to the fact that social policy is a domain of ongoing policy experimentation. Supra-national bodies can be in a better position than national Governments to assess the pros and cons of the various models, are not subject to pressures of local lobbies in benchmarking schemes, which better serve specific interests, and have typically longer horizons than national governments (and horizons are crucial in areas like pension reforms). Open coordination[8] Mechanisms, such as those devised at the EU level in fields like labour policies and social protection (mainly social inclusion), can play an important role in drawing from these experiments and highlighting best practices.

This type of coordination could be strengthened by assigning more relevance to (realistic!) quantitative targets such as those established in terms of employment rates at the 2000 EU Summit in Lisbon. The idea of New Maastricht for Labour is very much in this vein. This would also require a different timing and organisation of the review process. Under the so-called Luxembourg process, supra-national institutions set employment guidelines which offer the basis for the development of National Action Plans (to be delivered in Spring) by the Governments of the Member States. The plans and the achievements are subsequently verified by the means of an institutionalised procedure, selecting the 'best practices' (so-called 'benchmarking') and drawing up country specific recommendations. Stronger coordination should be explicitly directed to the Structural Spring Summits of the Council.

Another direction in which coordination could be extended is in assigning powers to the European supra-national authorities in imposing improvements in the

---

7   There are also arguments for imposing minimum standards to the accession candidates (see Boeri *et al.*, 2002 for a discussion).

8   Although not explicitly stated, open coordination is sometimes considered as a kind of preparatory stage for the 'enhanced cooperation', already mentioned in the Treaty of Amsterdam and now explicitly called for by the Nice Treaty: after a breaking-in period, a certain number of countries more interested and open to the idea of a federal Europe could move on from open coordination to enhanced cooperation; that is, greater integration as concerns substance and decision-making instruments.

administration of welfare policies in the various countries, e.g. in conditioning cash transfers to able-bodied individuals of working age on stringent work-tests.

This type of coordination can be supported by imposing more transparency in social policy expenditure accounts. Common standards are still far from being adopted in defining and estimating the debt of public pension systems, developing social policy expenditure projections and providing generational accounts that can best isolate the various (often improper) functions played by public pensions in the EU countries. Some progress has been made in this direction, for instance imposing on all countries the provision of long-term (lasting at least 50 years) projections of pension expenditure and making sure that these projections are based on explicit and internally consistent hypotheses, jointly agreed upon by a working group of the EU Economic Policy Committee.[9] But more ground has to be covered.

Finally, sheer pressures from supra-national European authorities can help in dealing with the politico-economic constraints discussed in the previous section. The fact that there are more citizens in favour of reducing pension spending in countries such as Italy, France, Germany and Spain than elsewhere, is not sufficient to yield reform pointing decidedly in that direction. Italy and, more recently, Germany have implemented parametric reforms of their pension systems. Parametric means that these reforms are just too slow and shy to free resources for the expansion of other social programmes. At most, they stabilise pension spending, while pension-to-GDP ratios should *decline* in spite of an ageing population in order to accommodate more welfare and family-friendly employment policies.

The reason why more radical pension reforms are not taking place in the high pension spending countries may be that there is a sort of status quo bias preventing the support for the retrenchment of these programmes to gain a majority. Political scientists, such as Pierson (1996), suggest that the citizens' preferences over the welfare state adapt to the status quo as voters suffer from a 'negativity bias': once they get something, they don't want to give it up. If so, the voters' psychology induces path dependence in politics. An alternative interpretation is that some powerful lobbies (e.g. employers and employees' organisations to start with) impose the status quo even when this goes against the preferences of a majority of citizens. Clearly, both of these political economic mechanisms – endogeneity in preferences and problems in the representation of voters – may be present, jointly obstructing reforms of those Social Europe(s) which would need heavier restructuring. Not only supra-national bodies may be in a better position to assess the pros and cons of the various models, but also they are not subject to pressures of local lobbies and have typically longer horizons than national governments (and horizons are crucial in areas like pension reforms). This suggests that the role of supra-national authorities in supervising and monitoring structural reforms in this area is indeed important.

---

9   For example, it is hypothesised that there will be a gradual convergence in growth of labour productivity among member states: as of 2025, the rate of growth of labour productivity will be the same throughout the European Union. This is important because small variations in future scenarios as regards the dynamics of labour productivity can generate considerable differences in spending projections.

Finally, there is another, more indirect, way in which supra-national authorities may support social welfare reforms going on the direction of improving EU citizens' welfare. EU citizens should be allowed to 'vote with their feet', arbitraging away some of the most undesirable differences in social policy models. This can only happen if citizens are allowed to gain access to the welfare of the country of destination at least on a flow, *pro rata*, basis. This *'Equal Treatment'* (of foreigners and nationals) principle in terms of access to social security is rarely enforced, although it is perfectly in line with EU rules.[10] Significant costs in terms of foregone social security entitlements are still associated with migration of EU workers. This occurs especially in three crucial areas:

(i)   lack of coordination of regulations concerning pension funds (notably in terms of length of vesting periods, indexation rules and bilateral agreements as to the actuarial valuation of accrued benefits);

(ii)   the presence of national restrictions in the allocation of the pension fund portfolios, and

(iii)   the absence of common rules as to the taxation of private pensions, e.g. specifying that the tax base is represented only by benefits and lump-sum payments (rather than contributions and capital gains). Although the enforcement of this principle is problematic in some areas,[11] it allows individuals to choose the welfare system, the combination of taxes and transfers, that they prefer. EU supra-national authorities have a crucial role to play in making sure that this happens. To begin with it is important that the draft directive on Pension Funds agreed under the Spanish Presidency of the EU is quickly approved by the Council and the European Parliament.

Final Remarks

The evidence collected and the arguments developed in this paper point decidedly in the direction of maintaining responsibilities over social policy at the national level, if not decentralising parts of these to regional bodies. Yet, this does not mean that EU supra-national authorities have no role to play in this context. Strengthening the 'open co-ordination' method, improving the monitoring of structural reforms, reviewing the policy enforcement mechanisms, introducing gradually pan-European safety nets and, last but not least, ensuring the actual portability of social security rights are just some of the examples of areas where this role is needed, and badly needed.

---

10 The *Equal Treatment* principle is stated by art 51 of the EC Treaty.

11 Difficulties arise for the defined benefit schemes, such as unemployment insurance and many occupational pension schemes. Even more serious problems arise for the non-insurance components of welfare systems, such as the unemployment assistance benefits offered to persons under long-term unemployment (the European plague) and social assistance, which is typically open-ended (in which case only the stock interpretation of the equal treatment principle is applicable).

References

Bertola, G. and Boeri, T. (2002) EMU labour markets two years on: microeconomic tensions and institutional evolution, in: M. Buti and A. Sapir (Eds) *EMU and Economic Policy in Europe: The Challenge of the Early Years* (Cheltenham: Edward Elgar).

Bertola, G., Boeri T. and Nicoletti G. (Eds) (2001) *Welfare and Employment in a United Europe* (Cambridge, MA: MIT Press).

Boeri, T. (2001) Introduction: putting the debate on a new footing, in: G. Bertola, T. Boeri and G. Nicoletti (Eds) *Welfare and Employment in a United Europe* (Cambridge, MA: MIT Press).

Boeri, T., Boersch-Supan A. and Tabellini G. (2001a) Would you like to shrink the welfare state: a survey of European citizens, *Economic Policy*, 32(4): 7–50.

Boeri, T., Brugiavini A. and Calmfors L. (Eds) (2001b) *The Role of the Unions in the Twenty-first Century* (Oxford: Oxford University Press).

Boeri, T., Boersch-Supan A. and Tabellini G. (2002) Pension reforms and the opinions of European citizens, *American Economic Review*.

Borjas, G. (2002) Comments on immigration and the US economy, in: T. Boeri, G. Hanson and B. McCormick (Eds) *Immigration Policy and the Welfare State* (Oxford: Oxford University Press).

Cameron, C. (1999) *Veto Bargaining: Presidents and the Politics of Negative Power* (Cambridge: Cambridge University Press).

Coe, D.T. and Snower, D.J. (1997) Policy complementarities: the case for fundamental labor market reform, *IMF Staff Papers*, 44(1).

Fatàs, A. (1998) Does EMU need a fiscal federation? *Economic Policy*, 165: 203.

Ferrera, M. (1998) The four social Europes: between universalism and selectivity, in: Y. Meny and M. Rhodes (Eds) *The Future of European Welfare: A New Social Contract*, pp. 81–96 (London: Macmillan).

McCormick, B., Brücker H., Epstein, G.S., Saint-Paul, G. and Venturini, A. (2002) Managing migration in the European welfare system, in: T. Boeri, G. Hanson and B. McCormick (Eds) *Immigration Policy and the Welfare System* (Oxford: University Press).

Oates, W. (1999) Fiscal federalism, *Journal of Economic Literature*.

OECD (1999) *Employment Outlook*.

Pierson P. (Ed) (1996) *The New Politics of the Welfare State* (Oxford: Oxford University Press).

Sapir, A. (2000) Who is afraid of globalization? The challenge of domestic adjustment in Europe and America. Conference on *Efficiency, Equity and Legitimacy: The Multilateral Trading System at the Millennium*.

Sinn, H-W. (2002) *The New Systems Competition, Yrjö Jahnsson Lectures* (Oxford: Basil Blackwell).

Chapter 10

Are Cross-border Mergers Paving the Way to European Firms and Institutions? Evidence from Franco-German Case Studies

Gilles Le Blanc and Delphine Corteel

Introduction: Outline and Rationale of the Research

AGF and Allianz merged on 1 April 1998. DaimlerBenz and Chrysler announced that they are going to bring their activities together on 7 May 1998. On 1 December 1998, Hoechst and Rhône Poulenc publicly declared their will to create Aventis, which will be the second largest group in life sciences worldwide. After numerous contradictory declarations, the German Dasa, the Spanish Casa and the French Aérospatiale Matra finally announced the merger of these three firms and the creation of EADS (European Aeronautic Defense and Space Company) on the 14 October 1999. On 4 February 2000, the board of Mannesmann approved the agreement reached the day before with Vodaphone Airtouch Vivendi-Seagram (June 2000), Usinor-Arbed (February 2001); this is not an exhaustive list.

The past few years have experienced a dramatic succession of mergers, whose number and financial magnitude have continuously kept on growing. One might consider that this phenomenon constitutes today the major industrial dynamics transforming the structures of contemporary economies. These mergers are traditionally pictured as the direct effect of the growing influence of the financial constraints and the dominance of 'corporate governance' in the firms. An increased profitability and shareholder value are actually the motives usually put forward to justify and motivate a merger. This perspective focuses on the relationship between management and shareholders, and employees are either not considered at all, or as a cost to reduce through restructuring and massive layoffs when firms face financial difficulties. In the literature, however, a larger approach of the firm has developed, bringing into the scope of corporate governance issues the firm's employees, its suppliers and customers, and the State of the country in which it is located. This stakeholder' framework allows new research and studies of the industrial structural changes and their socio-economic consequences.

Yet, most comparative research on corporate governance, whether centred on shareholders and financial markets, or whether based on a broader idea of the firm, including employees, has been embodied in the debate over varieties of capitalism.

Consequently, most of the comparative work has focused on the differences between the Anglo-Saxon type of corporate governance and the continental European one, discussing their possible convergence under financial markets' pressure. Few researchers have eventually been comparing different systems of corporate governance within 'one type of capitalism'. Considering the current construction of the European Union, it is however essential and urgent to start focusing on different forms of corporate governance within continental Europe, and especially comparing France and Germany. The shape of the future European model of corporate governance is actually still an open question: domination of one national model at the European level, a new configuration resuming the benefits of several national models, or original processes carried out by the firms themselves?

A transnational merger challenges traditional employees' participation models in two ways. First of all, by bringing together within a single structure different national systems of employees' participation, which provides a unique empirical base for comparing them. Secondly, every merger poses difficult organisation and restructuring problems, with major social consequences. Employees are clearly a key variable of these strategic decisions. Our central working assumption is that a merger in fact corresponds to the creation of a single firm out of two distinct entities. This shift from two firms to one requires a 'destructive creation' process, into which the effective participation of employees is a critical factor for successful implementation.

This paper is based on the EMEP research project we conducted in 2000–2001 with the support of the European Commission DG Research to analyse how transnational mergers in Europe impact employees' participation in the firms. The project combines bibliographic research with a joint industrial economy and industrial anthropology fieldwork research on four Franco-German cases with in-depth interviews of managers, workers and social partners. Franco-German mergers turn out to be quite relevant for our approach because German and French companies first differ, not by their respective ownership structure, but by the role of the banks and above all the relations between the firms and their employees. A Franco-German merger then confronts the French model of worker participation, representation and negotiation with the German 'co-determination' model.

This investigation was designed to assess and evaluate the role of employees' participation in the merger implementation and final outcome. The economic analysis actually faces great difficulties to identify and specify criteria explaining the success or the failure of a merger. Since classic economic factors, such as scale and scope economies, overhead cuts or technical, commercial and financial 'synergies', cannot be statistically demonstrated, one then evokes cultural incompatibilities, management mistakes, which are concepts hardly defined nor easy rigorously to compare.

Our objective is, on the contrary, to develop an explanation model of the reasons for success or failures of the transnational mergers, based on the role played by employees' participation in the merger implementation. The central working assumption of our work is that a merger in fact corresponds to the creation of a single firm out of two distinct entities. This shift from two to one firm requires a 'destructive creation' process, into which the effective participation of employees is a critical factor for successful implementation. The destruction of the former structures and the building up of new ones require strategic decisions in three key areas of the firm: production organisation, industrial and geographic location of its activities, and workforce adjustment. The employees are clearly a decisive variable of these choices, which will eventually define the economic model of the merged company. Their support and effective involvement in the merger implementation will largely depend on the participation and negotiation processes set up by the firms for the merger.

To analyse the links between corporate governance, mergers and workers participation, we will address the two following questions: what is the role of employees' participation in the final merger's outcome? And does cross-border mergers' experience in Europe allow us to identify a model for employees' participation in the future European firm?

Analytic References: Between the IO Merger Literature and the Studies on Varieties of Capitalism

Quite paradoxically, mergers remain a secondary research issue in social sciences (excluding economy). There is (still) no book or article dealing specifically with this issue, except for one chapter of a book published in 1983 (Aldrich and Sproule, 1983) about mergers in the United States, and for an article written by Tony Edwards (1999, see end of § 2).

Yet, most of the time, mergers are still indirectly examined through shareholder value and changes in ownership structure of the firms (Fairburn and Kay, 1989; OECD, 1994; Sudarsanam, 1995). According to this approach, employees are considered within broader terms and categories, such as cost minimization strategies, restructuring and synergies that lead, most of the time, to substantial redundancies. We will go back to this literature (see *infra*), but of course, the first obvious step is to look at economy analysis to provide useful insights into what determines mergers and their consequences.

The 1990s Wave of Cross-border Mergers in Europe

The 1990s experienced a merger and acquisition (M&A) wave with unprecedented levels in the number of deals and their value. We briefly present the main stylized facts and characteristics of recent merger activity. A simple way to do that is to compare the current wave with the previous ones over the last 50 years. One of the most consistent features of the huge empirical literature on mergers is actually that mergers occur in waves. One can then point out five historical peaks in merger activity during the 20th century: the 1900, 1920, 1960, 1980, and 1990 decades. While the first two waves are almost exclusively US-centric events, an increasing international dimension (mostly in Western Europe and Japan) marks the subsequent ones. However, the recent merger wave also exhibits the following specific features:

- first, its exceptional magnitude,

- the increasing number of very large so-called 'mega' deals,
- a strong clustering of mergers within industries and sectors,
- the increasing fraction of cross-border mergers.

These key trends noted by Pryor (2001) – industry consolidation through very large mergers – are confirmed and well illustrated in Table 10.1, which lists the largest mergers completed since 1998.

Although widely publicized, prominent transatlantic transactions like Vivendi Seagram (to form Vivendi Universal) and the much debated DaimlerBenz/Chrysler deal do not appear in this ranking because the amounts involved (respectively €34 billion and €45 billion) were slightly smaller than these top-ten records.

Table 10.1   Largest merger deals 1998–2000

Year	Companies	Deal Value	Industry
2000	America Online/Time Warner	€220 billion	Telecom
2000	Vodaphone Air Touch/Mannesmann	€210 billion	Telecom
2000	Pfizer/Warner-Lambert	€107 billion	Pharmaceuticals
1998	Exxon/Mobil	€92 billion	Oil
2000	SmithKline Beecham/Glaxo Welcome	€88 billion	Pharmaceuticals
1998	Travelers Group/Citicorp	€85 billion	Financial Services
1998	SBC/Ameritech	€73 billion	Telecom
1998	NationsBank/BankAmerica	€72 billion	Financial Services
1998	British Petroleum/Amoco	€71 billion	

The structural characteristics of the 1990s merger wave listed above can also be linked with the financing of the transactions. These deals were actually massively carried out through stock, at a time where stock market valuations reach an all-time high. This clearly contrasts with the previous merger wave just five to seven years earlier, driven by hostile takeovers in cash in a depressed stock market. Table 10.2 summarizes all these elements to pin down the distinct nature of the present merger intense activity.

However, the main point for our discussion is the impressive rise in cross-border mergers. As Figure 10.1 illustrates, the pace even tends to accelerate as the value of cross-border mergers and acquisitions completed in 2000 reached €1.2 trillion, nearly 50 percent higher than in 1999. As a result, cross-border M&As must be considered as a fundamental mechanism of industrial globalization. In particular, this is now the

Table 10.2   Characteristics of the last three merger waves

Period	Wave name	Rationale	Payment medium	Stock market valuation
1960s	Conglomerate	Build-up large diversified groups	Stock	Very high
1980s	Bust-up 'hostile' takeovers	Financial raiders acquire and split-up conglomerates	Cash	Low
1990s	Global	World or regional consolidation among major industries	Stock	Very high

major component and the driving force in foreign direct investment (FDI). However, this phenomenon remains highly localized within the OECD area and affects only marginally developing countries and North/South investment flows.

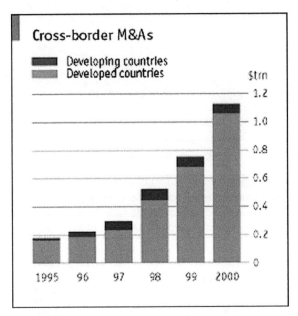

Figure 10.1   Value of cross-border mergers 1995–2000

For geographical statistical purposes, it is common to classify cross-border mergers as inward or outward, depending upon whether the merger consists of the sale of a domestic firm to a foreign acquirer or the purchase by a domestic firm of a foreign company. Figure 10.2 shows the number, in the European Union, of inward and outward cross-border mergers and acquisitions during the period 1991–1998, both in absolute and relative terms. EU figures add up the national inward and outward volume for each of the member states. Figure 10.2 shows that the European Union played a dominant role in worldwide cross-border merger activity, accounting on average for 36 percent and 47 percent of all inward and outward mergers during that period. It is interesting to note that the United States shares amount to, respectively, 27 percent and 23 percent. Given the dominance of the US in overall mergers – mergers between only US companies account for 47 percent of the value of all worldwide merger deals (Pryor 2001) – this means Europe is the indisputable centre of cross-border merger activity.

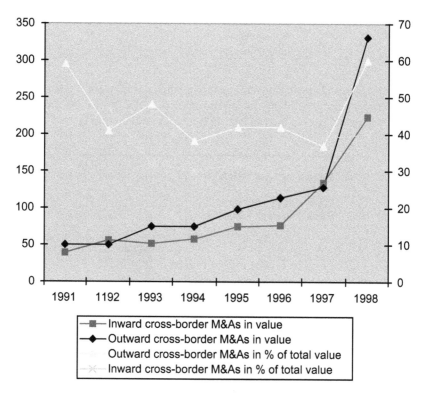

Figure 10.2   European Union cross-border M&As (aggregate value and worldwide share)

The major role played by the European Union is underlined when we get into the detailed picture of cross-border deals by country. The UK tops the charts in 2000, fuelled by Vodafone-Mannesman, the largest deal completed in the year at €210 billion. Total UK acquisitions amount to the value of €390 billion, a 120 percent increase from 1999. The next most acquisitive nations in 2000 are France (€160 billion), the US (€159 billion) and Germany (€72 billion). In 2000, Germany led the way in inward investment to the tune of €276 billion, a huge growth from the previous year (€65 billion), mainly due to the Vodafone-Mannesman giant takeover. Other main target countries were the US, which attracted €262 billion worth of inward investment, followed by the UK (€231 billion). The largest sector involved in global M&A activity unsurprisingly has been the telecommunications and broadcasting sector, which was the target in over a third of all deals. For example, the outward spend in 2000 by France Telecom in cross-border international acquisitions (€65 billion) is greater than the total inward investment by all countries into France (€55 billion)! The financial sector was the second major target attracting €183 billion worth of bids. However, it was the computers/electronic sector which took the biggest leap from €51 billion to €135 billion in 2000, whilst activity by traditional manufacturing businesses climbed by 22 percent to €118 billion. Chemicals and pharmaceuticals saw the biggest drop (−67 percent down to €42 billion), as the big deals of 1999, such as Zeneca Group–Astra and Rhone Poulenc–Hoechst, were not replicated.

A recent OECD survey provided interesting statistics of worldwide M&A activity:

- The value of cross-border mergers worldwide grew more than six-fold between 1991 and 1998.
- This trend even accelerates in recent years. In 2000 alone, outward investment by Western European countries alone increased by 40 percent to reach a record high of €370 billion, driven mainly by transatlantic takeovers (453 acquisitions of North American companies).
- As a result, cross-border deals represent a growing part of the total M&A picture in Europe far exceeding (1.5 ratio) domestic deals in terms of average value. It also represents an increasing proportion of the total value of all deals across the world (41 percent in 2000 compared with 24 percent in 1996).
- The total number of cross-border mergers also increases rapidly from 2900 deals completed in 1996 to 7300 in 2000.
- Between 1991 and 1998, the average size of cross-border deals increased about five-fold (to €120 million), drawn by the growing importance of very large-scale mergers. In 1998 and 1999, the first five deals made up more than 30 percent of global transaction values.

Another key feature of cross-border mergers is that they take place across all sectors, manufacturing as well as services industries. At the same time, empirical research evidence shows that most of the transactions involve firms from the same sector. Cross-border takeovers then appear as a major instrument of industry consolidation within increasingly globalized markets. Depending on the sector and countries involved, this consolidation and concentration process might be triggered by a number of reasons: increased competition, technological change, worldwide or regional excess capacity, concentration among clients or suppliers, regulatory reforms, investment liberalisation, and so on. We find here the main driving forces behind mergers worldwide, which we will discuss more extensively in the next part of the paper. What then are the specific reasons pushing firms to engage in cross-border mergers? Based on empirical evidence and existing business surveys, one can suggest that three factors, out of the usual merger's explanations, here play a particularly decisive role:

(1) Cross-border mergers are, first of all, an efficient and quick entry mode in foreign markets. The time factor is especially important for entering domestic markets recently opened up to competition, where the number of potential entrants is large and establishing a critical mass gives a strong competitive advantage. In such cases, a merger clearly appears as a superior strategy to greenfield investment, since it allows one immediately (after the average six-months delays for sorting the financial arrangement and the regulatory clearance) to seize the new market opportunity.

(2) Domestic government policies are a second fundamental factor determining cross-border mergers. More precisely, trade policies (elimination of trade barriers and customs distortions, liberalisation of capital movements and investments), regulatory reform (in telecoms, electricity, finance) and privatisation programs have contributed a lot during the last decade to cross-border merger activity, by creating new major growth opportunities for foreign companies. The continuous economic expansion between 1995 and 2000 also worked in favour of cross-border mergers, especially in the United States and in Europe. On the one hand, prolonged economic growth increases the financial resources at the disposal of domestic firms considering takeovers abroad (either through accumulated profits or by a favourable stock market environment pushing equity prices and available capital). On the other hand, favourable macro-economic forecasts contribute to secure the short-term profitability of the acquisition of the target firm.

(3) Regional integration policy. This was indubitably a key driving force behind cross-border mergers between European firms. The unification of domestic markets into a single one, the imminent prospect of a common currency, the definition of long-term credible public policies and targets (in the field of utilities regulation, competition and trade policy, budgetary and monetary restrictions) implemented across the entire continent (European directives mechanisms) promote and facilitate cross-border mergers.

It is likely that the economic slowdown in the US and Europe during 2000–01 will have a negative impact on merger activity. This will affect in particular cross-border mergers since these transactions are widely considered as the most hazardous investment for companies, and therefore the first to be cancelled or postponed when economic conditions deteriorate. Moreover, the current crisis in the telecom and high-tech industries, which have so far been major fields for cross-border mergers, is another strong adverse factor. Indications that the pace of worldwide mergers is slowing down emerged by the end of 2000, which last quarter recorded a 33 percent drop in announced cross-border deals compared with levels in each of the first two quarters for the year, according to Computasoft Research (CommScan). As a result, the total value of cross-border and domestic deals within the European Union will decrease for the first time in 2000, reaching €940 billion down from €1170 billion in 1999 (Thomson Financial Securities Data). There is also a growing concern among economists and business circles that the weak euro against the dollar, and the successive setbacks in the harmonization of national takeover codes and the legal definition of a European company, prompt capital flows to the US rather than within the EU. As the previous figures show, the former have, in 2000, exceeded the later on aggregate volume and in many individual countries (the UK, France, Germany).

The Economic Analysis of Mergers

The dramatic increase in the total value of mergers since 1995–96 has led many observers to talk about a 'merger mania'. Economists have not ignored this spectacular trend. Their interest in mergers, which dates back to the early days of industrial economics and competition policy, found there a new force and motivation. The structural transformation of the industry and the firms brought about by mergers actually raises a number of interesting issues. The first of them is without doubt: why? In other words, what is the rationale and the motivation in merging two or more companies? Then one might wonder: will the operation be beneficial to society or not? Should the government interfere with the process to clear or forbid the transaction? If so, on which legal justification and based on what kind of economic evidence and argument? Here, the main concern is that mergers could be used as an instrument to create legal cartels, since the merged firms will now be able to coordinate their actions and legally achieve joint-profit maximization. These public policy implications have given birth to a vast theoretical and empirical literature. The nature of competitive threats raised by mergers, the relevant distinction between mergers that are harmful for other firms and consumers and those that are not, the adequate antitrust policy with respect to mergers, are issues widely debated amongst financial, industrial organization and public economists. On all these points, there are no agreed-upon answers. The aim of this section is not to review systematically the existing theoretical and empirical economic literatures on the causes and consequences of mergers. Rather, we suggest investigating how the various existing economic models try to figure out the unique feature of a merger, in other words, what fundamentally changes when two formerly separate firms are joined into a single one? Therefore, we concentrate on the assumptions and the main hypothesis of the models, and leave aside their results and predictions. We will argue that the merger mechanism still remains to a large extent a black box for economic analysis. Most of the models actually clarify the motivation of a merger and display their predictable effects by assuming that the joint company gets a new or superior capacity that the merging firms did not enjoy separately before (increased market power, leadership role in the industry, scope economies etc). This new feature is central to the model resolution (price, quantities, corporate profits, social welfare compared prior and after the merger). However, these models give us very little clue as to why and how the merger confers to the joint firm such ability and feature. To sum up, the problem is simply shifted one step further but remains basically unresolved. The following brief review of the main merger models will help us illustrate this point and collect on our way the different assumptions used to capture the changes brought by a merger.

The first step of the analysis is to define exactly the nature of the transaction involved in a merger. Does the literature provide a useful and efficient classification of merger types? The basic approach consists of considering the nature of the relations that existed previously between the merging firms. This allows distinguishing three different kinds of mergers:

(1) between former competitors in the same product market: horizontal mergers (e.g. two food retail chains or two long distance telecommunications providers),

(2) between firms involved at different stages of one vertical production chain: vertical mergers (e.g. an oil producer and a refiner, a car manufacturer and a engine designer and producer). This category also extends beyond strict hierarchical links to include consolidation of complementary goods producers.

(3) between firms without a clear substitute or complementary relationship: conglomerate mergers (creating a diversified industrial group).

Economic theory lists many possible reasons for mergers:

- efficiency gains (as a result of scale economies or overall synergies between the merged companies),
- market power (to reach a monopoly position or form an oligopoly),
- market discipline (replace an incompetent management, and an inefficient firm),
- acquirer management will to grow (agency relation with shareholders),
- diversification (to exploit internal capital markets).

We could add many items to that list. The problem with this compilation of factors is their extreme heterogeneity and different relevant scope. The basic reason for that is that they have many different origins (theoretical, empirical or case studies research, IO, public economics, competition law, regulation economics, political or international economics and so on). To survey this vast existing literature on mergers, we then suggest sorting out the main contributions, arguments and models along two groups. The first one will consider the question: why do firms merge? It is useful to split it again between two different approaches of the determinants of mergers. A first approach interprets mergers as a reaction to exogenous shock to the industry structure. Contrasting with this somehow passive interpretation, the alternative view develops the strategic nature of mergers for competing firms. We may gather in a second group of references, all the research and studies analysing how firms may benefit from merging. Again a double perspective can be considered. The consequences of a merger can first be assessed in a welfare cost/benefit analysis. This is the point of view of competition regulators charged to clear or to block the proposed transaction (for antitrust literature, see for example Viscusi, 1995) The key variables to consider here are changes in market concentration, price, and innovation incentives, and the solutions found to the so-called 'merger paradox'.[1] For example,

---

1   The paradox also lies in the fact that, if a merger takes place, then it will directly benefit the non-participating firms, who without having to incur any costs see the elimination of one competitor. Their automatic relative share increase will dominate the fall in the total output, creating a clear gain.

Table 10.3   M&A strategies

Merger type	Strategic objectives	Major concerns	Frequency*
Overcapacity	Eliminate capacity, gain market share, improve operations' efficiency	Need to rationalize quickly, values differences, fight between management for control in a merger of equals	37%
Geographic roll-up	Geographical expansion	Impose processes and values from the acquirer	9%
Product or Market extension	Extend a company's product line or international coverage	Cultural and governmental differences, lack of understanding of markets	36%
R&D	Acquisitions replace in-house R&D	Evaluation of the target, cultural differences, retain key executives and staff	1%
Industry convergence	Build positions in a new emerging industry	Opportunities selection, adjust the right level of integration	4%

* Relative weight in the sample analysed.
Source: Bower (2001, pp. 94–95).

three factors: overcoming the problem of double marginalization, enhancing a supplier's ability to price discriminate, and facilitating market foreclosure, offer a clear economic rationale for vertical mergers. Another conceivable approach would focus on the firm level, the measure of merger's performance, trying to figure out the possible sources of total value increase (efficiency gains or merger's synergies, economies of scale, agency issues).

While economic and financial studies have so far rarely examined the merger process per se, merger implementation has rapidly become a major topic in the business and management literature. In addition, advice on merger and acquisition strategy is now an important market for consulting firms. To differentiate their offer in the very competitive environment of corporate advice, these companies then have clear incentives to formalize their diagnosis of the mergers' problem, and to exploit their bases of cases and experience to illustrate the argument with stylised facts and statistics. Despite an immediate commercial motivation, these contributions are worth considering for two reasons. First, they provide us with some statistical data and detailed case studies in a field largely constrained by confidentiality rules and secrecy (mergers remain highly strategic operations, supervised by a handful of senior executives). The second reason is that the argument developed and the key success factors identified by consulting firms often also mirror managers' beliefs and common knowledge on mergers.

Two contributions are of particular interest for our research. The first one (Bower, 2001) is based on a Harvard study of 1036 M&A deals over $500 million made between 1977 and 1999. It suggests a merger typology based on five distinct rationales, with specific strategic objectives, concerns and challenges for the deal success (see Table 10.3).

A second similar and complementary view is given by recent research reports by the consulting firm McKinsey. Again, the widespread use of the single concept of a merger to refer to very different situations is criticized. Such a generic view actually leads to several unsuitable approaches and methods. A good example is given by the excessive focus put on costs' synergies at the expense of post-merger revenue growth. But empirical studies demonstrate that, measured against industry peers, acquirers and targets have to face a significant slowdown. The problem is that shortfall in revenue growth can easily outweigh fluctuations in planned costs savings. And accordingly, a pursued momentum and higher growth rates than anticipated might offset a failure on initial (often over-estimated) costs targets. A McKinsey survey (Bieshaar *et al.*, 2001) of 160 mergers in 1995–96 across 11 sectors claims that only 12 percent of the acquirers achieved organic growth rates ahead of the organic growth of their peers over the next three years (to 1999).

Secondly, joining Bower's perspective, the need to specify the underlying strategic motivation to a merger is emphasized because it is argued that their relevance and chances of success will be very different. Stock market reactions and financial indicators are mobilized to demonstrate this point.

Global economic integration, the dismantling of barriers to trade and investment, the rapid homogenization of consumers' preferences worldwide, have paved the way during the last decade to a dramatic increase in cross-border activity. The level of tangible and R&D investment required and the pace imposed by products' reduced life cycle actually force companies to operate in the largest accessible markets. In this perspective, access to the world market becomes a key strategic objective, and cross-border mergers are a privileged instrument to preserve the firm's competitiveness and maintain its gained competitive advantage. The empirical distinction between mergers pursuing expansion strategies (such as the entry in new geographical markets or the creation of new distribution channels for its products and services) and mergers aimed at consolidating, restructuring and rationalising existing business is central to the management literature.

A recent McKinsey survey (Bieshaar *et al.*, 2001) of 231 transactions (mergers, acquisitions, joint ventures) achieved by 36 companies between 1994 and 1998, whose monetary value was announced publicly, examined the stock price movements a few days before and after the release of the deals. Within the hypothesis of financial markets' efficiency, this indicator actually captures all the information about the deal. Stock price reaction will incorporate an assessment of the expected future performance of the companies involved in the merger. The relative role of possible explanatory characteristics such as the industry, the deal size, the nature of the transaction or the company performance is discussed through a multivariate linear regression. The results illustrate (i) the preference given by financial markets to 'expansionist' deals relatively to 'transformative' takeovers. Combinations of two firms in the same industry (either for geographic expansion or consolidation) earned a 1.1 percent market premium in the 11 days surrounding the announcement, while creation of new distribution channels for the existing range of products and services resulted in a 4.2 percent premium. On the contrary, a refocus of a healthy portfolio of activities through the sale of divisions or subsidiaries, and mergers supporting a diversification in new lines of business destroyed on average 5.3 percent of the company's (i.e. the acquirer here) value. Logically, synergies tend to be much more concrete and predictable in a combination of similar assets rather than in the second type of transactions.

These management and consulting contributions make a strong case for the scope of our study since they anticipate the growing role of mergers with cross-border dimensions, which correspond to the 'transformative' or 'geographic roll-up' deals, whose chances of success are the largest. However, the analysis of the merger is once more limited to a single ex-ante dimension: the coherence between the company's strategy and the deal proposed. The rest is considered as a matter of execution, and management skills. Therefore, the implementation process is again often neglected. Or, which is equivalent, simply reduced to a 'people factor' or a 'cultural problem'. While there is no doubt that this is an important question for sociologists and even management research, we believe that this radical interpretation of implementation issues as strictly cultural or sociological factors is misleading and unsatisfactory. It is implicitly (or voluntarily?) a way to rule out the role of economic, financial or commercial elements in this critical process. Our empirical investigation on case studies aims to address this question.

Mergers, Shareholders, Management and Employees in Other Social Sciences

The analysis of firms' ownership structure, of the relation between management and shareholders and their evolution – that is everything, but limited to the study of mergers – gave rise to a vast literature, especially in the Anglo-Saxon political economy on corporate governance. It aims at identifying different – national and/or regional – models of corporate governance. The comparative advantages of those models are examined, particularly German versus Anglo-Saxon models (Windolf and Beyer, 1996; Kaplan, 1997; Vitols *et al.*, 1997; Mayer, 1998; Rhodes and van Apeldoorn, 1998; Jürgens *et al.*, 2000). It focuses on the ability for alternative corporate governance systems, such as the German one, to survive while the pressure for short term profitability affects more and more firms.

Of course, there is a specific field of corporate governance studies called 'stakeholder approach', not only focusing on managers and shareholders but integrating firms' clients, suppliers, employee representatives and a certain amount of state-controlled authorities. However, these studies usually concentrate on a macro and systemic level. Their authors sometimes evoke cross-border mergers, but as a symptom – not as a research topic – indicating a change in the corporate governance system, or announcing the domination of the Anglo-Saxon model. Employee representation structures are not examined as such but as an element of the entire system. Most of time they focus on the way employee representation structures impacts firms and national territory competitiveness.

Concerning forms of employee participation in trans-national companies – not necessarily arising from a cross-border merger – there are many articles on the implementation and operation of European Works Councils (EWCs). Most of these articles, published since the beginning of the 1990s, are based on case studies. The first ones (Streeck and Vitols, 1993; Turner, 1993) precede the European Directive on EWCs (Directive 94/45/EC, adopted on 22 September 1994), and examine the 'spontaneous' creation of supra-national information and consultation bodies within multinational firms, such as Volkswagen, Bull, Thomson or Europipe. Those supra-national employee representation bodies already existed in hundreds of firms, and some of them have been officially recognised by management, others not. In the absence of European legislation, their structures and functioning are rather heterogeneous. Turner (1993, p. 21) writes: 'it is really impossible to tell if what we are seeing is a groundwork for future progress or dead-end'.

The European Directive adopted in 1994 covers multinational firms employing at least 1000 workers in the member States, including at least 150 employees in two member States (*European Industrial Relations Review (EIRR)*, 250, November 1994). In 1998, 400 EWCs had been implemented (*EIRR*, 296, September 1998). Despite this quantitative success, studies on EWCs and their functioning point out the lack of information and consultation rights for employees at a trans-national level (*EIRR*, 317, June 2000). Those bodies are not used by national employee representatives as a tool that allows them to develop and coordinate a European solidarity, to decide joint minimum standards under which unions or employee representatives would refuse to negotiate locally. Moreover, EWCs work as an information forum under management control (Hancké, 2000).

A rare author to deal with the central topic of our research (Edwards, 1999) identifies three different consequences of cross-border mergers for labour and its representatives: (i) redundancies; (ii) management appealing to the principle 'divide and rule' in relation to labour representatives; (iii) the national effect: substantial differences remain in the nature of national business systems in which firms are embedded, and they lead to differences in the way management considers and deals with employee representatives.

To sum up the bibliography on our research topic, we will stress the four following points.

(1) Even if numerous social scientists mention the growing importance of mergers in general, and especially of cross-border mergers, very few of them really examine the specificity and the characteristic of these mergers and of their mechanisms.

(2) If we now turn to economic analysis, we must face a fundamental obstacle. Our review of existing models shows that neoclassical theory does not allow us to satisfactorily characterize the changes brought when two separate production units are joined and replaced by a single integrated one. This results from a larger weakness of the theory regarding the scope and the boundaries of the firm. That does not prevent it from deriving interesting results about the impact of mergers on competition and welfare, but little can be said about the merger process itself: what does common ownership permit the merged firms to do that could not be done before separately?

(3) On the one hand, legal forms of employee participation exist at European level, but they don't seem to be the occasion for different national union representatives to develop a collective strategy to defend European employee

rights.

(4) On the other hand, even if many studies focus on management and shareholders in trans-national firms and only consider employees through the number of lay-offs caused by the merger, the literature also shows some examples of information and consultation bodies created within multinational firms at the request of employee representatives. It sometimes occurred well before the adoption of the 1994 European Directive.

In order to go beyond the (too?) general debate on broad systems of corporate governance and varieties of capitalism, our research focuses on the process of creation of a trans-national company, with four detailed case studies of Franco-German mergers: Aventis, Europipe, Quante Pouyet, V&M Tubes (see annex). Unlike the observations and analysis made by academics on the functioning of EWCs in firms with a long multinational tradition, we assumed that a cross-border merger, in the current context of growing market internationalization and European economical integration – when according to Vallourec CEO 'industrials are making Europe' – would force management and labour representatives from different countries to face together concrete problems and issues. So we would see new dialog processes – formal or informal ones – emerging at a trans-national level. We assumed that these processes would depart from pre-existing national forms of employee participation. We expected therefore to witness the progressive disappearance of national challenges (at least on some issues), and the emerging feature of the European Society, whose status is still being debated.

Evidence from Mergers Case Studies: The Prevalence of the 'National' Issue

Surprisingly, our case studies show that national issues are still extremely present within firms arising from a cross-border merger, even if the merger occurred ten years ago. There are several ways for a national issue to be present. We will consider three of them: (i) firms care for a fair balance of the work load among different national territories; (ii) 'social' issues (wages, working time, holiday) are differently managed within the firm according to national territories; (iii) there is no dialogue among different national employee representatives within the trans-national firm. On this basis, the role of employees in the merger's outcome can be reconsidered. To illustrate and discuss these elements, we have included direct quotations from the interviews in the text with references to the cases, when this was allowed by the companies (in two cases, there will be no direct quotations but the results of the fieldwork research and the interviews conducted with their employees and managers is included and clearly fit with the argument developed).

The National Fair Balance Rule

In some cases, the management after the merger does not just decide according to the economic rationality. Some decisions, such as workload distribution, are ruled by a distinct logic, clearly identified by our interlocutors as a different logic than the economic one.

> There has been no change concerning physical flows. In case of low loading we tried to have a fair distribution of the orders, except in case of absolute specialisation. (V&M Tubes, 02. 2001) Italics are quotations from the interviews.

> The production planning committee makes sure of a fair distribution of the work load between France and Germany, partly based on costs and competencies, but not only'. (Europipe, 11. 2000)

One of the first objectives of the management of a trans-national firm is the search for a fair distribution of the workload among national territories, provided that technical constraints (*absolute specialization*) do not interfere. *Cost* and *competencies* criteria, which can be related to the economic rationality, constitute one of the decisive factors for the distribution of the production among plants. However, management does not only decide according to these criteria. As such, management does guarantee a so-called '*fair*' balance of the work load among national territories. This form of distribution is based on something else (partly based on cost and competencies, but not only).

> If we were willing to work, politically, we had to distribute the load in a fair way: on the middle run, however, we can be forced to take different decisions, this creates a very strong potential tension. (V&M Tubes, 02. 2001)

Besides economic rationality, the trans-national firm has to submit to the *political* rule in order to function. The political rationality that operates within the firm governs the relations among plants located on different national territories. It requires (*we had to*) a fair distribution of the work load. As a consequence, trans-national firms are not systematically free from national issues, they are not de-territorialized.

These two rationalities, the economical one and the political one, cannot be merged, they are distinct. If they are compatible, the workload is fairly balanced. As soon as they are no longer compatible, the economical rule prevails over the political rule (*we can be forced to take different decisions*) and this non-compatibility leads to imbalances regarding the workload distribution on the one hand, and eventually creates tensions on the other hand.

> The fair balance rule regarding work load among the two tube plants operated up to 1998, 1999. Since then Dunkerque has always had a lower loading than Mülheim. Dunkerque had to implement a flexible organization since the 1980s, and developed tools allowing to face dramatic changes in load. This is an advantage as well as a disadvantage: as the plant got this know-how, it is also required to implement it. In 2000 Dunkerque systematically operated with low loading (50% of its capacity) in order to preserve a full activity in Mülheim: as a consequence the rule does not exist any longer. (Europipe, 12. 2000)

The political rule leading to fairness can come to an end. As a consequence, in case of low loading, the logic at stake is a logic appealing to the different capacities national firms can use to face a lower loading. This logic is also related to the national issue but in a totally different way: the trans-national firm intends to mobilize the distinct resources given by different national laws regarding short-time working, fixed term contracts, temporary posting, etc. It is then a logic of differentiation (see the second section). The political rationality can already be implemented before the actual merger, during the preparatory negotiations:

> Concerning investment decisions the economic profitability prevails. Regarding this issue, certain points had been settled before the JV, attempting to equalize starting situations. (V&M Tubes, 02. 2001)

The aim is to establish a fair initial situation among the plants located on different territories that are going to be put together within the trans-national firm. As soon as the balance is reached, the economic rationality (*economic profitability*) is the only one at stake.

> The merger occasioned plant closures in France and in Germany, closures on both sides were one of the conditions for the merger. (Europipe, 11. 2000)

When the creation of the trans-national firms leads to layoffs, the political rule can apply as well. The implementation of the rule can even operate as one of the pre-conditions for the merger. Within the trans-national firm, the political – national – workload (or production) trio governs the relations among plants located on different national territories according to the fairness rule, provided that this rule is compatible with the economic rationality.

Management in trans-national firms sometimes submits to multiple logics and principles. This is everything but a naive understanding of the quotations. In the end, the firm is ruled by the economic rationality. However, this logic is not the only one to constrain management decisions. It does not only let there be room for manoeuvre but can temporary be confronted with other rationalities within the trans-national firm.

The political rationality, that is the 'fair balance rule', leading to a fair handling among national territories is provisional. It seems to be at stake at the very moment of the creation of the trans-national firm, and in some cases – especially horizontal mergers (Europipe, V&M Tubes) – it can go on for a long time. However, this fair balance rule is not permanent.

While (as we will see in the following section) most cross-border mergers must already cope with the fact that wages, social policy, work organization and conditions remain set on a national basis, the 'national fair balance rule' adds the two following economic constraints:

- the initial number of production sites in each country will not change,
- new orders and production are on average shared equally between the countries.

One might immediately question the economic viability of such a plan. How can one expect benefit from combining operations if you cannot exploit the increased size by rationalizing production and plants, nor coordinate on a global basis wages and labour costs? It is very important here to draw attention to the merger agreement, and in particular the actions undertaken during the pre-merger phase (i.e. the one–two year period between the very first informal contacts and the official public announcement of the transaction). The above mentioned plan can only be sustainable in an economic perspective if the productivity levels in the different sites are not too different. This requires, prior to the merger, and as a condition to its effective fulfilment, a levelling of the initial economic conditions. This was achieved through a simultaneous rationalization of each national industrial tool. In the cases studied, plant closures were actually decided before the merger (even if in some cases they really took place after it). With this starting point, one can reasonably contemplate that the status quo regarding the national number of plants and the equal share of workload is economically viable, at least for a while. Actually, if the initial agreement was soundly designed, the merged company can run its operations in a quasi steady state for some years (5, 7, 10?). However, as time goes by, the internal tensions are likely to grow, if productivity gaps between plants and national wages differences are not progressively brought down. This might eventually raise the issue of closing a plant. Such a decision would constitute a very serious challenge to the stability and future of the joint company. On the other hand, we can consider that this is the ultimate test to determine if the merger was just a temporary organization form, or if it has given birth to a truly new independent and self-sufficient firm.

Another key issue in the initial agreement is the location of the new headquarters of the merged company, in a subjective manner first for employees, because it eventually marks, in a symbolic way, the geographical rooting of the company. But also, since the mobility of employees remains very limited, it instantly indicates which nationality will predictably dominate the staff in the central functions of the merger firm. To avoid this kind of conflict as well as to improve management efficiency, a solution consists of setting up a very light and holding structure with a limited workforce (10–20) and decentralizing to the largest possible extent the management of operations at the individual site level (Europipe, V&M Tubes). If markets, technology and product characteristics, however, impose an important central structure, firms may choose to close their former headquarters and create a greenfield corporate HQ in a new geographic location (Aventis chose Strasbourg, which symbolically stands as a crossroads of France, Germany and Europe).

The 'Social Issue': Partition and Differentiation

The second way for the national issue to arise within trans-national companies appears in the 'social' topic (wages, working time, holidays, pension, etc). 'Social' themes are absolutely separated among the territories and lastingly rooted at the national level. This point constitutes the specificity of a cross-border merger. In the case of a merger between companies located on one and the same national territory, work contracts, wages, working time, etc, are subject to a harmonization. This process (can) lead(s) to tensed discussions or conflicts between management, employees and their representatives:

in case of merger or acquisition [in a national context] *the integration of employees is always a problem, especially when they lose some advantages.* (V&M Tubes, 02, 2001)

At the time of a cross-border merger, many activities tend to be coordinated: sales, marketing, management, relations with suppliers, quality, security, R&D, and so on. This process neither takes place immediately nor smoothly. However, the management of the trans-national company instigates an active policy regarding the harmonization of these issues. On the contrary, work contracts, wages, seniority, working time, holidays, pensions, are not supposed to be brought closer. Sometimes, those issues are not even re-negotiated:

the employees of the tube plant in Mülheim kept a Mannesmann work contract until 1997 [even if the plant belongs to Europipe since its creation in 1991]. (Europipe, 11, 2001)

The social issue is not an ordinary topic:

Social issues are very specific. Social issues are strictly a national problem, it's the specificity of social issues to be national, because of the legislation on the one hand and of the social practices on the other hand. (V&M Tubes, 02, 2001)

So that it is the proper typical feature of social issues – in comparison with other dimensions of the firm: technical, economical, financial, etc – to be strictly rooted at the national level. Social issues are ruled by their own logic, which is a national one whatever the geographical area of the firm's operations may be. The company may be trans-national, it has to submit to the different legal rules fixed at the national level. As a consequence, social issues are settled at national level, referring to other firms belonging to the same industrial sector:

There has been no unification of the pension, working time or wages regimes for Europipe employees. French subsidiaries still follow the rule fixed by Usinor and German production sites adopted the MRW rules. (Europipe, 11, 2000)

Moreover, there is no discussion about the different decision-making processes on this issue within the trans-national firm:

The wage issue is a black box on both sides. (Europipe, 12, 2000)

The human resource manager at Europipe France discovered at the beginning of 2000 that his German counterpart needed the approval of the works council to hire a new employee. This story is not only anecdotic. The partition of social issues treatment, and its national founding is absolute. Yet, this lack of communication does not prevent employees and union representatives from both sides having a rough idea of wages differences. For example, it is well known that the wage increase was nil or negligible in France in 1999, while in Germany branch negotiations resulted in an average 3 percent growth. There is also a wide consensus on a 25–30 percent difference between French and German gross salary (although comparisons are pretty complicated by very different qualifications and promotions systems).

Nowadays, French subsidiaries of trans-national companies are forced to negotiate over working time reduction to 35 hours a week. German firms still operate with a 35 hours week (since 1996), at least in metallurgy. When asking French managers, who are employees of a Franco-German firm, if they benefited from the German experience of working time reduction or at least if they talked with their German counterparts to know how they dealt with it, all of them answered with a no. Moreover, they considered the German experience to be of no help for them, the national practice is the only one that counts:

> In France the solution for the 35 hours week was well known, since 82 we have not reduced plants' utilisation time, but we introduced compensatory holidays, time accounts. (V&M Tubes, 02, 2001)

Regarding social issues, the experience that has been acquired on a national territory cannot be transferred into another. Social issues are ruled in a specific way for the national issue to be present, which excludes any possibility of exchange and connection within the trans-national firm on this topic. It acts as a factor of absolute differentiation and partition. Distinct social regimes lastingly coexist within one and the same entity.

> Concerning social issues, [...] each nationality continues to operate within its national context, social systems are considered as too different to be brought together. (Europipe, 12, 2000)

Social issues are not only related to *national* but also to *nationality*; that is, what legally rules and defines the membership of a national State. Regarding social issues, the national issue does not arise in a geographical sense but is related to Law and to the State. National States are present within the trans-national company through social issues.

Regarding social issues – that is, the way firms treat, count, pay their employees – the way for the national issue to present itself refers to national differentiation under the State's control. Employees of a trans-national company are still attached to a specific national territory. This pre-eminence of national patterns within the firm can also been understood as a result of weak shareholder control. In a 50 percent–50 percent merger, there is actually no clear dominant actor that could unanimously stand as the owner of the new firm (even though the merger agreement might give one of the shareholders the industrial control and daily management of operations). Since in most industrial mergers observed in Europe, the shareholders of the joint firm remain the parent companies (i.e. the former owner of the plants), the logical tendency for employees on every site is to stick to their previous employer. This is well illustrated by the common feeling shared by many of the managers we interviewed that in many plants the real owner of production facilities and the staff's employer still seem unclear.

Of course, trans-national companies use comparative advantages offered by different national legislation, as we saw with the case of the tube plant in Dunkerque with Europipe. However, this non-harmonization of social issues is not only rooted in objectives such as 'divide and rule'. Trans-national firms have to submit to the own logic of social issues embedded in the Law and the State that constrains them to implement distinct national solutions. In the absence of any social legal framework at the European level, social issues intrinsically lead to differentiations within the trans-national firm. This way for the national issue to be present, which is the presence of national States within the trans-national firm, is likely to last for a while. We can also turn the argument another way: even though firms are located on several national territories, national States still have influence on them.

The Employee Factor in the Cross-border Merger Outcome

The two previous sections illustrate the severe limitations associated with a cross-border merger in terms of production consolidation and wages coordination. As a result, the potential for production costs and labour costs reduction (often described as the primary source of economic benefits brought by a merger) is drastically restricted. This is the reason why we consider that the employee factor in the merger implementation is of key importance and should be central to the analysis of a merger's final outcome. Actually, any other source of economic synergy from the merger will necessarily deal with the internal organization of each former company (sales, marketing, R&D, accounting, finance, management control, computer system, and purchase units) in order to bring changes increasing overall efficiency. In such a process that implies intangible and information assets (such as working methods, rules, practices, standardization framework, software, etc), employees are likely to play a major role – either as a driving force, or as a powerful source of opposition.

How can these organizational changes be implemented? Our case studies offer interesting insights into this difficult problem. First of all, the unifying of the two existing systems is not considered as a credible solution. The main arguments raised against it are the cost, the internal resistance from employees on both sides, and a far too long precarious transition period. That leaves only two alternative means: the common adoption in the whole firm of one national system, or the creation of a new one. The first one seems to apply in situations:

(1) where there is a strong and clear commitment from the management to implement this solution (e.g. Europipe imposed the SAP accounting system used by Mannesmann to the French plants, which did not anyway previously share a common unified system), or

(2) when the system at work in one company emerges as indisputably superior. In the latter cases, reciprocal decisions could also help a smooth adoption: in V&M Tubes, the French management of the plant storage and cleanness and the German procedure regarding workplace security, unanimously viewed as superior, have been introduced in the counterpart plants. In some cases, we noted that the status quo (i.e. former company systems still run in parallel with minor changes while waiting for a new common standard system) is the only reasonable and feasible solution. The management must then wait for an opportunity to bring this change at the lowest possible cost and with the highest possible commitment and support from the affected staff. We noted in our cases two different factors that might bring such opportunity: a

technological change, that makes obsolete the old equipment, and a generation change (with the retirement of the majority of the employees in one unit). In each case, the introduction of new equipment and software, or the hiring of new employees (that do not share the historical heritage in terms of routines and practices from the pre-merger firm) can legitimate and make easier the adoption of a common shared system.

The interviews showed that there are three fields where these organizational changes are considered as particularly decisive but difficult: sales, accounting & finance, and computer systems. In any case, the final completion of these tasks far exceeds the period conventionally referred to as the merger and might require five to ten years. Information systems (IS) are obviously a critical issue in the merger because of their central role in the collection, processing and communication of information within a company. Therefore, a minimum level of integration must be rapidly achieved to implement the merger process, without disturbing too much the daily course of operations. This raises a number of technological problems, such as compatibility and redundancy of hardware and software, connectivity, standards, etc. Their resolution proves to be vastly time consuming and in most occasions the timetable planned initially for IS integration turns out to be severely underestimated, and even unrealistic. However, it would be misleading to only consider here the technical story. Actually, our case studies illustrate how these IS technical features are closely related to the specific work organisation in a company. This basically results from the three following factors.

(1) The organization of the IS department in the firm structure and its degree of centralization: is there a unique central department with all the staff or several teams working at the level of a division, a business line or a plant? Depending on the organization set up, the links and intensity of information exchanges between the production side, the sales and marketing, and the IS people will be very different.

(2) The level of autonomy and initiative given to divisions and/or plants to develop and implement their own products, software, solutions: this defines the degree of internal diversity of IS, but also the incentive in local innovation.

(3) The level of outsourcing of computer and communications systems operations, maintenance and upgrading: this is a strategic choice, usually decided by the management on the basis of careful cost/benefits analysis, but with serious consequences on the size, the skills and the mobility of the company's IS staff.

The first two points are not limited to IS but also apply to every central function, such as sales, accounting or R&D. Accounting and finance is another key field where the visible instrumental and practical differences mirror major discrepancies in the economic and industrial approach of the firm. Accounting classification, amortization rules, frequency and extent of financial planning are not only conventional rules that may be changed in a few days time. They ultimately refer to the strategic choices of the managers and the shareholders, and how they chose in the past years to financially picture the company and review its evolution. Any integration project of teams, software or methods must first deal with that problem and requires the prior definition of a common view on the merged company. Sales gives an example of how the organization chart shaped the skills and experience of employees and the resulting irreversibilities and obstacle to a major change. A sales department cannot immediately, without costs, loss of efficiency, and risk of losing the leading elements, be transferred to a new organization. We observed in our cases studies that this is a very slow process, mostly top-down driven with the managers experiencing and showing the example, and avoiding major frontal clashes (such as a direct mixing of national teams or direct competition). In some cases, for the most basic, disaggregated and repetitive tasks, such as order management and follow-up, the inertia and barriers to change inherited from decades of routine work and habits ensures that there is no other choice than to wait for the retirement of a significant fraction of the employees, and the hiring of a new generation to implement any change.

Unions and the National Issue

Within the context of a cross-border merger occurring in continental Europe, unions and employees representatives still have room for manoeuvre to impose their view on certain issues, especially for securing employment level or existing structures of representation. Yet, if Europipe is a firm ruled by the German law, with a supervisory board within which employee representatives and shareholders have an equal number of seats, this is incontestably due to the action of IG Metall. At the time of the creation of the company, the union feared that this merger would be an occasion for management and shareholders of the new firm to set a preceding case by escaping from the parity co-determination model instituted in the German steel industry (*Montanmitbestimmung*, 1951 law). At that time, management argued that Europipe was not producing steel but made tubes out of steel plates, and as a consequence did not fall under the 1951 law any longer. IG Metall threatened to mobilize the German workforce and put pressure on the management. In the end, Europipe agreed to implement a paritory supervisory board in accordance with the 1951 law (Turner, 1993, p. 33). However, contrary to this law, which requires appeal to a neutral arbitrator in the case of a blocked situation, shareholders have the last word, in accordance with the 1976 law on co-determination applying to firms of more than 2000 employees. On top of this, Europipe has no *Arbeitsdirektor*, who is a sort of a human resource manager, member of the management board, responsible for human resource issues, appointed by employee representatives (interviews, 11, 2000). Even though the participation regime of employee representatives at Europipe is noticeably different than the one that prevailed at Mannesmannröhren Werke AG, IG Metall succeed in preserving an important part of the role devoted to employee representatives.

Within German firms, employee representatives are given extended and co-determination rights by the law. When those firms are involved in a merger process, those strong national participation rights guarantee a certain influence of employee representatives over the merger process itself and a stability of the structures of employee's representation. Thus, the specific feature of the legal recognition of the role and place of employee representatives at national level significantly determines the supra-national representation structures.

Within the trans-national companies we studied, there are few (or no) exchanges and discussions among employee representatives coming from the different national territories on which the firm operates. Of course, supra-national representation structures, such as European Works Councils (EWCs) exist, but the different national groups of employee representatives seem to be weakly (or not at all) informed about the proceedings and decision-making processes of their counterparts. The French representative at Europipe's EWC has no information on German negotiations over wages. He declares:

> Even though employee representatives meet once or twice a year without management, those meetings are not the occasion for determining a joint strategy... (Europipe, 12, 2000)

This absence of dialog is also clear by the time of the creation of V&M Tubes. As members of the supervisory board and before giving their opinion about the merger project, German employee representatives came and visited French plants with which the tube department of Mannesmann was supposed to merge. They discussed with production managers, asked for detailed explanations about the production programme, the operations, the investments, etc, but they never expressed the wish to meet employee representatives of those plants. French and German union representatives sit together on the V&M Tubes' EWC nowadays, but they ignore each other much more than they talk.

Cross-border mergers are not used by unionists to create and implement a European solidarity. This conclusion meets the results of Bob Hancké (2000) in his study on EWCs in the car industry. Neither the challenge represented by the creation of a trans-national company, nor the existence of supra-national structures of employee representation constitute sufficient conditions for the implementation of an inter-national dialog among unionists. After all, the different unions are still strongly rooted in their own national framework.

Conclusion: Where is the European playing field?

In a research project on cross-border mergers focusing on the merger process, and the role of employees, we assumed we would find out new mechanisms, departing from national forms of employee participation on the one hand, and from former academic studies on European representation structures implemented in multinational firms, on the other hand. We thought that the arising of supra-national challenges within emerging trans-national firms would lead employees and their representatives to mobilize these issues in order to create new forms of dialog and participation that would coincide with management's need to make employees commit to the merger project. However, all through the interviews we have been conducting for this project, the remarkable presence of national issues within trans-national firms struck us. Hence, our own observations do not fundamentally diverge with the studies on multinational firms and the implementation of EWCs. However, our case studies bring to light an interesting phenomenon, never mentioned in the literature: the *national fair balance rule*, which is a very specific mobilization of the national issue under the fairness principle. Why do firms submit, even temporarily, to this logic? According to us, this question constitutes a highly interesting research track. We can already propose several potential answers:

- the intervention of national industrial shareholders having a close relationship with the trans-national firm (as suppliers of the firm for example) and interested in maintaining a certain activity level on the different national territories. This first hypothesis is rather insufficient, because those national industrial shareholders operate, and for a long time, all over the world, and do not depend any longer on national clients;
- a threat of employee mass protest in the case of substantial reduction of the workload, especially in countries such as Germany where unions are strong. However, the management also tries to maintain the activity on each territory, even those where unions are weaker, and management clearly knows the weakness of union coordination at European level;
- the need and the will of the young trans-national firm's management to get workers' support during the implementation and the construction of this trans-national firm.

Contrasting with the fair balance rule, the two other ways for the national issue to be present within the firms lead to differentiation, they are lasting and corroborate former studies' results. The merger as a creation of a trans-national firm rarely produces new forms of dialogue departing from the observed forms in supra-national structures implemented in companies with a long multinational history. The social issue and this absence of dialog among different national employee representatives are theoretically distinct and linked.

Yet, the European integration policy is, above all, an economic integration policy. However, the protection of employees vis-à-vis market integration still fundamentally rests on national States, in the absence of any European institution able to handle it (Streeck, 1998). As long as national States are responsible for carrying out social policy, trans-national firms will be forced to adopt distinct social regimes on different national territories and unions will turn to national States and continue to act within a strict national framework.

However, considering that national unions are embedded in the State's framework, the Europeanization of union organisations does not only mean redefining their strategy at a higher, supra-national level, but changing profoundly their own structures. There is no European State, and there will probably be none in a short as well as in a medium term. Rooting unions at a European level does not only mean federating different national unions but creating (inventing) absolutely new structures, as they are not going to negotiate with a European State, but with a European agency and with different European member States.

In conclusion, we would like to return to an argument that was briefly mentioned before about unions, but not developed. We actually said that unions were legal forms of employee representation coming from labour actions and strikes that aimed, among other things, at the recognition of structures responsible for representing labour. The paradox of the European structures is that they have been created without any labour action: without any mass mobilization of employees claiming their construction (Turner, 1996). There has been no European strike (except when Renault decided to close the Vilevoorde plant, see Didry, 2000). Moreover, the interviews with German workers in the car industry, conducted by Delphine Corteel,[2] showed that workers had few if no interest for European issues.

Considering the state and national nature of unions, in the absence of a real preoccupation of the employees themselves for European issues, it is reasonable to predict that employee representation structures created at European level will continue to be an information forum controlled by management and used by unions to preserve national forms of representation and participation. No European Directive will create a European mass labour movement.

Otherwise, even if Europe becomes an important issue of labour protest, and if, as a consequence, unions engage in a real and active Europeanization of their organizations, it may well be that the dialogue among employee representatives appear next to formal existing structures at the European level, as the example quoted in Turner (1996, p. 336) shows:

> EWC enthusiasts at DEC [Digital Equipment Corporation], in fact, viewed their unrecognised body as accomplishing the main positive function foreseen for EWCs in European firms: the exchange of information and the building of a cross-national network of plant activists. They argued that this outcome was in fact better than some officially recognised EWCs for which management paid the costs but also dominated the meetings, allowing little time for plant and union representatives to meet without management being present.

Beyond these institutional conclusions, it is worth pointing out the policy implications of our project in terms of future research. Our experience, built on the bibliographic research and empirical work on the case studies, indicates three main directions to be considered.

- The construction of a global database on European cross-border mergers, including social dimensions such as the evolution of jobs, production sites, brands, collective agreements, EWC. The lack of homogeneous, systematic, time series data on cross-border mergers in Europe is actually the major obstacle for further research using quantitative methods such as statistics, or econometrics. This is particularly important for having some temporal depth for reviewing the merger outcome and results. While significant information is produced at the announcement of the merger for financial markets and the review process by the European competition authority, it is extremely difficult to collect these data after some time. The systematic collection, processing

---

2   Individual interviews conducted with 30 workers at VW in Hanover, in October 1998, and with 25 workers at Leonische Drahtwerke AG, near Bremen, in April 1999. Fieldwork research for a PhD in industrial anthropology.

and follow-up over time of standardized information on the main operations could be the objective and the mission of a European Mergers Centre.

- Further research is clearly necessary on the significance, the scope, and the role of the 'national fair balance rule' we identified in our case studies. This actually constitutes a derogatory feature in economics and company management. It would be interesting to evaluate the extension of such a rule: is it limited to specific sectors? For what reasons? Is there any geographic concentration or is it widespread over European countries? Finally, the evolution of such a rule over time should be addressed: what is its average duration? What specific factors allow companies to be free from such a constraint? Is there some internal communication on that topic, particularly with employees' representatives, what is the assessment and influence of shareholders?
- The third key topic to be considered for future research is the analysis of the European dimension of employment in the coming European companies. Our study displayed very limited cross-border migration of employees at every management level of the companies involved. It also emphasized the persistent role and importance of face-to-face communications for management decisions (not only strategic but also standard operational ones), implying repeated, costly and time-consuming travels in each country. This demonstrates that the way companies can stimulate, encourage and train employees with an European dimension will play a major role in their future efficiency, growth and competitiveness. The associated respective role for the unions, the EWC, corporate initiatives such as universities or international training sessions, and public institutions either national or European, is for sure an open question. It therefore deserves careful attention since it might directly affect the future success (or not) of European companies and the design of efficient and relevant policies in that field.

Annex: Case Studies

Aventis

Creation	1999
Merged firms	Hoechst and Rhône-Poulenc
Employees	95,000
Products	'life science': pharmaceutical and agro business
Centralized activities	complete: R&D, marketing, production, administration
Lay-offs	no direct layoff but planned sale of the agro division and expected synergies of €1.2 billion between 2000 and 2002
EWC	EWC (April 2000) but an informal structure for employee representation at European level

Participation regime	Aventis is a French publicly traded incorporated company, headquartered in Strasbourg, and listed in Paris, Frankfurt and New York
Special remark	An ambitious worldwide stock purchase programme named 'Horizon' was launched in September 2000 in 56 countries. The chief of human resources argued that the preparation and the launch of an ambitious programme like Horizon just nine months after the creation of Aventis are contributing to the ongoing worldwide integration process. A total of 29,000 employees (34 percent of the eligible workforce) participated and will acquire 5 million Aventis shares. As a result, the employee ownership share amounts to 4 percent. High participation rates were recorded in France (42 percent), Japan (40 percent) and Germany (33 percent).

Europipe GmbH

Creation	1991
Merged firms	Mannesmannröhren-Werke, Bergrohr, GTS Industries, Usinor
Employees	1260 (in 1999)
Products	large diameter steel pipes
Centralized activities	sales, steel plates purchase, quality, production planning, R&D, investments, maintenance, accounting
Lay-offs	200 laid-off employees in Germany, 200 in France, closing of two tube plants, one in Germany, one in France
EWC	no officially recognised EWC, but an informal structure for employee representation at European level
Participation regime	holding located in Germany, rules by the *Montanmitbestimmung* law, softened by a company agreement: employee representatives have half of the seats at the supervisory board, but in case of blocked situation, shareholders have the last word.

Quante Pouyet

Creation	1998
Merged Firms	Quante AG, Pouyet SA

History	The Quante group had 66 percent of Pouyet shares since 1992 as it bought the shares held by a holding of employees: Pouyet Participation; in 1997, Quante AG tried to implement a joint strategy and to reorganize both firms but Acome, the minority shareholder of Pouyet, blocked this attempt, in 1998 the Quante group buys the rest of the shares of Pouyet.
Employees	2500 (in 2000)
Products	components and systems for communicative networks
Centralised activities	marketing, sales, R&D
Lay-offs	closure of a production site in United Kingdom
EWC	no EWC
Participation regime	holding located in Germany
Special remark	the Quante family decided to sell all its shares of the Quante group to the American firm 3M. Announced 1 February 2000.

V&M Tubes

Creation	1997
Merged firms	Vallourec, Mannesmannröhren-Werke AG
History	Mannesmann is the first external steel supplier of Vallourec; the two firms created a first joint subsidiary in 1990: IDPA and a second one with the Italian Dalmine, in 1994: DMW; those subsidiaries were already considered as experiences for a forthcoming merger
Employees	France-Germany: 6200 (in 2001), Brazil : 5000 (in 2001)
Products	tubes d'acier sans soudure
Centralised activities	reporting, suppliers, commercial departments, security, sales, R&D
Lay-offs	850 'lay-offs' in Germany managed by a social plan, most of those redundancies occurred through early retirement
EWC	officially recognized since April 2000
Participation regime	holding located in France

References

Aldrich, H. and Sproule Clare, P. (1983) The impact of corporate mergers on industrial and labor relations, in: W.H. Goldberg, *Mergers, Motives, Modes, Methods*, pp. 293–308 (Alderhot: Gower).

Althusser, L. (1995) *Sur la reproduction* (Paris: PUF).

Berle, M. and Means, G. (1932) *The Modern Corporation and Private Property* (New York: Macmillan).

Berndt, C. (1998) Corporate Germany at the crossroads? Americanization, competitiveness and place dependence, *ESCR Center for Business Research Working Paper 98* (Cambridge: University of Cambridge).

Bieshaar, H., Knight, J. and van Wassenaer, A. (2001) Deals that create value, *The McKinsey Quarterly*, No. 1, pp. 65–73.

Bower, J. (2001) Not all M&As are alike – and that matters, *Harvard Business Review*, March, pp. 93–101.

Breuer Jochen, P.(1999) Aufprall der Kulturen, *Mitbestimmung*, 12(99): 38–40.

Brouthers, K., van Hastenburg, P. and van den Ven, J. (1998) If most mergers fail why are they so popular, *Long Range Planning*, 31: 347–353.

Casper, S. and Vitols, S. (1997) The German Model in the 1990s: problems and prospects, *Industry and Innovation*, 4(1), pp. 1–13.

Clarke, T. and Bostock, R. (1997) Governance in Germany: the foundations of corporate structure, in: K. Keasy, S. Thompson and M. Wright (Eds) *Corporate Governance: Economic and Financial Issues* (Oxford: Oxford University Press).

Corteel, D. (1999) Flexibilité et post-taylorisme dans les usines automobiles allemandes, *L'Allemagne en chantier III* (Berlin).

Didry, C. (2000) La cause européenne de l'emploi, incohérences et potentiel du droit européen, de l'affaire Renault Vilvorde au contrôle des restructurations. Contribution to the Seminare 'les territoires de l'emploi. action publique et dialogue social', Florence, 5–6 May, 2000, manuscript, 33 p.

Edwards, T. (1999) Cross-border mergers and acquisitions: the implication for labour, *Transfer European Review of Labour Research*, no. 3.

Edwards, T. (2000) Multinationals, international integration and employment practices in domestic plants, *Industrial Relations Journal*, 31(2).

Fairburn, J.A. and Kay, J.A. (Eds) (1989) *Mergers and Merger Policy* (Oxford: Oxford University Press).

Fama, E. (1980) Agency problems and the theory of the firm, *Journal of Political Economy*, 88: 288–307.

Fligstein, N. and Freeland, R. (1995) Theoretical and comparative perspectives on corporate organization, *Annual Review of Sociology*, 21: 21–43.

Freeman, R. and Kleiner, M. (2000) Who benefits most from employee involvement: firms or workers, *American Economic Review*, 90(2): 219–223.

Golbe, D. and White, L.J. (1993) Catch a wave: the times series behavior of mergers, *Review of Economics and Statistics*, 75: 493–499.

Goyer, M. (1999) Boards, bankers and bureaucrats: corporate governance in France and Germany, 1980–1998. Paper presented to the conference on *Western Europe in an Age of Globalisation*, Center for European Studies (Harvard University), 26–28 February.

Griffith, V. (2000) The people factor in post-merger integration, in *Strategy + Business*, 20: 82–90.

Hancké, B. (2000) European works councils and the industrial restructuring in the European motor industry, *European Journal of Industrial Relations*, 6(1): 35–39.

Harbison, J., Viscio, A. and Asin, A. (2000) Making acquisitions work: capturing value after the deal, in: *Viewpoint Serie* (Booz Allen & Hamilton).

Hartz, P. (1994) *Jeder Arbeitsplatz hat ein Gesicht, die Volkswagen Lösung* (Frankfurt am Main: Campus).

Hitt, M.A., Hokisson, R.E. and Kim, H. (1997) International diversification: effects on innovation and team performance, *Product-Diversified Firms'*, *Academy of Management Journal*, 5: 1207–1251.

Hopt, K. (Ed) (1998) *Comparative Corporate Governance – The State of the Art and Emerging Research* (Oxford: Clarendon Press).

Hubbard, N. (2001) *Acquisition Strategy and Implementation*, revised edition, (Basingstoke: Palgrave).

Industrial Relations Europe (1994–2000)

Jensen, M. and Meckling, P. (1974) Theory of the firm: managerial behavior, agency costs and ownership structure, *Journal of Financial Economics*, 3: 305–360.

Jürgens, U., Naumann, K. and Rupp, J. (2000) Shareholder value in an adverse environment: the German case, *Economy and Society*, 29(1): 54–79.

Kaplan, S.N. (1997) Corporate governance and corporate performance: a comparison of Germany, Japan and the US, *Journal of Applied Corporate Finance*, 9(4): 86–93.

King, S. and Aisthorpe, P. (2000) Re-engineering in the face of a merger: soft systems and concurrent dynamics, *Journal of Information Technology*, 15: 165–179.

Kissler, L. (1988) La cogestion en République fédérale d'Allemagne: modèle et réalité, *Droit social*, No 12, December: 857–870.

Lattard, A. (1987) *La réduction du temps de travail en Allemagne fédérale, Etudes allemandes contemporaines* (Paris: CIRAC).

Lazarus, S. (1996) *Anthropologie du nom* (Paris: Seuil).

Lecher, W., Nagel, B. and Platzer, H.W. (1998) *Die Konstituierung Europäischer Betriebsräte - Von Informationsforum zum Akteur? Eine vergleichende Studie von acht Konzernen in Deutschland, Frankreich, Großbritannien und Italien*, Schriften der Hans-Böckler-Stiftung Band 35 (Baden-Baden: Nomos Verlagsgesellschaft), 290 p.

Lecher, W. and Rüb, S. (1999) The constitution of European Works councils: from information forum to social actors, *European Journal of Industrial Relations*, 5(1): 7–25.

Linn, S.C. and Zhu, Z. (1997) Aggregate merger activity: new evidence on the wave hypothesis, *Southern Economic Journal*, 64: 130–146.

Mayer, C. (1998) Financial systems and corporate governance: a review of the international evidence, *Journal of Institutional and Theoretical Economy*, 154: 144–165.

Mentre, P. (1994) *France et Allemagne les enjeux industriels*, Rapport de mission, Paris, Ministère de l'industrie, des Postes et Télécommunications et du Commerce Extérieur, p. 100.

Meschi, M. (1997) *Analytical Perspectives on Mergers and Acquisition: a Survey*, Centre for International Business Studies (London: South Bank University research paper 5-97).

Moerland, P.W. (1995) Corporate ownership and control structures: an international comparison, *Review of Industrial Organization*, 10(4): 443–464.

Mueller, D.C. and Sirower, M.L. (1998) *The Causes of Mergers: Test Based on the Gains to Acquiring Firms' Stakeholders and the Size of Premia*, Working Paper (Vienna: University of Vienna).

Müller, F. (1996) National stakeholders in the global contest for corporate governance, *European Journal of Industrial Relation*, 2(3): 345–368.

Mussati, G. (Ed) (1995) *Mergers, Markets and Public Policy* (Dordrecht: Kluwer Academic).

OECD (1994) *Merger Cases in the Real World, a Study of Merger Control Procedure*, p. 200 (Paris: OECD).

Piazza, E. (1999) Les *fusions transfrontalières, Aspects juridiques et fiscaux*, (mémoire de DEA).

Pryor (2001) New trends in U.S. industrial concentration, *Review of Industrial Organizations*, 18(3), May.

Rhodes, M. and van Apeldoorn, B. (1998) Capital unbound? The transformation of European corporate governance, *Journal of European Public Policy*, 5(3): 406–427.

Richter, A. (1997) *Restructuring or Restrukturierung? Corporate Restructuring in Britain and Germany* (London: London School of Economics, Center for Economics Performance).

Schweiger, D. and Denisi, A. (1991) Communication with employees following a merger: a longitudinal field experiment, *Academy of Management Journal*, 34(1): 110–135.

Silvia, S.J. (1999) Every which way but loose: German industrial relations since 1980, in: Martin Andrew, Ross George, *et al.* (Eds) *The Brave New World of European labor, European Trade Unions at the Millennium*, pp. 75–124 (New York, Oxford: Berghahn Books).

Soskice, D. (1999) Divergent production regimes: coordinated and uncoordinated market economies in the 1980s and the 1990s, in: H. Kitschelt, P. Lange, G. Marks, J.D. Stephens (Eds) *Continuity and Changes in Contemporary Capitalism* (Cambridge: Cambridge University Press).

Streeck, W. (1998) Gewerkschaften zwischen Nationalstaat und Europäischer Union, *WSI-Mitteilungen*, 1: 1–14.

Streeck, W. and Vitols, S. (1993) *European Works Councils: Between Statutory Enactment and Voluntary Adoption*, WZB Discussion Paper, 64 p. (Berlin: FS I 93-312).

Stylianou, A., Jeffries, C. and Robbins, S. (1996) Corporate mergers and the problem of IS integration, *Information & Management*, 31: 203–213.

Sudarsanam, S. (1995) *The Essence of Mergers and Acquisitions*, 303 p. (London: Prentice Hall).

Thelen, K.A. (1991) *Union of Parts, Labor Politics in Germany* (Ithaca and London: Cornell University Press).

Turner, L. (1993) *Beyond National Unionism? Cross-national Labor Collaboration in the European Community*, WZB Discussion Paper, 50 p. (Berlin: FS I 93-203).

Turner, L. (1996) The Europeanisation of labour: structure before action, *European Journal of Industrial Relations*, 2(3): 325–344.

Viscusi (1995) *Economics of Regulation and Antitrust*, with John Vernon and Joseph E. Harrington, Jr. (Lexington: D.C. Heath & Co, 1992), Second Edition (Cambridge: MIT Press, 1995), Third Edition (Cambridge: MIT Press, 2000).

Vitols, S., Casper, S., Soskice, D. and Woolcock, S. (1997) *Corporate Governance in Large British and German Companies*, Report of the Anglo-German Foundation for the Study of Industrial Society.

Waline, P. (1970) *50 ans de rapports entre patrons et ouvriers en Allemagne*, Tome 1: 1918–1945, Tome 2: depuis 1945, Cahiers de la fondation nationale des sciences politiques (Paris: Édition Armand Colin).

Windolf, P. and Beyer, J. (1996) Co-operative capitalism: corporate networks in Germany and Britain, *British Journal of Sociology*, 47(2): 205–227.

Chapter 11

The European Central Bank and the 'Economic Government of Europe'

Jean Paul Fitoussi and Jérôme Creel

Introduction

The scope of this chapter is to assess and evaluate the 'Economic Government' of Europe; in particular, it will focus on monetary policy, whose relevance has enormously increased since the creation of the Euro.

We will argue that, for a complete assessment, we cannot limit our analysis to efficiency considerations, which have been a priority in the design of European institutions, but instead consider the (until now) neglected principle of equity and democratic legitimacy.

The argument will be that a deficit of democratic legitimacy has, until now, been a flaw in the institutional design of Europe, so that the only direction that could be undertaken was towards a free-market oriented system, in which the principle of equity was in fact neglected. We will then focus more specifically on monetary policy, discussing the institutional design behind the creation of the European Central Bank (ECB), and the differences with other central Banks, namely the Fed and the Bundesbank (Buba); we will see that the 'democratic deficit' is statutory. We will then give an evaluation of the policy actually followed by the ECB. Although it is too soon to judge, the overall judgement ought to be positive, even if many choices in the past three years can be criticized. In particular, the decision to set the target rate of inflation at the excessively low level of 2 percent might have had an influence on the low growth of the Area. Finally, we will advance some proposals for reform that address the problem of legitimacy and of the neglect of the equity principle.

Democracy and Efficiency

Given the political difficulties linked to the process of unification, the European construction has until been driven by economic forces. The creation of a free trade area, and the set-up of a common policy for competition and regulation (in the hands of the European Commission) have pushed towards a unified goods market, further developed by free circulation of goods and capitals.

The 1990s have seen an important step forward in this unification process, with the creation of a common currency area (the Euro Zone) including 12 of the 15 members of the European Union. The successful introduction of Euro notes and coins in 2001 was a turning point of undeniable symbolic importance.

For history and culture, European countries were (and are) not ready to proceed towards stricter forms of political association. As a consequence, the process of unification has happened along the only possible dimension, namely the economic one. At present, even if it is not usually presented that way, we can say that there exists a 'Federal Economic Government' of Europe; this government is in charge of monetary policy (the ECB), of competition policies and regulation (the Competition Directorate of the European Commission) and, although only in an indirect way, of fiscal policies (through the Stability Pact). The defining characteristic of this government is that its (considerable) power is not in the hands of politically accountable bodies (such as national governments and parliaments), but rather of 'agencies': The European Commission, which has legislative power on competition policy and is involved in fiscal policy, can be dismissed by the European Parliament, but only under exceptional circumstances. Similarly, the ECB has its task defined by the international treaties, but is free in setting targets and objectives within these tasks; and, contrary to the vast majority of national central banks, it is not directly accountable for its actions before any political body.

Since the very beginning, an ambiguity has characterized the successive steps that have brought about the Union, creating a strange 'Political Object': national states have lost some sovereignty (as is inevitable in any process of federation); but this sovereignty, together with democratic legitimacy (and accountability), has not been transferred to Europe, because of the reluctance to push towards a supranational sovereign entity. National states, in spite of losing some of their prerogatives, are still a barrier between European institutions and citizens.

This ambiguity is at the root of the widely perceived problem of 'democratic deficit' of the European economic government. On many important matters decisions are made by a body that has no democratic accountability, and hence has no choice but to push towards free market reforms. The legitimate and desirable protection of market functioning and efficiency has been the sole criterion for judging the economic government. The tension between market principles and 'democracy principles' (equity and collective choice) has seen the latter completely subordinated, when in principle the contrary should hold. Over 20 years ago, Usher (1981) proposed substituting the economic efficiency criterion with another that seems particularly appropriated nowadays: a law, a policy, an institutional project, should be primarily evaluated by asking whether it reinforces democracy. 'Europe' has often been seen by citizens as an alien and bureaucratic entity, whose decisions were increasingly seen as affecting everyday life.[1] The only way to try to close this gap is to adhere to Usher's principle when redesigning the European institutions.

In light of these considerations, European institutions clearly appear biased as they stand. The criticism, nevertheless, has to be downscaled, being the whole European edifice is still under construction. In fact, it might seem too easy to criticize a project

---

1   This perception is certainly one, even if not the most important, reason for the growth of consensus for inward-oriented, anti-European right-wing movements, across all of Europe.

that is still incomplete, and in this sense the judgement should be suspended. The European convention, which has been given the task of proposing a 'Constitution' for Europe, is certainly an occasion to address the democratic deficit that affects European institutions, thus making them more effective and more accountable.

Macroeconomic policy is a crucial factor behind success (or failure) of an economy. Far from being able to bend market forces, it has nevertheless an important role in accommodating them, and in creating the conditions for certain outcomes that, for a variety of reasons, may be more desirable than others.

Recent developments in macroeconomic theory have gradually shifted attention from fiscal to monetary policy, which is nowadays seen as having a more active (and reactive) role in stabilizing economic activity and hence in the pursuit of the objectives of employment, growth, and low inflation. This is why this chapter focuses on monetary policy.

The next section will describe the institutional design of the ECB, and evaluate its behaviour in its first few years of existence. The unprecedented characteristics of the creation of the euro, and the short life of the ECB, make such a task harder, so that a comparison with other experiences (the US Fed, and the German Bundesbank) becomes crucial. Fiscal policy issues (in particular the stability pact) will be analysed in their relationship with monetary policy, in particular regarding the problems of coordination between an independent central bank, and 15 national fiscal authorities.

The European Central Bank: Design and Policy

The two acts designing the institutions of Europe, as they are at present, are the 'founding Treaty' signed in Maastricht in 1991, and the Amsterdam treaty, signed in 1997, which completes the set-up with the Stability Pact.

The Maastricht Treaty does set the objective of the Union in very general terms:

> The Community shall have as its task, by establishing a common market and an economic and monetary union and by implementing the common policies, [...] to promote throughout the Community a harmonious and balanced development of economic activities, sustainable and non-inflationary growth respecting the environment, a high degree of convergence of economic performance, a high level of employment and of social protection, the raising of the standard of living and quality of life, and economic and social cohesion and solidarity among Member States. (Art. 2)

But already in the immediately following Article 3a, the priorities become clear when it is stated that the community defines and will conduct 'a single monetary policy and exchange rate policy, the *primary objective of both of which shall be to maintain price stability* and, without prejudice to this objective, to support the general economic policies in the Community' (emphasis added). The Treaty further defines the famous 'Maastricht criteria' that countries had to fulfil in order to be enclosed in the single currency area.

Institutions: Fiscal Policy

The Amsterdam Treaty (Stability and Growth Pact) contains further provisions regarding fiscal policy, which have the scope of increasing transparency and control on public finances: each member country has to present annually a *'Stability Plan'* reporting forecasts about growth, and about public expenditure and revenues. These plans are examined by the European Council, which may subsequently provide 'recommendations', in cases where a country deviates from the plan. The pact further establishes what deviations from the 3 percent budget deficit target are acceptable (basically in case of strong recession), and gives the Council the right to sanction the country not respecting the limit. It is important to notice that the sanction is not automatic, but has to be decided by a qualified majority (two thirds) of the council members.

Institutions: Monetary Policy

The conduct of monetary policy is attributed to the European System of Central Banks (ESCB, or Eurosystem), composed of the ECB and the national central banks (NCBs) of the 15 Member States (only the central banks of the Euro Area are in charge of monetary policy, though). The primary objective of the Eurosystem is, as stated in the Maastricht Treaty quoted above, to maintain price stability. Only when it does not prevent the fulfilment of this objective, can monetary policy be directed towards other objectives.

Two bodies are in charge of decision making:[2]

(a) the *Governing Council*, which defines the guidelines of monetary policy, and is composed of the members of the Executive Board of the ECB (European Central Bank) and the governors of the Euro Area NCBs. It decides by simple majority. The President is chosen for 8 years by National governments;

(b) the *Executive Board* has to implement monetary policy in accordance with the guidelines laid down by the Governing Council. It comprises the President, the Vice-President and four other members, 'all chosen from among persons of recognised standing and professional experience in monetary or banking matters' (www.ecb.int).

A distinguishing feature of the ESCB is that it is independent, as, by statute, neither the ECB, nor an NCB, nor any member of their decision-making bodies, may take instructions from any external body, including Member States. The ECB has to present a yearly report to the European Parliament, which auditions its President quarterly. However, contrary to what happens at a national level, including for the US Congress with respect to the FED, the Parliament does not have the power to modify

---

2   A third body, the General Council has a temporary character, being composed by the President and Vice-President of the ECB, and the governors of the NCBs of all 15 Member States. Its main task is to coordinate monetary policies of the Euro Area and of the other Member States.

the statute of the ECB, nor to have a saying on its objectives. Finally, transparency is limited, as the secrecy of debates and votes is also assured by the statute.

Coordination

At the European level, the coordination of fiscal and monetary policy is a serious issue. The main problem is that a unique and centralized monetary policy is confronted with 12 (or 15) different fiscal policies, each responding primarily to national interests. The institutional design only provides for limited means of coordination. The treaties state that the President of the European Council and a Commission member participate in the ECB Governing Council meetings, and that, in turn, the ECB President attends to those meetings of the European Council that deal with monetary matters.

Coordination between countries is limited to the working of *Ecofin* (the group of finance ministers), where national policies are discussed, and that has the power to warn member states whose conduct is deemed potentially dangerous. Besides Ecofin, the *Eurogroup* is supposed to help disseminate information and coordinate national fiscal policies; this group is nevertheless consultative and informal.[3]

This lack of institutional means to coordinate fiscal policies among the Member States, and with a monetary policy, has a serious and potentially harmful consequence: in fact, it is probably at the root of the strictness of the emphasis on convergence (especially regarding fiscal policies). With coordination being attained by strict targets, economic policy loses the flexibility it needs to be effective.

Monetary Policy in Practice

Since the transfer of monetary policy to the ECB, in January 1999, the Macroeconomic situation has changed significantly more than once. As a first approximation, it can be said that the ECB has well accommodated these changes, and succeeded in keeping inflation low while not suffocating growth. In the three years 1999 to 2001, we can distinguish three different phases.

- From January to autumn 1999. The European economy was still under the influence of the Asian crisis, and the Bank stance has accordingly been rather accommodating (the refinancing rate has been 2.5 percent from April to November 1999).
- During the following year, the stance became progressively more restrictive, with the rate attaining the level of 4.75 percent in autumn 2000. After that moment, and until the following May, the rate did not change, despite expectations by the markets (one-year interest rates dropped below short-term ones) that seemed to be discounting a more expansive policy.
- After two small revisions (from 4.75 percent to 4.5 percent and then to 4.25

---

3   The *Broad Economic Policy Guidelines*, prepared annually by the Commission and adopted by Ecofin, are supposed to be another instrument of coordination. Even in this case however, these recommendations are non-binding.

percent in May and August 2001 respectively), the ECB considerably lowered the rate in the autumn of 2001, following the September 11 events. The rate was brought to its actual (June 2001) level of 3.25 percent. In the meantime, nevertheless, the Fed acted more rapidly and with larger changes. This has brought many to accuse the ECB of excessive inertia.

A closer look at this behaviour raises doubt that the ECB tended to overreact to inflation changes, and hence that growth could have been higher in the Euro Area (see Figure 11.1).

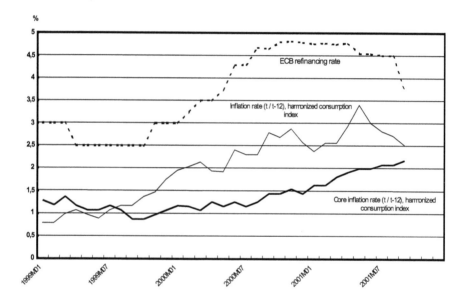

Figure 11.1   Inflation and interest rates in the Euro Zone

Source: Eurostat.

Note: Figure 11.1 reveals that the ECB began (November 1999) to raise rates, in response to actual, rather than core inflation. In fact, the latter did not seem to show a tendency to increase, the critical 2% level being only attained in the summer of 2001. This leaves room for a doubt: Was the ECB correctly forecasting the future increase of core inflation? Or did it actually contribute to that increase, by depressing growth and hence contributing to the Euro weakness and to imported inflation?

A look at the growth rate of the Euro Zone, and to its components (Figure 11.2), allows us to suggest a choice between these options; it shows that the slowdown begins in the first quarter of the year 2000, and that it is caused by a sharp fall in domestic demand. So, throughout the year 2000, we observe a monetary tightening in spite of weakening demand and basically stable (core) inflation. The timing just outlined induces us to believe that monetary policy was in fact procyclical over the years 2000–2001, strengthening the slowdown.

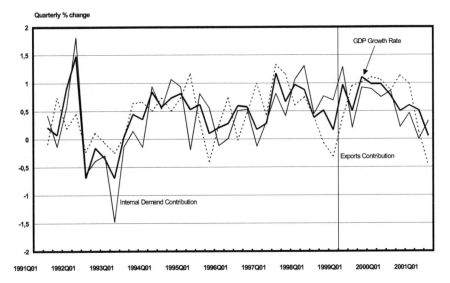

Figure 11.2   Contribution of demand components to Euro Zone GDP growth

Source: Eurostat.

It is worth noticing that the period of slow growth begun in early 2000 was the first of the Euro era, and that it was managed with a strong anti-inflationary bias.

The timing of monetary policy decisions in the year 2000 also raises the doubt that monetary policy in Europe was 'done in Washington'. In fact, between the summers of 1999 and 2000, the Fed tightened monetary policy, in a contest of domestic inflation acceleration. The same could not be said in Europe, where as we said core inflation was roughly constant, and where the overheating of the economy was less visible. This does not mean of course that the ECB was blindly following the Fed; simply, the fear of imported inflation (due to the synchronization of business cycles, and to tensions on the energy markets), had an important role in the decision to raise interest, even without a direct internal cause.

The inertia of the ECB can nevertheless be justified when we look at levels, and not only changes. The Fed happens to manage an economic environment close to full employment, in which it was therefore easier to react to changes in inflation or unemployment. The ECB instead, had to deal with a structural rate of unemployment considerably higher, and hence had lower freedom of action. And it is certainly not the task of the central bank alone to bring the 'natural' level of activity close to full employment.

In principle, the European Central Bank follows a rule called 'the two pillars': The bank is supposed to target, on one side, money growth (the M3 aggregate does not have to average more than a 4.5 percent yearly growth rate); on the other it targets inflation. In fact, it is increasingly evident that this strategy is artificial. The first pillar, money growth targeting, has (luckily) not been pursued, and the bank has substantially followed an inflation targeting rule. The continued reference to both pillars, has nevertheless allowed the bank to be less transparent in stating objectives and instruments linked to its inflation targeting strategy; this opacity, while sometimes keeping down the pressure, has contributed to the perplexity of markets about the conduct of monetary policy.

Once acknowledged that the bank has in fact followed an inflation targeting rule, we can ask how its behaviour compares to the rule followed by the Bundesbank. Creel and Fayolle (2002) estimate the Bundesbank reaction function using data from 1981 to 1998, and conclude that the bank did not overreact to changes in inflation. In fact, increases in inflation caused less than proportional changes in nominal rates, and hence lower real rates: output stabilization clearly was a concern. Creel and Fayolle conduct an experiment computing a 'Buba rate' with the Euro zone data since 1999, and compare it with the rate effectively set by the ECB. They conclude that the ECB has in fact conducted a less restrictive policy (lower rates) than the one that would have been followed by the Buba, had it been confronted with the same macroeconomic environment.[4]

To summarize, the assessment of monetary policy by the ECB gives us contrasting signals when we observe it in detail and compare it to the Buba and Fed behaviours:

(a) The ECB skilfully managed the recovery from the Asian/Russian crisis in 1999. It kept rates at a rate lower than the one that would have plausibly been chosen by the Buba in analogous circumstances.

(b) In autumn 1999 it did not react to the beginning to the slowdown; even more, it overreacted to an increase of prices not accompanied by higher core inflation. At that moment, it probably contributed to limit European growth.

(c) Since the beginning of 2001 it has reacted slowly, and marginally, to changes in the macroeconomic conditions. It has followed the Fed but less decisively. It looked as if the ECB was accumulating information on which to make a decision, but this inertia raised the doubts of markets about its capacity to manage the business cycle

As stated above, a series of justifications can be invoked to defend this behaviour, among which are the necessity to learn, for a young institution, and the situation in Europe, both institutional and macroeconomic (higher structural unemployment, problems of coordination with fiscal policy by 15 member states).

Credibility

The other crucial issue in evaluating a central bank action is the one of credibility. The agreement in the literature on a definition of credibility and consequently on the means of reaching it is far from settled (see Walsh, 1998, for a complete survey of the issues at stake). Here we will focus on two issues: the first is the ability of

---

4   Faust *et al.* (2001) conducted an analogous experiment, and pushed the argument even further, concluding that the weight on the output gap of the ECB is higher than in the case of the Buba.

the ECB to create (mainly affecting expectations) the conditions for a durably low inflation rate; the second is the issue of transparency in its action.

Regarding the first issue, the need to establish its own credibility as an 'inflation crusher' might explain the insistence of the ECB on controlling inflation even in periods when it was evident inflation was not a danger. The necessity for a young institution to build credibility through reputation could have induced it to pay the price of depressing growth.[5] Regarding the issue of transparency, its necessity is evident in an ideal case, in which the Bank operates with efficiency to reach correctly defined (and stated) objectives; i.e. when it follows a rule.[6] When it is not such a case, transparency may actually harm credibility by showing errors, divisions, and opacity in the decision process. However, the practice of Central Banking is often based on a certain degree of discretionary decision making (for example in the much celebrated case of the Fed); the issue of transparency then becomes non-trivial, as some secrecy is necessary for efficacy.[7] The ECB seems to have opted for the second strategy, and in fact releases the minimum of necessary information. Transparency is further hampered by the already discussed reference, in official documents, to a money growth objective (the first pillar), that is in fact neglected.[8]

In conclusion, it is certainly too soon to judge whether the ECB is correctly operating in order, on one hand, to manage macroeconomic fluctuations, and, on the other, to establish its credibility. We have offered many criticisms of its action, but we also acknowledged that its task is very hard, and that it faces institutional difficulties never experienced by other central banks. By weighting these two arguments, we can cautiously express an overall positive judgement.

In one crucial respect, however, we feel the action of the ECB should be criticized, and that action should be taken to correct it. The inflation target rate (2 percent) initially chosen by the ECB, probably influenced by the low inflation experienced in 1998, is certainly too low; this has caused growth to be lower than it could have been, and risks in the long run even affecting potential economic growth. A higher target, or equivalently the allowance of some discretionary deviations from the target would certainly not harm credibility, and, on the other hand, give (much needed) oxygen to the European stagnating economy.

---

5   Corsetti (2000) argues that in doing so the ECB did cause a depreciation of the Euro, and consequently imported inflation; this caused a shift of the short run Phillips curve, and consequently an increase (or a lower decrease) of structural unemployment.

6   This could be the case for the Bank of England, which follows a strict inflation targeting rule, and whose decision process is public.

7   Think for instance of the publication of the minutes of the meetings. Publicity may prevent members of the board from speaking openly, and/or show that some choices are not taken with due conviction. On the other hand, Buiter (1999) argues that publicity helps agents better understand the decision process.

8   Notice that the Bundesbank, which was supposed to follow a monetary target, did in fact also follow a Taylor rule (Clarida *et al.*, 1998; Faust *et al.*, 2001; Creel and Fayolle, 2002).

Reforming the European Policy Mix

The Euro Zone is composed of 12 countries that, in many respects, are still heterogeneous. This calls for differentiated economic policy measures that the actual policy mix is unable to warrant. In the previous section we discussed at length the working of the ECB, and the difficulties in coordinating with 12 fiscal policies. We also observed that the solution to this problem has been to tie the hands of the national states by means of the stability pact. In this section we will first return shortly to the problem of accountability for the ECB; we will then focus on the Stability Pact, showing the theoretical weakness of its raison d'être, and advancing some proposals for reducing its negative impact on the European economy.

Embedding the European Central Bank within European Democracy

As it stands, the ECB is not accountable in front of any political institution. We said above that, overall, the judgement on its work has, up to now, been positive. But if it were not (or if it were not in the future), no means of pressure would be available to contrast its action. Within very strict limits, every central bank is constitutionally made accountable for its action in front of democratically elected bodies.[9] The ECB is, in this sense, is a notable and inexplicable exception. The problem of accountability is even more stringent if we consider that the ECB follows a precise doctrine, repeatedly enunciated: reduce the government size and presence in the economy, and make the system more flexible by reducing labour market rigidities and cutting welfare-related public expenditures. By keeping the interest rate at high levels, the bank can actually sanction governments that do not follow its prescriptions, but this sanctioning power is not symmetric, as national governments have no instrument to punish the bank if it did not follow what they believed to be the right monetary policy.

In summary, the bank is free to chose its objective (the Maastricht treaty generally speaks of price stability), and to chose the instruments to pursue it. Furthermore, in its relationship with national governments, we observe an asymmetry in sanctioning power. This situation is not satisfying, not only because it changes the ranking, by submitting democratically elected bodies to an agency not accountable for its actions. But also because in doing so it exposes the ECB to criticisms that would be unwarranted had it a stricter relationship with governments.

This institutional and political disequilibrium could be tackled by giving to the European Parliament the power to modify (by qualified majority) the precise definition of price stability. This definition would be given after consulting with the bank itself, and other experts, among which are extra-European central bankers. A sufficiently high majority (e.g. two thirds) would avoid short-term thinking, and confer to the act the solemnity of a constitutional change. As a desirable side effect, such a change would also somehow alter the balance of power between the

---

9   The fact that the power to change the central bank statute is almost never utilized by parliaments does not mean it is useless. Its very existence, in fact, suffices for the bank to internalize the collective concerns, and act accordingly.

Parliament, the Commission and the Council, which is at present skewed in favour of the latter.

The Policy Mix and the Stability Pact

The Stability Pact puts in place sanctions for 'excessive deficits', and furthermore it constrains national fiscal policies to a (not better defined) medium-run balanced budget.

We believe that the Pact has flawed theoretical foundations, and furthermore it is not credible. We will analyse both issues in turn.

The theoretical foundations of the Stability Pact repose on an externality argument: excessive deficits by a country imply higher interest rates that negatively affect growth for the whole area. The externality would induce national governments to run budget deficits, allowing them to make the other countries 'pay the bill'. Furthermore, in case one country became insolvent, the ECB would be forced to monetize its debt, losing all credibility.

The argument could nevertheless go in the opposite direction, by showing that a positive externality may arise.[10] Suppose a budget deficit expansion occurred in one country. If this were unwarranted, it would result in inflationary pressure, and hence in reduced competitiveness. If it responded to a slump in production it would sustain demand and hence income. In both cases, demand for the other countries' production would increase, and their deficit (thanks to increased revenues) would be reduced. As for the risk of insolvency, its scarce plausibility in the present context, is apparent. So, the theoretical foundations for the Stability Pact, even assuming that their practical relevance was significant, appear to be rather shaky, and can be easily contrasted by a symmetrical argument showing that budget deficit can create positive externalities.

The other argument against the Pact relies on credibility considerations. In the present conditions it will most plausibly imply a restrictive stance of fiscal policy for the Euro Zone in the next 2 to 3 years. As this happens in conditions of weak growth, it implies pro-cyclicality of fiscal policy, i.e. that it will retard the recovery from this period of low growth. Mainly because of high interest charges,[11] the three largest countries, Germany France and Italy, do not have room for the automatic stabilizers to play, so that fiscal policy is (and will be) ineffective even facing transitory shocks.

Having lost the monetary instrument, the national governments find themselves forced by the Pact to use the fiscal one in an opposite sense to the one they would wish. The result of such an excessive constraint is a series of acts (creative accounting, overestimation of growth and fiscal revenues and the like) that affect their credibility, and create a permanent conflict with the Commission and the ECB.

---

10 We can also make a quantitative point, by noting that a 1 percent increase in the national fiscal deficit would imply a 1 or 2 tenths increase at a European level – barely significant, and unlikely to cause a change in the interest rate.

11 In 2001, interest charges were 2.7, 2.9 and 5.7 percent of GDP for Germany, France and Italy respectively.

The limits of the Pact were evident when the strictness of the rule forced the Commission to issue early warnings to three countries (Ireland, Portugal and Germany) whose problems were totally different (overheating economy in the first case, and excessive deficit, but with totally different causes, in the other two).

A unique monetary policy, which may prove too restrictive for some countries and too expansive for some others, requires compensating fiscal policies that have to have room to operate. In front of asymmetric shocks, and of different initial conditions, the increase in budget deficit dispersion would be desirable (Fitoussi, 1999), in order to allow a faster reabsorption, of the disturbance. The Stability Pact prevents this necessary differentiation, by forcing budget deficits to converge.

The Pact as it stands has three shortcomings: it prevents automatic stabilizers from acting countercyclically; it penalizes public investment, the most volatile and easily manageable item of public expenditure; it prevents poorer countries increasing public investment in order to sustain their catch-up (the case of Ireland is paradigmatic).

To avoid these contractionary effects, a reformed Stability Pact should impose convergence of the structural deficit net of public investment. This would ensure long-term soundness of public finances, leaving room for short-term countercyclical policies (at least by letting automatic stabilizers operate freely), and for investment aimed at increasing potential output.[12]

Considering public investment poses a problem that can nevertheless be turned into an opportunity: the definition of what to include in the category necessarily implies a degree of arbitrariness, that risks generating endless bargaining when discussing national stability plans. The task of precisely defining what belongs to the category should be given to the Council; it might use this defining power for pushing towards types of expenditure that it deems useful for enhancing growth and competitiveness (R&D, new technologies, human capital formation, and so on). More than laws and directives, such a power would put in place a system of incentives and hence could push towards a real European Policy on crucial issues.

Finally, a reformed stability pact would improve the policy mix, by increasing the room for monetary policy. National governments, not affected by strict constraints, would release their pressure on the ECB. The burden of pro-growth policies would fall off its shoulders, where it does not belong, and the bank could focus on managing short term fluctuations.

References

Buiter, W.H. (1999) Alice in Euroland, *Journal of Common Market Studies*, No. 37.
Buiter, W.H., Corsetti, G. and Roubini, N. (1993) Excessive deficits: sense and nonsense in the Treaty of Maastricht, *Economic Policy*, No. 16.

---

12 A really optimal rule should also consider interest payments (focusing on primary deficit), to avoid more indebted countries having to follow a systematically more restrictive fiscal policy. But, in the actual conditions, imposing such a rule would allow some countries to run deficits of up to 8 percent, and hence would be practically equivalent to no limit at all. The case for focusing on a structural deficit had already been made in 1993 by Buiter *et al.* (1993), who wanted precisely to allow the full deployment of automatic stabilizers.

Clarida, R.M., Gali, M. and Gertler, M. (1998) Monetary policy rules in practice: some international evidence, *European Economic Review*, 42: 10033–67.

Corsetti, G. (2000) Perspective on the Euro, *CESifo Forum*.

Creel, J. and Fayolle, J. (2002) La BCE ou le Seigneur des Euros, *Revue de l'OFCE*, March.

Faust, J., Rogers, J. and Wright, J.H. (2001) *An Empirical Comparison of Bundesbank and ECB Monetary Policy Rules, Papers*, No. 75, August.

Fitoussi, J.P. (ed) (1999) *Rapport sur l'état de l'Union européenne 1999* (Fayard et Presses de Sciences-Po).

Usher, D. (1981) *The Economic Prerequisites of Democracy* (Columbia University Press).

Walsh, C. (1998) *Monetary Theory and Policy* (MIT Press).

Part 3

Chapter 12

Economic Policy Coordination and Policy Regimes in the European Union

Stefano Micossi

Introduction

In the European Union, policy coordination amongst member states takes different forms, with varying participants, legal bases and degrees of coercion of public and private actors. However, one recurrent feature is that the goals and the balance of interests of the member states and other actors are embedded in the institutions and procedural rules that govern decision-making and the implementation of Community law. The peculiar balance of laws, implementing rules, sanctions and jurisdictional remedies defines the policy regime in the different areas.

Policy coordination is a broad expression. It has often been used to mean member states undertaking the same (discretionary) action – e.g. an expansionary fiscal policy – at the same time. However, it is not very likely that this kind of coordination will occur in the Union (although there have been examples) since decision-making is slow and powers are dispersed among independent authorities (the member states and their diverse institutions). Rather, coordination of policies will normally involve:

(i)   Shared goals, that is agreement on the common direction and end-result;
(ii) Community rules and procedures to force/encourage progress towards those goals in a medium-term perspective;
(iii) Different institutions and policy approaches for the implementation of common decisions in the member states.

In this context, the coordination of policies may entail a gradation of constraints on member states, from weak requirements of compatibility – not working at cross-purpose – to stronger conditions of consistency of policies and policy tools, up to the imposition, or prohibition, of certain actions (European Commission, 2001c).

Moreover, rules and procedures created for one purpose are subject to erosion and reinterpretation, and evolve in response to the interests of the different actors and their bargaining power, sometimes with radical deviations from the original intentions. Consequently, within each policy regime it is necessary to consider the tensions emerging between the actors and the ensuing modifications of goals and procedural rules.

This chapter discusses three regimes for the coordination of economic policies in the EC Treaty – 'pillar one' of the European Union – namely the Single Market, macro-economic policy coordination, and the Open Coordination Method increasingly applied to a broad range of social policies to foster their 'convergence'. For each regime, the paper highlights the relationship between policy goals and institutional design, and the evolutionary forces at work. An overall assessment of their interaction in shaping 'pillar one' economic policies concludes the chapter.

Integration in the Internal Market

The Single Market is the paramount example of 'negative' integration – following Jan Tinbergen's well-known definition – that is, integration achieved by removing obstacles to the operation of market forces and 'creating an area without internal frontiers in which the free movement of goods, persons, services and capital is ensured' (Article 14 of the EC Treaty).

The institutional design is relatively straightforward. The 'motor' is the principle of mutual recognition of national laws and regulations, first established by the Court of Justice with its famous 'Cassis de Dijon' decision in 1979. Mutual recognition may be denied, on a non-discriminatory basis, for legitimate reasons of public interest when it can be shown that the national rules of another member state do not afford 'equivalent protection'.

In such case, the Community can intervene and issue a directive establishing a common platform of protection – through 'minimal harmonisation' – to eliminate the restriction and undesirably low national standards. Accordingly, 'new approach' directives only determine the 'essential requirements' of protection and not the technical details of implementation; once the essential requirements are met, mutual recognition cannot be refused and becomes an 'absolute' principle.

Competition policy completes the system by preventing anti-competitive practices in the enlarged European market and restraining member states' ability to support 'national champions' with state aid.

Two aspects of this system are worth stressing; in a way they are the two sides of the same coin. On one side, the system requires the Community to intervene only when there is a threat to the principle of free circulation but otherwise lets different national rules coexist. It is thus a flexible system that – unlike other parts of the Treaty – contains intrinsic safeguards of subsidiarity.

On the other side, as a result of the principles of 'direct effect' and 'supremacy' of Community law, established by the Court of Justice in the early 1960s,[1] and the Commission's 'own' powers to prosecute infringements of Community law,[2] the binding force of negative integration on member states is quite strong. Mutual recognition implies that national rules for the protection of safety, health, consumers, savers and the environment, will compete with each other; with the result, it has been

---

1   Case C-26/62, Van Gend Loos v. NDL Administratie der Belastingen, *ECR* 1963 p. 1, and Case C-6/64, Flaminio Costa v. Enel, *ECR* 1964 p. 585.

2   Articles 211 and 226, and the specific powers for the implementation of competition policy under Title VI of the EC Treaty.

claimed, that fear of driving away the mobile factors of production may lead to a regulatory 'race to the bottom'.

Scharpf (1999), for example, has argued that the balance between the goals of an integrated market and a cohesive society has been skewed unduly in favour of the former by this 'constitutionalisation' of integration and competition rules. He refers, in particular, to member states' inability to use macro-policies to fight unemployment, to tax mobile factors of production for re-distributive purposes, and to grant monopoly power to public utilities for reasons of general interest.

In reality, the first and second of these restrictions are more a consequence of globalisation and capital mobility than a specific effect of Community policies, and the third may be overrated, as will be discussed. Scharpf himself is ready to acknowledge that a regulatory 'race to the bottom' has not occurred in critical policy areas such as the environment.

But the indictment is more serious: it is that Community policies of market integration (with majority voting) have caused a permanent loss of control by member states over the fundamental direction of their economic policies.

It seems to me that this contention is contradicted by actual developments in important policy areas. I will provide examples from financial services and public utility services, and discuss some recent changes in decision-making in the Single Market.

Financial Services

Basically, the free circulation of services in the Single market rests on the same principles as apply to goods. Freedom to provide services is listed, along with the other Single Market freedoms, among the fundamental objectives of the Community. Financial services fall within the general category of services (Articles 49–55 on the freedom to provide services and Articles 43–48 on the freedom of establishment). However, in 1981, the Court of Justice ruled that these provisions were not 'directly applicable' and had to be implemented by directives (Story and Walters, 1997). The member states were thus able to retain control of the content of Community legislation.

In principle, mutual recognition (of national licences) and 'minimal' harmonisation (of prudential rules) are fully applicable to financial services (O'Keeffe and Carey, 2002). A (non-discriminatory) restriction on the provision of services may be justified by a legitimate ('general good') interest of a non-economic nature, as in 'Cassis de Dijon', where 'that interest is not safeguarded by the rules to which the provider of the service is subject in the member state of its establishment',[3] and the restrictions are necessary and proportionate for the purpose.[4]

In practice, however, mutual recognition in financial services has not worked and the market for financial services has remained segmented along national lines; so much so that the European Council in Cardiff (1998) deemed it necessary to launch

---

3　Case C-279/80, Criminal proceedings against Webb, *ECR* 1981 p. 3305 §9.

4　Case C-55/94, Gebhard v. Consiglio dell'Ordine degli Avvocati e Procuratori di Milano, *ECR* 1995 p. I-04165.

a new Financial Services Action Plan (FSAP) and adopt special decision-making procedures for its implementation (cf. the Report by the Committee of Wise Men 2001). The main reason is that countries with higher standards of investor protection and business conduct wanted to prevent their erosion by the free supply of services by providers from other member states. 'Single passport' rules for providers of financial services have thus had to coexist with host-country business conduct and investor protection rules, which have hampered integration and effective competition.

The prevalence of host-country rules was implicitly recognised by Article 11 of the Investment Services Directive (93/22/EC), which enumerates objectives of minimal protection that do not preclude member states from enacting more stringent rules (Tison, 2002). While these may not lead to unjustified restrictions on the free movement of services or financial firms, in practice large differences in national rules have been deemed compatible with the Treaty even when serving similar purposes.

Accordingly, this is an area where member states have not relinquished control and national preferences have delayed and muted integration. Quite clearly, progress has been dictated by the needs of the financial industry much more than the Treaty rules on integration (Story and Walter, 1997). Rules and procedures have accommodated national preferences rather than bending them.

Public Services and the Application of Article 86

Public services constitute a sensitive aspect of public policy. Since the late-1980s the Commission has gradually tried to apply competition rules to this area, which is dominated by large state-owned companies. At the outset the Commission was careful not to propose a general liberalisation programme and proceeded instead on a pragmatic step-by-step basis.

The rationale for the liberalisation and privatisation of public utilities was self-evident. In most instances, public ownership of utilities had resulted in expensive and low-quality services, slow innovation and large financial deficits; the interests of politicians, managers and employees had prevailed over those of consumers. Experience in the UK indicated that the liberalisation of telecommunications and gas had brought substantial benefits. From a European perspective, the fragmentation of utilities markets came to be seen as a major obstacle to innovation and growth. Meanwhile, technology had started to erode the 'natural monopoly' justification for public ownership, especially in telecommunications.

The Treaty provisions concerning Single Market policies for public utilities are contained in Article 86 of the EC Treaty. Paragraph one provides that member states may not adopt measures contrary to the Treaty, notably as regards non-discrimination and competition rules. Paragraph two balances the previous provision by requiring that the application of the Treaty in this area does 'not obstruct the performance, in law or fact, of the particular tasks assigned' to public utilities. Paragraph three entrusts the Commission with the task of overseeing the application of these principles and gives it the power – 'where necessary' – to address appropriate directives or decisions to member states.

This last provision is the most contentious since it gives the Commission 'own' powers to issue directives without Council and Parliament approval. However, while upholding the use of these powers against member states on various occasions, the Court of Justice has ruled that their scope is defined by the norms that the Commission is trying to enforce. In other words, directives issued under Article 86 cannot be used to introduce new general obligations on member states.

For its part, the Commission has clarified that Article 86 only applies to services of economic interest and companies that are engaged in commercial or industrial activity, and has declared that it will respect the following principles:

(i) neutrality with regard to the (public or private) ownership regime (under Article 295 of the Treaty);
(ii) freedom for member states to define public service and public service obligations; and,
(iii) proportionality of measures restricting competition and internal market freedoms, in the sense that they may not exceed what is necessary for effective fulfilment of the mission entrusted to the public utility company (European Commission, 2001a).

Thus, the goal of market opening finds a limit in public service obligations. Member states may maintain privileges and exclusive rights for public utilities or special funding arrangements to ensure that these obligations are met. Restrictive measures must respect principles of transparency, necessity and proportionality, but they are by no means excluded.

Moreover, in a public speech in October 1996, the then competition commissioner, Karel van Miert, explained that 'whenever the Commission has to adopt measures on the basis of Article 86, it always takes care to carry out extensive consultations with the European Parliament, the Council, the Member States and the parties concerned to reach the broadest possible consensus'.

Early experience with the application of competition policy in this area did produce controversy and friction with some member states. Their concerns found their way into the Treaty on the occasion of the revision in Amsterdam. The new Article 16 (formerly 7d) of the EC Treaty provides that 'the Community and the Member States . shall take care that such services operate on the basis of principles and conditions which enable them to fulfil their missions'.

The application of these principles is reflected in the uneven pace of liberalisation, most advanced in telecommunications and air transport, less advanced in postal services, railways, and gas, where it is feared that the market would not ensure adequate services throughout the country, and the technology and infrastructure lend themselves less readily to a multiplicity of providers. Decisions to proceed or delay are taken at the highest level by the European Council, as recently shown again in the case of energy market liberalisation.

Changing Decision-making Procedures

The Single Market legislative programme was, by and large, completed by 1993 and soon after started to make its impact felt. Under its rules, the Community has acquired extensive powers of scrutiny and oversight of national legislation. Council

Directive 98/34/EC (previously 83/189/ECC) requires all technical measures liable to affect the free circulation of goods and services to be notified to the Commission; in 1996, the Court of Justice ruled that measures that had not been notified would be null and void.[5]

The Commission is charged with ascertaining whether technical measures are compatible with the free movement obligations; it may issue a 'reasoned opinion', demanding appropriate changes and, if the member state concerned refuses to comply, it may take the case before the Court of Justice. It may also ask the member state to suspend adoption of the national measure (standstill).

On the other hand, as mentioned earlier, member states may adopt restrictive measures to the extent that they can show that there is a 'sufficient' public interest. Safeguard measures are explicitly allowed under Articles 30, 46 and 95 of the EC Treaty, on various grounds of 'imperative need', and may also be provided for by individual liberalisation directives.

The post-1992 balance between the Community goal of liberalisation and member states' ability to protect public health and safety was questioned following the 'mad cow' food scare in 1997. Member states complained that Commission powers interfered unduly with national prerogatives. The result was that Article 95 – the principal legal basis of Single Market legislation – was amended to correct the balance of powers in favour of member states.

Accordingly, Paragraph Four now provides that member states may maintain national measures – on grounds of major need referred to in Article 30, or relating to the protection of the environment or the working environment – even after the adoption of harmonised legislation; and Paragraph Five allows member states to introduce new measures in a harmonised area based on new scientific evidence or specific problems that have emerged after the adoption of harmonised legislation. After a national measure has been notified, the Commission has six months (12 in exceptional cases) to decide whether it is compatible with the Treaty – a very tight time constraint in view of the complex procedures. In the absence of a decision, the measure is deemed to be approved. If a restrictive national measure is found to be legitimate, the Commission must immediately propose new legislation.

Thus, member states' powers to maintain national measures and to take protective action for reasons of public policy have been enhanced, and the Commission's powers to oppose them have been curbed. The Council has shown that it is fully capable of changing the Commission's powers when these are found to interfere excessively with national prerogatives.

Two other developments in recent legislation are worth discussing for their effects on the content and quality of Union legislation and the balance of power within the 'institutional triangle' of Union institutions.

The first development is the adoption – by the European Council in Göteborg in June 2001 and the European Parliament in February 2002 – of the new 'Lamfalussy' procedures for decision-making in the field of financial services.

These procedures have been designed to speed up implementation of the FSAP; however, a side-effect has been an increase in the scope of primary legislation and

---

5   Case C-194/94, CIA-Security International, *ECR* 1996 p. I-2211.

the relative weight of national governments, the Ecofin and the Commission in shaping financial market rules. The reason is simple: the responsibility for primary legislation (Level 1 legislation) has been assigned to the Ecofin Council (with co-decision with Parliament), assisted by a new Council Committee – the European Securities Regulatory Committee (ESRC) made up of member state officials. The task of enacting implementing regulations (Level 2 legislation) has been assigned to the Commission assisted by the Securities Committee under standard 'Comitology' procedures. Financial market regulators – such as the British FSA, the Italian Consob and the French COB – are consulted and may give their views on legislation and implementing rules; however, their formal task has been narrowed to ensuring the consistency of implementing measures at national level (Level 3). The Commission has also acquired strong powers of enforcement of common rules.

As may be seen, the first two legislative proposals under discussion with the 'Lamfalussy' procedures – the Directives on market abuse (COM(2001) 281 of 30 May 2001) and on the single prospectus for security issues (COM(2001) 280 of 30 May 2001) – are characterised by very detailed and complex harmonising prescriptions in areas normally left to secondary legislation in national regulation. It appears that member states officials and the Commission are exploiting their new place in the legislative process to regain ground at the expense of national agencies; as is usually the case, hard bargaining leads to complex legislation that will be more difficult to implement.

The Coordination of Macro-economic Policies in the European Union

Under Title VII (Articles 98-124) of the EC Treaty, the framework for the coordination of macro-economic policies rests on three pillars:

(i) A single monetary policy geared mainly to maintaining price stability and entrusted to an independent central bank (the ECB), which may support the general economic policy of the Community when this does not endanger the primary target of price stability;[6]

(ii) Decentralised fiscal policies, which, however, have to respect the twin constraints of the Excessive Deficit Procedure (Article 104 of the EC Treaty, forbidding deficits in excess of 3 percent of GDP) and the Stability and Growth Pact (SGP, aimed at achieving a balanced budgetary position in the

---

6 The Community does not have an explicit exchange rate policy. Article 111 of the Treaty leaves open the possibility for the Council, 'acting unanimously', to conclude agreements on an exchange rate system (Paragraph One) and, lacking such an agreement, to formulate by qualified majority general orientations for exchange rate policy in relation to third currencies. Any such action must be 'consistent with the objective of price stability' and may be taken only in 'exceptional circumstances' such as an 'evident misalignment' of the euro exchange rate (Council Resolution on the Co-ordination of Economic Policies in Phase Three of EMU and Articles 109 [now 111] and 109B [now 111§2] of the EC Treaty).

medium term);[7]

(iii) A procedure for mutual surveillance of economic policies – which member
states 'shall regard as a matter of common concern' – entrusted to the Ecofin
Council and implemented by the latter by agreeing and jointly monitoring
the Broad Economic Policy Guidelines (BEPG).

The first two pillars do not entail coordination to achieve a specific aggregate fiscal
policy stance, although the Council has the power to act in special circumstances.[8]
The policy mix is the indirect result of the independent actions of the ECB and the
national governments. Thus, here the policy approach displays features of 'negative
integration' and subsidiarity, as in the Single Market.

The rationale of the SGP mainly lies in the possibility that EMU may loosen the
financial constraint on deficit spending due to member states' ability to borrow on a
broader capital market and at cheaper rates that no longer incorporate a risk premium
for exchange rate depreciations.

The status of the BEPG is less clear. According to Article 99 of the EC Treaty,
'the Council shall, acting by a qualified majority on a recommendation from the
Commission, formulate a draft for the broad guidelines of the economic policies
of the Member States and of the Community, and shall report its findings to the
European Council' (Paragraph One). In turn, the European Council shall 'adopt a
recommendation setting out these broad guidelines' (Paragraph Two). The Ecofin
Council monitors the consistency of economic policies with these guidelines
(Paragraph Three) and, when it finds that they are not consistent or 'risk jeopardising
the proper functioning of economic and monetary union', may issue a recommendation
to the member state concerned (Paragraph Four). The Commission is empowered to
obtain all the necessary information from the member states, and has the initiative in
proposing the draft guidelines and preparing periodic assessments of performance.
Council decisions in this area, including recommendations, are not legally binding,
although they do carry considerable weight.

In the three years since the inception of EMU, the present approach has worked
satisfactorily. The ECB has acted cautiously but on the whole effectively in the face
of incipient inflation in 2000 and the economic slowdown in 2001, and its record
of independence has been good (Alesina et al., 2001). Public debts and budget
deficits have been coming down, as a ratio to GDP, and automatic budget stabilisers
provided desirable support for economic activity in 2001 (some 0.5 percent of GDP,
according to Commission estimates). The overall policy-mix is regarded as having

---

7   The SGP consists of a European Council Resolution (97/C 236/01) adopted in
Amsterdam on 17 June 1997, two Council Regulations – both of 7 July 1997 – n. 1466
on strengthened surveillance and coordination of economic policies, and n. 1467 on the
clarification of excessive deficit procedures, and a Code of conduct on the content and
presentation of stability and convergence programmes, adopted by the Ecofin Council in 1998
and revised in July 2001 (cf. European Commission, 2002a).

8   For example, in October 1999 the Ecofin Council approved a directive to let member
states temporarily lower (for three years) the VAT rate on certain labour intensive services, if
they so wished, in order to cushion the cyclical impact of a sharp downturn of activity in Asia
(cf. Directive 1999/85/EC of 22 October 1999).

been broadly appropriate, although not as aggressively counter-cyclical as in the United States (European Commission, 2002a; ECB, 2002).

And yet, some of the member states and the Commission would like a radical change. In a widely-publicised pamphlet, Jacquet and Pisany-Ferry (2001) have advocated strengthened macro-policy coordination that would encompass joint determination of the fiscal stance and the policy mix, as well as 'positive ECB reaction to structural reforms that boost output'.

They argue that coordination to prevent destabilising behaviour by some actors (regime-preserving coordination) does not necessarily ensure policy-optimising coordination, that is 'the best possible distribution of fiscal policy decisions', notably in view of the increased interdependence brought about by EMU and the Single Market programme. In their view, policy coordination at the euro-zone level would provide support for national reform policies and 'relieve the ECB from the excessive burden of being viewed as the sole policy actor within the area', thus reinforcing, rather than weakening, its independence.

This argument for 'positive' coordination mainly relies on the existence of fiscal policy spillover across countries, due to the (positive) interest rate effects of expansionary demand policies and other inflation and productivity effects of the public sector budget. However, empirical evidence of such spillover effects is scanty (Gros and Hobza, 2001; Wyplosz, 2002). In addition, the desirability of discretionary anti-cyclical fiscal policy finds little theoretical and empirical support (Taylor, 2000; Balassone and Franco, 2001).

A different case for coordinating public spending policies has been made by Melitz (2000), who has argued that – while the effects of automatic stabilisers are on the whole rather weak[9] – public spending in the Union suffers from a systemic tendency to increase more rapidly than taxation because of aging and other structural reasons, and that opportunistic governments will exploit periods of rapid economic growth to relax spending constraints. Korkman (2001) agrees that 'there is nothing in the SGP ... to prevent member states from undertaking pro-cyclical expenditure increases and tax reductions during periods of strong growth'.

In reality, a majority of member states already have some sort of medium-term framework for keeping public expenditure and the overall deficit in check, including internal stability pacts to keep local government spending in check (Fischer, 2001). Furthermore, empirical evidence indicates strong disciplinary effects of the public debt on the size of the deficit (Melitz, 2000 and Wyplosz, 2002), and no evidence of asymmetrical behaviour of the deficit in downswings and upswings (Wyplosz, 2002). Sapir and Buti (2001) find that EMU has passed the early credibility test since 'pre-emptive co-ordination aimed at reducing policy-induced shocks and enhancing adaptability to shocks has worked fairly well'.

The main criticism, however, is one of excessive rigidity of the SGP rule, especially in view of the protracted slowdown of economic activity in the European Union since 2001 that is pushing a number of member states against the 3 percent deficit ceiling. It is argued that the Union is confronted with an exogenous shock and that the SGP rule is unduly constraining countries' ability to take growth enhancing measures.

---

9   The same result is obtained by Wyplosz (2002).

Accordingly, it is proposed that growth-enhancing investment should be excluded from the deficit ceiling (the so-called *golden rule* of public finance). The problem is that the notion of public investment is ill-defined and exposed to manipulation by 'opportunistic' politicians (Balassone and Franco, 2001). Furthermore, the golden rule may open the way to the excessive growth in government debt that the SGP was meant to avoid.

In order to meet this objection, Pisany-Ferry (2002) has proposed that a 'debt sustainability pact' be substituted to the current deficit-based SGP as a 'sound finance' criterion; but the definition of the debt would have to include all government liabilities, including unfunded pension liabilities and any other off-balance sheet items. The proposal makes good economic sense, since it would allow greater flexibility to accommodate growth-enhancing investment and, over time, favour high-return public investments. However, given that most Union member states have large pension liabilities, in practice the increase in budgetary flexibility would be limited.

While a compelling analytical and empirical case for change has not been made, the Ecofin Council and the Commission are pressing for strengthened coordination through the BEPG. In February 2001, the Ecofin Council addressed a recommendation to the Irish government, under Article 99§4 of the EC Treaty. The Irish budget was criticised for being pro-cyclical and 'inconsistent with the BEPG adopted by the Council in 2000', in spite of a sound government budget and the stellar performance of the Irish economy over the previous decade. Soon afterwards, in March, the Ecofin Council and the Commission sent a Report to the European Council in Stockholm on 'The contribution of public finances to employment and growth'. The report posits additional requirements for sound public finances, namely:

(i)   The need to avoid pro-cyclical fiscal policies, notably by imposing strict expenditure controls;
(ii) Criteria for sustainable tax cuts in the medium term, including 'an appropriate balance and sequencing ... between running down public debt, cutting taxes, and financing public investment in key areas'; and
(iii) A strategy for tackling the economic and budgetary consequences of an aging population, including pension reform.

The European Commission's (2001b) Communication provides an ambitious blueprint for overhauling the content and procedures of policy coordination within the Ecofin Council. Many of the suggestions in that document have been retained in the Commission's proposals to the European Convention convened to prepare the institutional reforms of the Union (European Commission, 2002b).

The Commission wants to develop 'activity indicators to provide a synthetic view of the euro area' and, on that basis, 'as an exact an evaluation as possible of the stance of the policy mix', prepared twice a year. It also intends to elaborate, in consultation with the ECB, detailed rules on the appropriate policy response to changing economic conditions – including rules for the general conduct of policy, policy responses to particular shocks, and the instruments necessary for the implementation of these responses. And it would propose fully specified common policies for the Union and the Euro Area.

Strengthened coordination on all macro and structural matters would require appropriate institutional and procedural changes. The Commission proposes the following: the Euro-zone Council should be given formal decision-making powers; the Commission should be given 'own' powers in the drafting and implementation of the BEPG, including the possibility of issuing warnings addressed directly to member states that the Council could only reject by a unanimous vote; there would be regular formal meetings between the presidents of the ECB, the Euro-zone Economic Council and the Commission so as 'to strengthen the European view of the assessment of national policies';[10] and, finally, national policy-making processes would be strictly coordinated with decision-making at Union level.

The position of the Ecofin Council on these proposals is not yet known. However, they are surely determined to have the last word on the substance of policy decisions. This was apparent in their decision in February 2002 to reject a Commission proposal to address an early warning to Germany and Portugal with regard to their failure to comply with the budgetary objectives in their stability programmes.[11] In June 2002, in Seville, the European Council decided to relax somewhat the SGP obligations by requiring member states to aim at a budgetary position 'close-to-balance' over the medium term, rather than 'balanced', and by deferring (by one year) the deadline for achieving that goal by the countries that were out of line.

These procedural changes would undoubtedly strengthen Community institutions and their capacity to intrude into national policies enormously. Whether in practice this would be feasible and effective is an open question. However, some of the changes seem to be already taking place without any serious discussion of their desirability or much evidence of the need for them.

Positive Integration and the 'Open Coordination' Method

Historically in the European Community, every step in the integration process has been accompanied by measures of 'positive integration' designed to facilitate adjustment and maintain economic and social cohesion while strengthening market forces and competition. These polices were mainly of a re-distributive nature[12] and

---

10 The possibility of a formal participation of the president of the ECB in the meetings of the Eurogroup has been envisaged in the Nice Treaty revisions. As has been noted, while an exchange of views may always be useful, there is a risk that institutional meetings of this type provide an officially sanctioned forum for fiscal authorities to put undue pressure on the ECB (Alesina *et al.*, 2001).

11 The Commission inserted a statement in the official minutes of the meeting declaring that Germany's and Portugal's policy commitments 'respond to the substance of the concern of the Commission Recommendation for an early warning', and reaffirming the essential role of the early warning procedure in the SGP. But the damage was done.

12 The Common Agricultural Policy and the Structural and Cohesion Funds are the paramount examples; but the complete list is much longer and comprises such things as research and industrial policy, the trans-European networks, consumer protection, the environment, assistance in institution building (as in the present enlargement exercise), and more.

designed to gain acceptance of the 'core' integration goals of the Community, but over time they have proved ineffective, expensive, and a source of major distortions in the economy. Moreover, the policy consensus in the Union has increasingly stressed flexibility, investment in human capital and incentive-compatible social policies rather than protection.

With the Amsterdam revision, a new tool of policy coordination has found formal recognition in the Employment Title of the EC Treaty (Articles 125-30), following early experiments in labour market policy coordination within the Labour Ministers Council (the 'Luxembourg' coordination process). Other 'processes' were added in the subsequent years by the European Council, with coordination extending to structural reform policies (the 'Cardiff' process), macro-policies (the 'Cologne' process), and a comprehensive programme for innovation and human capital (the 'e-Europe' programme adopted in Lisbon). The new approach was baptised the 'open coordination method' (OCM) by the European Council in Lisbon.

At the outset, explicit recognition of employment as a positive goal of policy, notably with the introduction of quantitative targets, was meant to operate as a counter-weight to the Maastricht criteria for sound financial policies. However, along the way it has evolved into a 'soft' coordination tool for the implementation of the new strategy to adapt the Union's social model to the requirements of a more flexible and dynamic economy (cf. European Council, 2000).

The institutional balance of responsibilities for economic policies has also been modified following the decision – also taken in Lisbon – to devote, each semester, a special meeting of the European Council to economic and social questions. While previously the responsibility for setting goals and reviewing progress on the various fronts basically belonged to the Ecofin Council, with the BEPG,[13] it has now been taken over by the heads of state and government in the European Council. They have also instructed the Ecofin Council to take account of the opinions of the different Council formations in formulating the BEPG. This explicit role of the European Council goes beyond the tasks of arbiter and strategic motor of the Union; it involves genuine decision-making on economic and social policies and monitoring their application (Commission, 2001c; De La Porte, 2002).

The ingredients of the OCM were spelled out in Lisbon by the European Council and include:

(i)   Fixing common guidelines for national policies in various policy areas – e.g. employment policies, education and training for employability, flexible labour markets, aging and sustainable pension systems, social exclusion – with dates for their implementation.

(ii) Developing indicators (benchmarks) of national performance as a means for comparing best practice.

(iii) Asking countries to adopt national action plans to implement the common

---

13 Cf. European Council Resolution on Economic Policy Coordination in Phase Three of EMU of 13 December 1977. The legal basis of the BEPG is provided by Article 99 of the EC Treaty.

guidelines.

(iv) Undertaking joint monitoring and review of results, thus bringing peer pressure to bear in order to sustain progress.

Two features worth stressing concern the role of the Commission and subsidiarity. While these coordination exercises involve areas of policy that are not within the competence of the Union, almost inevitably the Commission has taken on an important role in proposing policy guidelines, developing indicators and providing comparative analysis of results. Thus, the Commission is emerging as a main player in shaping overall economic policy in the Union alongside the European Council and outside the normal Community framework.

For their part, member states retain considerable freedom to adapt policy guidelines to national contexts and decide their preferred approach to implementing them. On the other hand, while not legally bound by the Treaty, de facto, member states face new constraints on decision-making since they are obliged to debate and decide their national plans in time for the meetings of the European Council. This also means that they all carry out the exercise at the same time. Furthermore, their performance, relative to the other member states, is regularly exposed and compared in public reports prepared by the Commission, thereby putting pressure on governments to match best performance.

The European Council has also stressed the importance of involving a broad range of stakeholders in consultations at all policy stages, from the formulation of guidelines to their implementation and review. Thus, national Parliaments, social partners and other national players are increasingly involved in the discussions on European policies. Their legitimacy and acceptance are likely to benefit from these features of decentralisation and involvement.

Thus, while the working methods are decentralised, their goal is increasing 'convergence' of economic structures and social institutions. Use of the OCM does not mean that convergence of national policies will be painless. The goal of the Lisbon agenda – to make Europe 'the most competitive and dynamic knowledge-based economy in the world' by 2010 – entails radical market-friendly reforms. Labour market and welfare systems differ widely within the European Union; as has been observed (De La Porte, 2002), policy convergence will entail greater structural changes in 'corporatist' systems in the Centre and South of the Union.

The formal equality of obligations and parity of positions in coordination exercises cannot conceal substantial inequalities in the distance that the different member states will need to travel. The effectiveness of the OCM in muting political opposition and legitimating the new ambitions of economic and social 'convergence' is still untested.

There is also the question of the consistency of the new coordination framework with the traditional Community legal framework. Scott and Trubeck (2000) note that new forms of governance such as OCM entail 'a breakdown of the distinction between rule making and rule application'. The success of EU integration has been predicated on direct effect, supremacy and uniform interpretation of Community law, which is the constituent element of its supra-nationalism. There is a risk that the emerging modes of governance will change the perception, and later also the reality, of the institutional balance of powers, with unpredictable effects on the dynamics of integration.

The Commission is aware of the problem and is developing principles to circumscribe application of the OCM. It considers that its use should be limited to cases where harmonising legislation and binding Union intervention would be inappropriate, because the subject matter touches closely on national identity and culture, or national arrangements are so diverse and complex that harmonisation would be 'out of all proportion to the objectives'. It stresses that resort to the OCM should observe the principle of proportionality, be decided on a case-by-case basis, and not made when there is room for Community intervention under the Treaty (European Commission 2001c).

On the other hand, the Commission does not exclude the possibility of bringing policy areas into the Treaty where the OCM has proved successful and 'where the member states are not ready to embrace common legislation ... immediately but do have the political will to take very concrete steps towards an identified common objective'.

The OCM, thus, may become a precursor of further transfers of tasks to the European Union in very sensitive areas of national sovereignty and, over time, modify the institutional balance and modes of governance in economic policy making – a 'grey area' of Union activity where powers and procedures are shaped by political bargaining within the European Council without any clear definition of legal boundaries.

Elements for an Overall Assessment of Policy Coordination

The approach to economic policy coordination embodied the EC Treaty has a fairly simple and logical architecture. Mutual recognition, based on minimal harmonisation of public policy requirements, is to govern integration and the elimination of technical barriers that prevent free circulation among national markets.

The common good of macro-economic and financial stability is entrusted to an independent central bank, with a set of constraints on national budgetary policies designed to limit free riding and opportunistic behaviour by member states. But the latter are to remain free to decide their own policies and choose how much to spend and tax through the budget and how to design their welfare and social safety-net.

Recent developments in the balance of powers and decision-making procedures indicate substantial changes to this model, reflecting the reaction by the member states to a feared loss of control over the fundamental direction of their economic policies. The main emerging changes concern the following aspects.

(i) The balance between Community law and national policy goals in the Single Market and economic policy coordination seem to be tilting in favour of the latter; member states display a growing preference for discretionary decisions that override clear and simple coordination rules.

(ii) Policy coordination at Community level shows increasing ambitions, gradually extending to all aspects of economic and social policies.

(iii) Within Union institutions, decision making is moving 'upwards', from specialised committees to ministerial fora and from ministerial fora to the European Council, with ever-more encompassing goals and procedures.

These trends are not based on the results of an explicit debate over policy design. Indeed, there is little analytical reasoning or empirical evidence in supporting the changes that are taking place. Rather, the process is the result of political opportunism, administrative interaction (as in Maurer *et al.*, 2000) and ad-hoc Council agenda that fail to appreciate the institutional and policy consequences of individual decisions.

The main risk is that, while creating high expectations amongst the public, this ever-more complex and encompassing policy-approach will reveal its ineffectiveness and at the same time blur the responsibilities for policy failures. As a result, Union institutions could be further discredited while national policy makers would find it easier to avoid hard choices and eschew attendant political costs.

References

Alesina, A., Blanchard, O., Gali, J., Giavazzi, F. and Uhlig, H. (2001) Defining a macro-economic framework for the Euro Area, *Report on Monitoring the European Central Bank* n. 3, (CEPR March).

Balassone, F. and Franco, D. (2001) EMU fiscal rules: a new answer to an old question?, *Fiscal Rules* (Rome: Banca d'Italia).

Committee of Wise Men on the Regulation of European Securities Markets (2001) *Final Report* (Brussels: February).

Council of the European Union (2001) *Report on the Contribution of Public Finances to Growth and Employment: Improving Quality and Sustainability*, No. 6997/01, March.

De la Porte, C. (2002) Is the open method of coordination appropriate for organising activities at European level in sensitive policy areas?, *European Law Journal*, March.

European Central Bank (2002) The operation of automatic fiscal stabilisers in the Euro Area, *Monthly Bulletin*, April.

European Commission (2000) *The Contribution of Public Finances to Growth and Employment: Improving Quality and Sustainability* (COM 846 of 21, December).

European Commission (2001a) *Services of General Interest in Europe* (Communication from the Commission, OJ 2001/C 17/04 of 19 January).

European Commission (2001b) *Communication on Strengthening Economic Policy Co-ordination within the Euro Area* (COM 82 of 7 February).

European Commission (2001c) *Involving Experts in the Process of National Policy Convergence* (Report by Working Group 4a, June).

European Commission (2002a) Public finances in EMU, *European Economy*, March.

European Commission (2002b) *A Project for the European Union* (COM 247 of 22 May).

European Council (2000) *Presidency Conclusions* (Lisbon: March).

Fischer, J. (2001) *National and EU Budgetary Rules and Procedures: an Evolving Interaction*, Workshop (Rome: Banca d'Italia).

Gros, D. and Hobza, A. (2001) *Fiscal Policy Spillovers in the Euro Area: Where Are They?* (CEPS Working Document 176, November).

Jacquet, P. and Pisani-Ferry, J. (2001) *Economic Policy Co-ordination in the Eurozone: What Has Been Achieved? What Should Be Done?* (CER Essays, January).

Korkman, S. (2001) Fiscal policy coordination in EMU: should it go beyond the SGP? In: A. Brunila, M. Buti and D. Franco (Eds) *The Stability and Growth Pact: the Architecture of Fiscal Policy in EMU* (Hampshire, UK: Palgrave).

Maurer, A., Mittag, J. and Wessels, W. (2000) Theoretical perspectives on administrative interaction in the European Union, in: T. Christiansen and E. Kirchner (Eds) *Committee Governance in the European Union* (Manchester: University Press).

Melitz, J. (2000) Some cross-country evidence about fiscal policy behaviour and consequences for EMU, *European Economy*, No 2, February.

O'Keeffe, D. and Carey, N. (2002) Financial services and the internal market, in: G. Ferrarini, K.J. Hopt and E. Wymeersch (Eds) *Capital Markets in the Age of the Euro* (Kluwer Law International).

Pisany-Ferry, J. (2002) Balancing the stability pact, *Financial Times*, 28 June.

Sapir, A. and Buti, M. (2001) *EMU in the early Years: Differences and Credibility*, (CEPR Paper 2832, June).

Scott, J. and Trubeck, D.M. (2002) Mind the gap: law and new approaches to governance in the European Union, *European Law Journal*, March.

Scharpf, F.W. (1999) *Governing in Europe. Effective and Democratic?* (Oxford: Oxford University Press).

Story, J. and Walters, I. (1997) *Political Economy of Financial Integration in Europe* (The MIT Press).

Taylor, J.B. (2000) Reassessing discretionary fiscal policy, *Journal of Economic Perspectives*, 14(3): 21–36.

Tison, M. (2002) Conduct of business rules and their implementation in the EU Member States, in: G. Ferrarini, K.J. Hopt and E. Wymeersch (Eds) *Capital Markets in the Age of the Euro* (Kluwer Law International).

Van Miert, K. (1996) Public utilities, liberalisation and consumers: comprehensive explanation of the commission position, *International Forum on Public Utilities, Liberalisation and Consumers*, Rome, 4 October.

Wyplosz, C. (2002) *Fiscal Discipline in EMU: Rules or Institutions?* Paper for the meeting of the Group of Economic Analysis of the European Commission, April.

Chapter 13

The Lisbon Strategy to the New Economy. Some Economic and Institutional Aspects

Pierluigi Morelli, Pier Carlo Padoan and Lisa Rodano

Introduction

There is a general consensus that the main factor behind the exceptional performance of the US economy over the past decade has been the introduction and diffusion of new information and communication technologies. Increasing sophistication of financial markets as well as flexible labor markets are also considered important supporting factors in the exploitation of the new technologies. Conversely, the 'new economy' has barely found its way into the European countries, although here are some notable exceptions. After the successful introduction of the euro, the European Union, at the urging of the Portuguese Presidency and of the Commission, launched a new strategy, at the Lisbon European Council in march 2000, aimed at accelerating the transition towards the new economy in Europe, while simultaneously taking into account the institutional specificities of the European Union and the goal of combining market efficiency and social cohesion and making Europe the 'most dynamic, knowledge-based economy in the world by 2010'.

The Lisbon Strategy (LS) is based on three (implicit) assumptions:

(a) higher growth requires structural reforms;
(b) the benefits of reform in one sector (e.g. labor markets) are enhanced by reforms in other sectors (e.g. product markets), this is especially relevant in order to exploit the positive impact of ICT on growth;
(c) political incentives to undertake reforms in the EU must be strengthened while preserving the EU social model.

This chapter looks at some economic and institutional aspects of the LS. The economics of the LS are analyzed by looking at the set of economic and social indicators singled out to identify the targets and assess the performance of the European economies. The institutional (political economy) aspects relate to the structure of the decision making processes and the incentives to implement the measures identified in the LS (the 'Open Method of Coordination'). The rest of the chapter is organized as follows. The next section looks at the economics of the LS by performing a principal component and a cluster analysis. We identify groups of countries with similar characteristics and explore a possible convergence process towards a higher growth and employment. We also consider the early experience of the LS two years after the Lisbon summit. We then discuss the institutional aspects of the strategy, based on the so-called 'Open Method of Coordination', and we ask to what extent the LS will be successful in achieving the Lisbon goals. In so doing we compare the LS (which covers mainly microeconomic and structural issues) with the Maastricht Strategy (MS) to monetary union which, instead, deals mainly with macroeconomic issues.

The Economics of the Lisbon Strategy

In order to make Europe the 'most dynamic, knowledge-based economy in the world by 2010' the EU Commission has selected a number of structural indicators – listed in Table 13.1 – to form a framework for the guidance of national policies. These indicators, grouped into four areas – employment, research and development, economic reforms, and social cohesion – are ideally based on an economic model that, once implemented, should lead to sustained and sustainable growth. The underlying principle is that economic growth is associated with growth in employment and in innovation activities. At the same time, the principle of cohesion requires that the benefits of growth have to be shared by all the countries (and regions) of the European Union. Finally, growth must be achieved through, and is supported by, macroeconomic and financial stability as assured by the respect of monetary stability and the principles of the Stability and Growth Pact.

The indicators (Table 13.1) offer a framework for national economic policies based on the comparison of national performances among EU member states, as well as with non-EU economies, so as to identify best practices and benchmarks to guide national policies. The effectiveness of the method in guiding national policies will be discussed in the next section. Here we discuss the economic logic that supports the choice of the indicators.

While the long-term economic goals have been clearly identified at the Lisbon summit, the relationship between the indicators and the targets set in terms of employment and growth remains unclear.[1] A number of questions can be asked in this respect. Are all indicators equally relevant for the long-term strategy? What is the relationship between policy and performance indicators? Is the relationship between indicators pointing to a common economic model for all EU countries, or are national specificities more relevant? The analysis that follows offers tentative answers to these questions.

Three main conclusions emerge from our analysis:

(a) not all the variables identified by the indicators show a clear correlation with output and employment growth; there is, however a common 'framework

---

1   The Lisbon summit has also set an overall target for the employment rate of the EU at 70 percent in 2010. The rate of growth consistent with this target has been set at 3 percent per year.

Table 13.1 Performance and policy indicators

Structural Indicators	Type
Employment	
1. Growth rate of Employment	Performance
2. Women's employment rate	Performance
3. Employment rate of the elderly	Performance
4. Unemployment rate	Performance
5. Tax rate on low wages	Policy
6. Life-long learning	Policy
Research and innovation	
1. Public expenditure in education	Policy
2. Expenditure on R&D	Policy
3. Expenditure on ICT	Policy
4. Internet access	Performance
5. Patents	Performance
6. High tech exports	Performance
7. Venture Capital	Performance
Economic reform	
1. Trade integration	Performance/Policy
2. Business investment	Performance
3. Relative prices and price convergence	Performance
4. Prices in Network industries	Performance/Policy
5. Public procurement	Policy
6. Sectoral state aid	Policy
7. Capital raised in the stock exchange	Performance
Social cohesion	
1. Income distribution	Performance/Policy
2. Poverty rates before and after social transfers	Performance (before transfer); policy (after)
3. Persistence of poverty	Performance
4. Jobless families	Performance
5. Regional cohesion (variation in regional unemployment rates)	Performance
6. People leaving school early and are not in training programs	Performance/Policy
7. Long term unemployment	Performance

model' based on a correlation between growth, employment and innovation activities;

(b) nonetheless, EU countries display a high heterogeneity in their growth models, to the extent that these models are captured by the Lisbon indicators. To some extent at least, national economies can be classified into different groups. Cluster analysis identifies three groups. One group (strong structure) includes the large continental economies and the UK, where the employment rate and R&D investment are above average. A second group (weak structure) includes the Mediterranean countries and Belgium, where employment performance has been much less satisfactory. A third group (followers) includes the small Nordic countries and Ireland;

(c) In spite of significant differences, a process whereby the weaker countries converge to the more dynamic ones can be identified. This last result offers reasons for moderate optimism for the success of the LS.

Principal Component Analysis

Principal component analysis has been applied to a number of variables for the 15 EU countries and some other OECD economies (US, Japan, Canada, Australia, and Norway) over the period 1980–2000, with the aim of identifying a 'common growth model' as captured by the Lisbon indicators. Data availability has prevented us from using all the Lisbon indicators included in Table 13.1 so in some cases proxy variables have been used. The variables we have chosen, in addition to real GDP growth (g), are referred to the four 'pillars' (in parenthesis). They are the following: (employment) the activity rate of the population between 15 and 64 years of age (lr); (innovation) the ratio of R&D expenditure to GDP ($gerd$), the employment rate in the R&D sector (lrd), productivity of R&D expenditure as proxied by the ratio between patents and R&D expenditure ($tpat$), FDI inflows as a share of GDP ($fdii$); (economic reform) rate of growth of real labor costs ($drlc$), rate of growth of labor productivity ($dprod$), social contributions as a percentage of GDP (ssc), ratio of public investment over GDP ($ginv$), debt to GDP ratio (d), deficit to GDP ratio (def), degree of trade integration (xm); (social cohesion) unemployment rate. All variables have been considered in levels and in growth rates (when applicable).

The first result to consider is that four of the 23 factors (the number of factors is equal to the number of variables introduced) capture most of the information and up to 40 percent of total variability and the first two factors alone account for 30 percent of total variability.

Figure 13.1 describes the relationship between the variables. Real GDP (g) is positively correlated with the growth of the activity rate (dlr) and both variables are negatively correlated with the rate of growth of unemployment (du) and of social contributions ($dssc$). Output growth rates are positively correlated with growth in the activity rate, and negatively correlated with unemployment growth. Somewhat less intuitive, but nevertheless relevant, is the negative correlation with the rate of growth of social contributions.

Figure 13.1 points to other results. Variables in the fourth quadrant are positively correlated. These are the activity rate and a number of innovation indicators, such

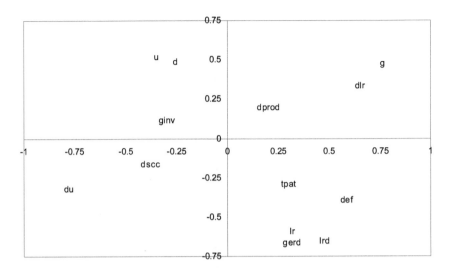

Figure 13.1   Relationship between the variables

as the relation of R&D to GDP (*gerd*), R&D productivity (*tpat*) and employment in the innovative sectors (*lrd*). All the above variables are negatively correlated with the unemployment rate (*u*). In sum, factor analysis leads to a first tentative answer to one of our questions. The extent to which the Lisbon indicators are based on a common economic model is limited, and it is circumscribed to a relationship between employment, growth and innovation activities.

Cluster Analysis

Cluster analysis identifies three groups of countries that share common features in their economic models. The three groups of countries are described in Table 13.2.

Group 1. Strong structure. Countries in this group – the US, Japan, the large continental EU countries, and the UK – share a common strong structure identified by variables in their *levels*. Important common features are a favorable employment outlook both in terms of activity ratio and employment in the innovative sectors, a low rate of growth of unemployment (and a high rate of growth of real labor costs), a strong innovative position, as well as a sound public finance situation.

Group 2. Followers. Countries included in this group – the small Nordic countries and Ireland, as well as Australia and Canada – share similar values in the *rate of change* of variables rather than in their levels. Growth rates of both employment and GDP are higher than average. Unemployment grows less and so do social security contributions. Level variables above average are also productivity in R&D, and foreign direct investment as a share of GDP.

Table 13.2   Cluster analysis

	Above average	Below average	Countries
Group 1: Strong structure	* Activity rate (in % of pop. 15-64) * R&D expend (in % Gdp) * Employment rate in R&D sectors * Growth of real labor costs	* Growth of unemployment rate * deficit (in % Gdp) * Govt public debt (in % Gdp)	Germany, France, Luxembourg, Austria, Finland, Sweden, UK, Norway, US, Japan
Group 2: Followers	* Growth of activity rate * Gdp growth * Productivity of R&D expenditure * FDI inflows (in % Gdp)	* Growth of unemployment rate * Growth of social contributions * Public investments (in % Gdp)	Netherlands, Denmark, Australia, Canada, Ireland
Group 3: Weak structure	* Unemployment rate * Govt debt (in % Gdp) * Public investment (in % Gdp) * Govt deficit (in % Gdp)	* Activity rate (in % of pop. 15-64) * Employment rate in R&D * R&D expenditure (in % Gdp) * Productivity of R&D expenditure	Belgium, , Greece, Spain, Italy, Portugal

Group 3. Weak structure. The remaining countries – the Mediterranean countries and Belgium – share a weak structure of the economy, associated with unemployment above average, low activity rate as well as low employment in innovative activities, low R&D expenditure and low R&D productivity. Public finance is also less sound than average.

These results are not surprising and, in many respects, they are consistent with the view that in the EU there coexist small dynamic economies that are able to exploit the benefits of innovation and a number of economies, including some large continental countries, that are somewhat lagging behind and/or display both weak public finances and low employment opportunities.[2] It would be misleading, however, to consider the classification above as static, and not subject to change over time. As we all know, it is a feature of integration processes, not least the EU one, to see significant catching-up processes, as well as cases in which countries 'fall behind' the top performers. After all, the basic philosophy of the LS is precisely to upgrade the overall level of economic performance in the EU and to encourage the effort of followers to catch up. Indications in this sense are offered by the analysis of convergence.

Some evidence about a different, yet related, aspect is worth recalling at this point. Boeri *et al.* (2000) consider the OECD countries according to the degree of labor and product market regulation. They identify four clusters of countries:

(a) countries that combine strict regulation in both labor and product markets (France, Italy, Greece and Spain);

(b) continental European countries with relatively restrictive product market regulation but with different employment protection legislations (Germany, Austria, the Netherlands, Finland, and Portugal being more restrictive than Belgium and Denmark);

(c) common law countries characterized by a relatively liberal approach in both labor and product markets (US, UK, Canada, Ireland, Australia and New Zealand);

(d) Sweden which, together with Japan, combines relatively restrictive labor market regulation with relatively few product market restrictions. It is not surprising that the countries with most restrictive regulations are, to a large extent, the same countries that are included in the 'weak structure' cluster, while countries included in the 'strong structure' and 'followers' groups display less restrictive regulation. The authors also find that better performance in terms of non-agricultural employment is associated with less restrictive regulation.

Economic Convergence

Convergence of lagging economies towards higher per capita GDP levels is a very well known phenomenon, both within and outside the EU. The following analysis does not add much in this respect. What it offers is some evidence that countries

---

2 See for example Commission of the European Communities (2000).

Table 13.3   Transition matrix

| | Target Cluster | | |
Cluster of Origin	1	2	3
1	81%	18%	1%
2	24%	74%	2%
3	0%	13%	88%

classified as followers, or weak performers, may have the opportunity to catch up. As mentioned, this is an encouraging sign for the success of the LS.

The exercise is based on the analysis of the probability of transition from one cluster to another. We have estimated the probability of transition between the three clusters over the period 1980–2000. Probabilities have been computed relating the frequency with which each country shifts from one cluster to another to the total movements from the originating cluster.

Results are reported in Table 13.3. Values in the main diagonal are very high, indicating a strong inertia. The probability of remaining in a cluster at the end of a period is large. In spite of a large inertia, the probability of weak structure countries (group 3) moving on to the group of followers (group 2) is 13 percent. While followers have a probability of 24 percent of moving on to the strong structure group (group 1). (The probability of moving directly from group 3 to group 1 is zero). Once a country leaves group 3 it is practically impossible to fall back into it while there is a high probability of falling back from group 1 to group 2.

Table 13.4   **Progress towards Lisbon goals and indicators of best performance**

	Lisbon	Barcelona	EU Best 3 Performers	EU 2010 target
1. General economic background				
a. GDP p.c. PPS, US=100 (99/01)	65.1	65.1	96.0	
b. GDP Growth r. 1995 prices (99/01)	2.6	1.6	4.9	
c. Productivity/empl in PPS, US=100 (99/01)	74.0	72.2	106.0	
2. Employment				
a. Overall (% of active pop.) 99/01	63.2	63.9	73.6 **	70 (67 in 2005)
b. Women 99/01	52.8	54.7	69.0	60 (57 in 2005)
c. Older workers (55-64) 99/01	37.2	38.3	66.0	50
3. R&D				
a. Total (public and private) R&D expenditure as % GDP 98 / 00	1.87	1.90	3.1	
b. Share of total R&D exp. financed by industry (%) 98 / 99	55.1	55.9	68.1	
4. Education and training				
a. Public spending on education as % GDP 99/00	5.0	5.1	6.7	–
b. Early school leav (% not in further ed.) 99/01	18.7	17.7	7.2	9.4
c. Lifel. Learn. (% part. adults) 99/ 01	8.2	8.3	21.4	–
5. Internet Penetration				
a. EU homes (% homes) 00/01	18.4	37.7	60.6	
b. EU broadband (% homes,) Year 01	2.5	5.8	14.9	
c. EU schools (% all schools) Year 01	–	89	99	100 end 2001
6. Public Procurement				
a. Value of tenders published in EU Official Journal (% of GDP) 98/00	1.8	2.4	3.9	–
7. Venture Capital				
a. Early stage (% of GDP) 99/01	0.038	0.036	0.079	–
b. Expansion (% of GDP) 99/01	0.104	0.099	0.192	–
8. State Aid				
a. Aid as % GDP Years 95–97/97–99	1.1	0.9	0.5	–
9. Social Cohesion				
a. Risk of poverty (after social transfers) 97/98	18	18	10	

Source: Eurostat

Table 13.5 Number of presences in the top 3 (T3) or bottom 3 (B3) performers in the extended list of performance indicators, by group of indicators

	Global Economic Outlook		Employment		Innovation		Economic Reform		Social Cohesion		Total		
	T3	B3	T3	B3	T3	B3	T3	B3	T3	B3	T3	B3	T3-B3
A	1	3	2	3	1	2	1	4	3	–	8	12	-4
B	2	1	1	2	1	–	–	4	–	1	4	8	-4
D	–	2	–	1	5	–	3	4	–	2	8	9	-1
DK	2	3	1	2	1	1	2	1	3	–	9	7	+2
E	3	2	–	8	1	8	7	2	–	4	11	24	-13
EL	1	5	–	3	1	7	4	4	2	3	8	22	-14
F	1	–	6	1	1	1	–	2	1	1	9	5	+4
FIN	2	1	2	–	6	2	7	6	1	–	18	12	+6
IRL	9	1	1	2	1	–	4	1	1	1	16	5	+11
I	1	1	–	9	–	4	2	4	1	6	4	21	-17
L	6	–	10	–	3	1	1	5	1	–	21	6	+15
NL	1	1	10	–	3	1	4	–	5	–	23	2	+21
P	–	6	1	2	–	8	3	6	1	2	5	24	-19
S	–	1	2	2	9	–	5	2	1	1	19	7	+9
UK	2	2	4	–	2	–	6	3	2	2	16	7	+9

Given the values of the transition matrix we have conducted a simulation exercise. Cluster analysis allocates 58 percent of the countries into group 1, 14 percent in group 2, and 29 percent in group 3. Given these initial values and the transition probabilities we have checked whether the Markov process leads countries to converge towards one single cluster or towards increased diversification. Results are reported in Figure 13.2. They indicate that a convergence process takes place.

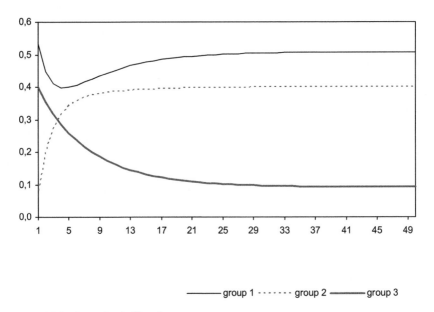

Figure 13.2   Results indicating a convergence process

At the end of the process, the percentage of group 2 countries rises to 40 percent while the weak structure group falls to 10 percent. Group 1 initially shrinks to 44 percent and eventually rises back to 50 percent.

In general, the overall structure of EU economies improves as the share of weak structure countries falls by two thirds. However, there is not necessarily a full convergence towards a strong structure. This last result is telling of the problems underlying the LS. Spontaneous convergence may not be enough to fully upgrade the EU economy.

The Lisbon Strategy. Early results

Although the LS began in 2000, and given that its time horizon spreads up to 2010, it is probably still premature to look for results. Some initial evidence, however, is available and it is briefly discussed below.

Table 13.6   **The CER Barcelona scoreboard**

Issue	2002 (2001)	Heroes	Villains
Innovation			
Information Society	C+ (B+)	NL, S, DK,	F, D,
R&D	C+ (B-)	S, FIN, D,	I, E, EL, P
Liberalization			
Telecoms	B- (B+)	FIN,	D. UK, A,
Other utilities and services	D- (D)	UK, FIN, DK, S, NL,	F, D, EL
Financial services	B- (C+)	UK, E,	D
Enterprise			
Business start-up environment	D (D)	DK, UK, IRL,	A, I, B,
Business regulation	C- (D+)	FIN,	I, F
State aid and competition policy	B- (B-)	UK, D,	FIN, P,
Social Inclusion			
Bringing people into workforce	B- (B-)	S, E, IRL, UK, DK, NL	I, EL, A
Upgrading skills	C- (D)	S, DK, FIN, UK,	F, D, EL, P, L
Modernizing social protection	C+ (C+)	UK, D,	E, I, B,
Conclusion			
Overall assessment	C- (C+)		

Let us, first, look at some evidence from Commission sources. Table 13.4 (CEC, 2002) offers some quantitative evidence of progress over the period from Lisbon to Barcelona, as measured by some of the Lisbon indicators. The table compares EU averages at the Lisbon and Barcelona summit dates and the unweighted average of the three best performers in 2000–2001. The distance between EU averages and best performers is evident all across the board. The 'Best Performance Indicators' are useful in providing an indication of what can and should be achieved, although they only serve to measure progress towards EU-wide targets and do not set binding targets for individual Member States.

Table 13.5 offers another assessment of the initial phase of the Lisbon strategy, also derived from Commission sources. It is based on an extended list of 63 performance indicators (CEC, 2002, Annex II)[3] pertaining to the four pillars of reform as well as to macroeconomic performance. The Commission document does not provide precise values but only a ranking, so figures reported in the table indicate the times a country is included in the top three (T3) or bottom three (B3) performers in the EU for each of the five pillars. A rough overall assessment of country performance according to the extended list of indicators is the difference between the total number

---

3   The 63 indicators considered form an extended list with respect to the indicators presented in Table 13.1.

of T3 less the total number of B3. Results suggest a ranking of countries that is not very dissimilar from the one identified by cluster analysis above, as well as by Boeri *et al.* (2000). Top performers include 'strong structure' countries such as Sweden, the UK and Finland, and 'followers' such as the Netherlands, Denmark, and Ireland, while all 'weak structure' countries show up as bottom performers. If anything, this preliminary evidence suggests that while followers are in a good position to catch-up with countries in the leading cluster, weak countries are still lagging behind.

Table 13.6 offers an assessment of the Lisbon strategy carried out by the Center for European Reform. It is a qualitative judgment of the reform process based on the actions taken by individual member countries. The selected areas do not correspond to the four pillars according to which the indicators are classified. Nevertheless, they closely follow the 'spirit' of the LS and the aim is to see overall results while identifying countries leading the process (heroes) and countries lagging behind (villains). Two main messages can be derived from the table. The LS, as seen from Barcelona (2002), has lost steam somewhat and countries leading the process are, to a large extent, those identified by the previous analysis, i.e. countries with strong structure and limited regulations. However, some clarifications are appropriate. While weak structure countries are almost systematically identified as 'villains' this group also includes, in many cases, the large continental economies, such as France and Germany. 'Heroes', on the other hand, include small northern countries previously included either in the 'strong structure' or 'followers' groups.

Institutional Aspects

As we know from theory and ample empirical evidence there are several channels through which catching up takes place. The two most relevant ones are the accumulation of capital and the transfer of technology. Capital accumulation takes place in backward regions because initial capital shortage increases return to investment with respect to advanced regions. Capital is accumulated both through domestic investment and through capital flows from abroad. Technology transfers also take place through different channels including trade, capital flows as well as patent transfers, as returns to the application of technologies that are new for the entrant but old for the incumbents are higher in the former.

Growth convergence can be absolute or, more likely, conditional. In addition, convergence can involve only parts of the laggard countries (regions) and, finally, convergence is likely to affect regions more than countries in their entirety. For instance, Padoan *et al.* (2000, ch. 8) find that convergence among regions of EU15 excludes some of the poorest regions in some of the Mediterranean countries, thus suggesting the presence of 'convergence clubs', it is conditional rather than absolute, and it depends on sector specific rather than country specific characteristics. Padoan (2000, ch. 8) also finds that convergence is faster in regions where there is a strong presence of both advanced industrial sectors and well-developed financial and banking sectors.

The Open Method of Coordination

The LS implicitly assumes that market led convergence is not sufficient to reach the targets of growth and employment set out in Lisbon and it calls for an explicit role of policy based on the so-called 'Open Method of Coordination' (OMC). The basic principle underlying the OMC is that, contrary to monetary and fiscal policy as envisaged in the MS, in many of the policy areas considered by the LS it is not possible, or desirable, to identify common goals or, even less, common instruments and guidelines. Rather, as a form of 'soft coordination', the OMC is based on a process of learning and exchange of best practices.

The OMC is based on the following steps:

(a) the definition of guidelines at the EU level and the fixing of deadlines for their fulfillment,
(b) the definition, whenever possible, of quantitative or qualitative targets based on benchmarking vis-à-vis the best world practices,
(c) the 'transposition' of EU guidelines into national (and regional) targets that take into account national specificities,
(d) a process of monitoring and peer review. In a nutshell, the OMC is a process of convergence towards best practices, the outcome of which should be the catching-up in terms of performance (growth and employment).[4]

The Lisbon indicators should be seen as instrumental to the OMC as fostering catching-up in that they include variables that are directly connected to knowledge accumulation (the variables included in the innovation pillar) and to capital accumulation (the economic reform pillar). In addition, variables related to labor market reforms are also conducive to faster catching-up to the extent that they allow for higher productivity growth as well as improving the potential for innovation diffusion through human capital accumulation and better organization.

The OMC should be seen as a set of instruments additional to the legislative instruments associated with directives and EU legislation. It basically follows a 'bottom up' approach where competition among rules is set in motion, rather than the identification of a common rule (top down).

The Lisbon summit has also clarified the more formal aspects of the coordination process. The key element in this respect is the Broad Economic Policy Guidelines (BEPG) as defined by the Treaty (art. 99). The BEPG is the key document that defines the basic guidelines of economic policy and coordinates the three processes (Luxembourg, Cardiff, and Cologne). Every year, BEPG are designed so as to provide a coherent framework for four areas: the macroeconomic framework, public finances in the Stability and Growth Pact, structural reforms (the Cardiff Process), labor markets (the Luxembourg Process).

The mechanism was strengthened in 1999. The Spring Meeting of the European Council, in 1999, was put in the position of reviewing the process and setting

---

4   Hodson and Maher (2001) discuss the OMC as a new model of governance in Europe

the policy guidelines for the Union in a medium term perspective, including the framework for the definition of the National Stability Programs and the National Action Plans within the Luxembourg process. The Cologne European council in 1999 added a social dialogue dimension to the process.

The Council of Economic and Financial Ministers (Ecofin) is at the center of the coordination mechanism.

While the design of the institutional structure is sufficiently clear, it remains to be seen whether it is also effective, i.e. whether it generates pressures and incentives that will deliver the necessary policy action. There is no clear cut answer to this question, mainly because there are significant differences among the components of the policy process envisaged in the LS and the incentives and policy mechanism that are involved in the policy areas are also largely different. This suggests that to cope with policy complexity some form of simplification is necessary, given that the LS is both about economic convergence and policy convergence.

What kind of governance mechanism does the LS need to be successful? In discussing this point some insight can be obtained by comparing two institutional processes that have characterized EU integration over the recent past: the move to the single currency and the 'Luxembourg process' coordinating employment and labor market policies, which can be taken as an early, and possibly the most advanced, example of OMC.

While the LS is largely, if not exclusively, about microeconomic and structural issues, it is in the macroeconomic domain (that, from now on, we will refer to as the 'Maastricht Strategy', MS) that the most significant progress in policy convergence has been achieved in the EU. The aim of both strategies is to change the relevant policy regime. It is useful to explore, therefore, what lessons, if any, can be drawn from one domain towards the other, keeping in mind the relevance of different mechanisms and rules, in the two policy regimes.

Change in Policy Regime 1. The Maastricht Strategy to Monetary Union

In looking at policy regimes, one question to ask is, are they stable? That is, are regimes based on a structure of incentives that leads to mutually consistent behavior by the actors involved, both policy and market agents? The move to monetary union offers important insights in this respect. As we have discussed elsewhere (Padoan, 2002), according to the endogenous currency approach area, monetary integration generates pressure to change both in markets and in policies, in a way that may support monetary union itself. This stems from two factors. First, the creation of a supranational institution in one policy area generates pressures for change in other policy areas. Second, to the extent that a 'mixed' model of economic policy emerges, it must be based on a coherent set of policy incentives to produce consistent and stable outcomes. To see the point let us recall that one of the main (economic) justifications for the move to a single currency (EMU) and away from a fixed exchange rate regime (EMS) has been that the latter was becoming increasingly unsustainable in the presence of full capital mobility.

The EMS can be described as a 'weak hegemonic regime', based on different (asymmetric) policy incentives in the key country and in the periphery. The incentives for the latter were to import monetary discipline, or the exploitation of the public good of monetary stability provided by the center economy. The incentive for the key country to participate in the regime was the control of monetary stability and the support of its international competitiveness by preventing, or limiting, exchange rate devaluations in the periphery. The stability of the regime was assured to the extent that national policies converged towards the German policy stance. The regime collapsed when, after unification, the core country was not willing or able to bear the cost of supporting the weaker (more inflation prone) economies and the periphery was not willing to make the (deflationary) adjustment necessary to support the exchange rate regime required to cope with the consequences of full capital liberalization. The policy regime proved to be effective as an anti-inflationary mechanism, but it produced limited, if any, policy spillovers towards other areas (especially fiscal policy). Its crisis showed that policy convergence had to extend to areas beyond monetary and exchange rate policy, if it were to pass the judgment of the markets. As long as it succeeded, it proved that an 'intergovernmental' approach to macroeconomic policy requires leadership but that there are limits to such an approach when market integration deepens beyond some critical threshold.

The move forward from the EMS to EMU – based on the MS – has led to a major change in the policy regime. Policy convergence has affected both monetary and fiscal policy but, what is perhaps more important, it has shifted towards a more symmetric configuration. The greater symmetry, however, has required two additional conditions for the system to be effective:

(a) the move from a national (hegemonic) leadership structure to a supranational one;
(b) the imposition of high entry costs (fulfillment of the Maastricht convergence conditions under the threat of exclusion) as well as high exit costs (the costs associated with the possibility of one country leaving the single currency). In this respect monetary union can be described as a club good (Padoan, 1997).

Change in Policy Regime 2. The Luxembourg Process for Employment Policies

The Stability and Growth Pact guarantees that, once monetary convergence has been obtained and a single monetary policy becomes feasible, national fiscal policies are managed according to common guidelines. However, the sustainability of monetary union requires that adaptation towards the configuration of an optimum currency area is also obtained, involving adjustment in both product and labor markets. As one cannot rely on market forces alone to produce such a convergence, a well functioning monetary union requires the adoption of appropriate micro (structural) policies to overcome labor and product market rigidities. In this respect, the LS serves a double purpose: to make Europe a dynamic knowledge-based economy and an economy that is better fit to the operation of a monetary union. This is the purpose of the OMC.

As mentioned, the Luxembourg process represents an early example of the OMC dealing with labor markets and employment, an area that is crucial for the operation of monetary unions. Briefly, the Luxembourg process operates as follows. Every year, each EU Member State sets out its National Action Plan (NAP), which contains the policy actions that have been taken towards the improvement of employment opportunities. The philosophy of the approach is that flexibility in European labor markets can be increased by moving away from 'passive' employment policies towards 'active' policies, such as welfare-to-work schemes and active learning and retraining. Within the process, however, a wide range of polices are considered, including policies targeted at supporting small and medium enterprises.

Policies are implemented at the national level, as national governments only have jurisdictions over such policies, and are classified according to a (long) list of 'policy guidelines' set out by the Commission and grouped under four headings: employability (employment polices in a strict sense such as the implementation of placing agencies), adaptability (polices aimed at adapting workers to the new market conditions such as retraining policies), entrepreneurship (policies aimed at improving the demand side of the labor market, such as incentives for small business), equal opportunity (policies aimed at increasing the employment opportunities for women).

Every year, NAPs are presented to the Commission and reviewed by member states through a 'peer review' procedure. A final 'score' is assigned to each government identifying the degree of fulfillment of policy guidelines as well as the identification of best practices. Policy recommendations are then directed to each member country by the Commission and the Council.

As national governments retain full control of policy, they are not subject to any explicit obligation,[5] and failure to follow recommendations is not associated with any punishment and/or exclusion threat, as is the case with the MS. As a consequence, moving away from areas in which the supranational element prevails, the pressure for convergence and adjustment weakens.

It would be inappropriate, however, to jump to the conclusion that in areas where there is no explicit obligation to adjust to an EU wide rule there are also no incentives for national policies to change. Two distinct incentive sets can be seen at work in such a case: a 'competition' incentive and a 'cooperation' (regime building) incentive. The competition incentive derives from both the policy arena and from the market. A country performing poorly in, for example, improving its employment policies, would see her reputation weaken and, consequently, her leverage in the design and implementation of EU policies at large would decrease. This would be particularly worrying whenever the intergovernmental dimension is relevant. In addition, markets would punish a poor performer to the extent that inefficient policies would make that country less attractive for investment, while good performers would enjoy larger investment as their perceived profitability would be enhanced. The evidence, discussed above, of a relationship between economic performance, regulatory tightness, and success in policy implementation lends some support to this conjecture. This aspect, in addition, will be increasingly relevant in a world of high capital mobility. In short, institutional competition may well produce a healthy

---

5 In some areas, of course, national governments must fulfill obligations emanating from Commission Directives, such as those related to the prohibition of implementing state aids.

improvement in EU and EMU economic performance as long as it takes the form of exchange of best practices and provides content to the principle of subsidiarity (Hodson and Maher, 2001).

The cooperation incentive is relevant to the extent that poor performance in any member of EMU weakens the performance and attractiveness of Euroland as a whole vis-à-vis the rest of the world. In other words, poor policy and economic performance in any one member of the club decreases the quality of the club good, generating a negative externality on the other club members. This would presumably lead to a strengthened peer pressure on the poor performer from the rest of the club members (and from the Commission). In this case, the supranational, rather than the intergovernmental, dimension would prevail. To the extent that such an incentive structure strengthens, therefore, policy convergence could well be the result of the interaction between inter-governmentalism and supra-nationality.

The Maastricht and Lisbon Strategies compared

Let us now compare the Maastricht and the Lisbon Strategies so as to clarify to what extent lesson can be drawn from the former towards the success of the latter. The comparison can be based on five criteria: leadership, best practice, economic logic, control over outcomes, and incentive structure.

Leadership

Institutional change in international systems requires leadership, the action of one or more leading actors providing political and institutional drive to the project. Progress towards monetary union was initially based on German leadership, during the EMS, to achieve monetary stability, and Franco–German leadership in the transition from the EMS to EMU. The LS lacks such a clear leadership, as the best EU performers in the move towards a new economy, both in terms of innovation efforts and market reform, are the small Nordic countries (and Ireland) while the large continental countries are, as we have seen, lagging behind in many respects. If anything, the Commission has been playing a leadership role in pushing towards market reform and innovation efforts.

Best Practices

EMU has been set up having in mind a clear institutional model, based on the central role of monetary stability and on the independence of the Central Bank, made popular by the German experience. The very nature of the Lisbon goals makes it very difficult to identify one single model of the 'new economy' that can be taken as institutional and economic best practice.[6]

---

6   Unless such a model is to be found in the US experience.

Economic Logic

The MS was based on convergence of monetary and fiscal variables that reflected a clear economic logic, and on the assumption that once convergence was obtained it would have signaled the achievement of monetary and fiscal discipline in member countries. The analysis carried out above suggests that, to some extent at least, the economic indicators at the base of the LS reflect the familiar paradigm of a relationship between innovation, employment, and output growth. One could therefore argue that in both the MS and the LS the policy strategy is based on a reasonable and widely accepted economic logic.

Control over Outcomes

In the case of the MS, fiscal variables are directly under policy control, and so is the choice of the exchange regime. Less so in the case of inflation and interest rates, but the fiscal variables have proved to be the crucial ones, precisely because they signal the degree of policy commitment . As Table 13.1 shows, variables considered in the LS include both policy and performance indicators. While in this respect the two strategies can be put on the same ground, an advantage of the MS is the smaller number of variables involved.

Incentives

The MS is based on a clear inclusion/exclusion mechanism. Entry in monetary union is subject to meeting critical values in the relevant variables. Only once these conditions are met is a member admitted to the new policy regime. The LS, based on the OMC and on peer pressure, does not envisage any exclusion mechanism. Both the prize for the good performers and the punishment for poor performers remain unclear. Meeting targets for the Lisbon parameters does not imply that the country enters a different policy regime.

In sum, the MS has been a success because it was based on strong leadership, a 'best practice' to look to, a clear economic logic, control over outcomes for the relevant variables, and a transparent and effective incentive structure. In the case of the LS, leadership is weak and dispersed, there is no obvious best practice to look to, the economic logic is apparently clear, and policy has control over outcomes in some cases (but the number of variables to consider is higher), however the incentive structure is much weaker.

Conclusions

The 'new economy' is not based only on the exploitation of information and communication technologies. It also requires changes in labor and product markets. The Lisbon Strategy aims at making Europe the 'best knowledge-based economy in the world by 2010'. To the extent that it will improve the functioning of labor and product markets, the LS will also improve the operation of monetary union.

EMU has been introduced thanks to a policy strategy and institutional design that remain, to a large extent, unique. While that strategy – the Maastricht Strategy – can teach useful lessons for the process of EU integration, the Lisbon goals have to be achieved through a different strategy.

To this end, the EU has identified a set of indicators to provide benchmarks and suggest best practices for policies by member states. As our preliminary analysis suggests, these indicators are, to some extent, based on a widely accepted economic model, which relates output growth to innovation and employment growth. Our analysis also shows that not all EU countries have, so far, experienced the same performance in this respect. Rather, they can be grouped as strong, weak, and catching-up economies.

Economic convergence towards a strong structure for all countries is possible, yet it requires appropriate policy action by EU member states in microeconomic and structural areas. As these policy domains are not governed at the supranational level (as the common monetary policy is) and as there are no binding obligations for countries to adopt specific policies (as is the case of the MS), some form of policy coordination is needed. This is the role of the Open Method of Coordination, which is based on soft incentives, exchange of best practices, benchmarking, and peer pressure. This policy regime is not as strong and compelling as the one that has led to monetary union, and it remains to be seen whether it will lead to convergence through a combination of market and policy incentives. The early experience of the employment policies (the Luxembourg Process) allows for some moderate optimism in this respect.

References

Boeri, T., Nicoletti, G. and Scarpetta, S. (2000) Regulation and labor market performance, in: G. Galli and J. Pelkmans (Eds) *Regulatory Reform, Market Functioning, and Competitiveness* (Aldershot: Edward Elgar).

Commission of European Communities (2000) *Competitiveness Report*.

Commission of the European Communities (2002) *The Lisbon Strategy. Making Things Happen*, Communication of the Commission in the Spring European Council (Barcelona).

Hodson, D. and Maher, I. (2001) The open method of coordination: the case of soft economic policy coordination, *Journal of Common Market Studies*, 39(4), pp. 719–746.

Padoan, P.C. (1997) Regional agreements as clubs, the European case, in: E. Mansfield and H. Milner (Eds) *The Political Economy of Regionalism* (Columbia University Press).

Padoan, P.C. (Ed.) (2000) *Monetary Union, Employment and Growth* (Aldershot: Edward Elgar).

Index